Making
OUTREACH
VISIBLE

A Guide to Documenting Professional Service and Outreach

by AMY DRISCOLL
and ERNEST A. LYNTON

companion volume to
Making the Case for Professional Service

American Association for Higher Education

**MAKING OUTREACH VISIBLE: A GUIDE TO DOCUMENTING
PROFESSIONAL SERVICE AND OUTREACH**

by Amy Driscoll and Ernest A. Lynton

For more about AAHE, see pp. 46-47.
Additional copies of this publication or Ernest Lynton's
Making the Case for Professional Service are available from:
  AMERICAN ASSOCIATION FOR HIGHER EDUCATION
  One Dupont Circle, Suite 360
  Washington, DC 20036-1110
  Ph: 202/293-6440 x11, fax: 202/293-0073, email: pubs@aahe.org
  Website: www.aahe.org

ISBN 1-56377-045-8

DEDICATION

This publication is dedicated to Ernest Lynton, whose vision and spirit guided the work of all who contributed to the thinking and wisdom evident herein. Ernest, who died while we were working on this manuscript, had devoted these last years to advocacy of recognition and reward for the scholarship of professional service/outreach. His writing promoted a national understanding of professional service and its importance for the future of higher education. His words — "It is the increasing responsibility of the university not merely to be a principal source of new knowledge but also to be instrumental in analyzing and applying this knowledge and in making it rapidly useful to all societal sectors" (1983: 53) — inspired a growing movement in universities and colleges across the country.

In response to his ideas and those of his contemporaries, among them Ernest Boyer, Donald Schön, Russ Edgerton, Gene Rice, and William Greiner, institutions of higher education are reframing priorities, rethinking faculty roles and rewards, and reconceptualizing outreach and community service as important scholarly activities. Ernest Lynton has been called a "gentle giant" by those who collaborated with him on this work to promote and document the scholarship of professional service. He brought wisdom and strength to our collaboration, and as a leader left deep footprints for higher education to follow.

— *A.D.*

The Authors

Amy Driscoll is director of teaching, learning, and assessment at California State University, Monterey Bay. Previously, she was director of community/university partnerships and professor of education at Portland State University. She has presented extensively at conferences of the American Association for Higher Education and the American Educational Research Association and has published on the topics of assessment of service-learning and the scholarship of service, including articles in the *Michigan Journal of Public Service*, the *Journal of Public Service and Outreach*, *Metropolitan Universities*, and the *Journal of Adult Learning and Higher Education*.

Ernest A. Lynton was Commonwealth Professor and senior associate of the New England Resource Center for Higher Education, at the University of Massachusetts at Boston. He had previously been senior vice president for academic affairs for the University of Massachusetts. He was a longtime advocate for greater attention to professional service, publishing and presenting extensively on that topic. He worked on both *Scholarship Assessed* and *Scholarship Reconsidered* with Ernest Boyer.

In his first book with the American Association for Higher Education, *Making the Case for Professional Service* (1995), Ernest Lynton laid out his central thesis: that the key to elevating the status of professional service was to capture evidence of its "scholarship" for review by peers. The current volume takes the next step, reporting the experiences of faculty and campuses that undertook to make such documentation of service/outreach part of their reward structures and offering guidance to others that would attempt to do so.

Their work on this publication was supported by the W.K. Kellogg Foundation and the New England Resource Center for Higher Education.

CONTENTS

FOREWORD

by R. Eugene Rice

In 1983, Ernest Lynton began writing and speaking about the "crisis of purpose" in the American university. I was particularly struck by his contention that many universities are striving to be what they are not, and "falling short of being what they could be." His special concern was with the disconnection developing between the academic knowledge generated by faculty in the university and the growing needs for applied knowledge in a society increasingly dependent on its citizens' intellectual capital and capacity to learn.

Ernest Lynton led the way in recognizing that in order to reconnect the generating of academic knowledge to the needs of a knowledge-dependent society we would have to broaden our understanding of what counts as scholarly work for faculty and what is rewarded. Ernest was a major contributor to the development of the Carnegie report *Scholarship Reconsidered* and played a key role in launching AAHE's Forum on Faculty Roles & Rewards. He resolutely devoted the latter part of his life and career to one critical aspect of the scholarly role of faculty — professional service, its recognition and reward.

Publication of Lynton's *Making the Case for Professional Service* set forth the dimensions of the debate, began to define key terms, and established an action agenda for us to follow. This guidebook with Amy Driscoll is the next logical step. The professional service and outreach of faculty will never be fully honored as legitimate scholarly work until the hard, pragmatic task of documenting this form of applied academic scholarship is completed. This *Guide* shows faculty and administrators, departments and schools, the way. It is a concrete, practical guide that, with its detailed examples of exemplary work from distinguished universities we all know, breaths vitality into a process that could be blandly mechanical and bureaucratic or abstractly philosophical.

The discussion of the criteria to be used in making judgments about the quality of the scholarly work of faculty found in Chapter Three will be especially helpful to institutions developing fresh guidelines for tenure and promotion. The examples from Michigan State and Indiana University Purdue University Indianapolis demonstrate that we are already moving toward a consensus.

The power of the individual faculty statements found in Chapter Five introduces us to new ways of thinking about theory and practice, research and community development, policy analysis, technical assistance, and faculty involvement in program development and evaluation. This *Guide* will not only help us recognize and document scholarly work of faculty that has for years gone unappreciated; it also can lead to greater appreciation of the special contribution the university makes to society, which continues to be largely unacknowledged and both underdeveloped and underutilized.

One of the purposes of this *Guide* is to contribute to making the professional service of faculty a scholarly activity that is publicly shared, as is the case now with traditional research. Just as Lee Shulman, Pat Hutchings, and others have aspired to make teaching "community property," so Driscoll and Lynton's work is intended to make the professional service and outreach of faculty a matter of public debate and rich intellectual exchange. The faculty statements in this *Guide* demonstrate that this is already happening.

The work of this guidebook is grounded in a fundamental challenge to what Donald Schön referred to as the "institutional epistemology" that has dominated the American university since the opening years of this century. Its overarching assumption is that theory and research have precedence over the applied — practice is regarded as secondary and derivative. *Making the Case for Professional Service* and the current volume press for the righting of this imbalance in the assessment and rewarding of the scholarly work of faculty. What is being called for is a new honoring of practice and the applied. In this endeavor the support of the W.K. Kellogg Foundation is much appreciated. We are also indebted to the New England Resource Center for Higher Education and the leadership of its director, Zelda Gamson.

Amy Driscoll brings to this *Guide* her rich experience at Portland State, where pioneering work in establishing university/community partnerships has been advanced. Her direct, hands-on experience with faculty grappling with the challenge of documenting professional service complemented nicely Ernest Lynton's broader, national effort to "make the case."

A personal word: Ernest Lynton, to whom this guide is dedicated, will be sorely missed. He cared deeply about faculty and their role in the university and society, and was a cherished colleague and friend.

R. Eugene Rice is director of the AAHE Forum on Faculty Roles & Rewards.

ACKNOWLEDGMENTS

This *Guide* represents the thinking of four campuses and numerous individuals therein who participated during the three years of a project to document the scholarship of professional service/outreach. The sixteen faculty who contributed the documentations reproduced in this volume and whose work is the heart of the *Guide* contributed much more than their portfolios. Their tireless reflections and inspired revisions yielded much wisdom for the profession, as higher education struggles to acknowledge and respect a new form of scholarship. We honor them as pioneers in that struggle.

Their colleagues at Indiana University Purdue University Indianapolis, Michigan State University, Portland State University, and the University of Memphis supported their work and provided thoughtful and critical input to their documentation process. At each of the institutions, a key administrator or two mentored the faculty members and at intervals engaged as part of the group in its collaborative thinking. We are grateful to them — Lorilee Sandmann, Ivan Legg, Robert Bringle, Michael Reardon, William Plater, and James Votruba — for their support to the faculty members, for their perspectives, and for their role in the involvement of their campus.

The process of documenting the scholarship of professional service was costly and intensive. We are indebted to the W.K. Kellogg Foundation for funding and recognition and for the encouragement and wisdom of Betty Overton, its director of higher education.

The leadership of the New England Resource Center for Higher Education provided multiple forms of support for the work of this *Guide*. Our colleagues Zelda Gamson, Deborah Hirsch, and Cathy Burack shared their insights, provided a forum, and contributed budgetary and other logistical structures for the project.

We acknowledge the significant contribution of KerryAnn O'Meara, for thoughtful research and synthesis of campus materials and resources to support this *Guide*.

At the American Association for Higher Education, we have been the recipients of consistent encouragement and brilliant support. Its access to faculty and administrators from across the nation has provided a national forum for the thinking and framing of a scholarship of professional service. At AAHE's annual Conferences on Faculty Roles & Rewards, at each session at which we presented our ideas about documentation, attendees enriched the contents of this *Guide*. The leadership of AAHE communicated the value of our process to its membership and continues to inspire them and other followers to think broadly about scholarship and the importance of professional service. The insights of Russell Edgerton (AAHE president 1977-1997, now at the Pew Charitable Trusts) and R. Eugene Rice (director, AAHE Forum on Faculty Roles & Rewards) were influential throughout the documentation and contributed to the potential for changing higher education's reward system with recognition of professional service and outreach. Bry Pollack (AAHE's director of publications) enhanced the manuscript's form and the quality of its presentation.

A special thanks to Carla Lynton, who was our constant friend and listener

ACKNOWLEDGMENTS *continued*

through the long hours of collaboration and difficulties of documentation. She nurtured our spirits and eased the fatigue of writing and revision. She continues to mentor and inspire the work of professional service.

This *Guide* represents the thinking, questions, writing, values, and documentation struggles of more individuals than we can possibly acknowledge. The *Guide* has truly been a collaborative venture — one that provides wisdom, guidelines, and examples for higher education. The hope, and vision, of those who struggled with us is for recognition and rewards to accrue for a new form of scholarship — a scholarship that makes visible to the higher education community the work of faculty who engage in community service and outreach. This *Guide* is a beginning, intended to prompt new struggles at other campuses and to engage a wider audience in the thinking and documentation that began here.

INTRODUCTION: BEYOND MAKING THE CASE FOR PROFESSIONAL SERVICE

As early as 1983, we were writing about the concerns of leaders in higher education over the substantial neglect of institutional outreach and the need to reinforce the "responsibility of the university . . . to be instrumental in analyzing and applying [new] knowledge and in making it rapidly useful to all societal sectors" (Lynton 1983: 53). Acknowledged with that responsibility was the pivotal role of faculty and the need for their involvement in community service or other outreach to be recognized, rewarded, and reconsidered "as parts of a broad spectrum of important scholarly activity" (53).

Fortunately, higher education began to take on that responsibility to society and to consider broadening its conception of scholarly activity to include such outreach. These new notions of scholarship received widespread attention with the publication of Ernest L. Boyer's best-selling *Scholarship Reconsidered* (1990), by the Carnegie Foundation for the Advancement of Teaching. Its publication led directly to the launch in 1991 of AAHE's Forum on Faculty Roles & Rewards, which has been an important venue for discussion of these issues. (For more about AAHE, see **Appendix D**.)

More recently, higher education has given growing attention to the work that faculty do when they become directly involved in societal problems such as social and economic development and the improvement of primary and secondary schools. All sectors, most particularly the universities, have begun to acknowledge their responsibilities to become so engaged. The implication of their institutional response is the engagement of substantial numbers of their faculty members in professional service/outreach.

AAHE's 1995 release of *Making the Case for Professional Service* (Lynton), a monograph advocating institutional outreach by means of faculty professional service, increased the momentum for a number of institutional changes. Across the country, colleges and universities began to revisit and revise promotion and tenure guidelines and hiring practices, and to engage in discussions of mission. Faculty service/outreach traditionally has been touted by almost all colleges and universities as one in a triad of institutional responsibilities: teaching, research, and service. In reality, however, service has been the scholarly stepchild of the three, receiving inadequate attention and even less recognition. *Making the Case* prompted the growth of awareness of the external as well as internal importance of such outreach, and it triggered discussions on many campuses about how to integrate professional service appropriately into systems of faculty roles and rewards.

Beyond Making the Case: Need for a Guide

With the institutional changes prompted by *Making the Case for Professional Service* came a different dilemma and new questions: How do faculty document the scholarship of service/outreach? What evidence demonstrates such scholarship? What criteria should be used to judge that scholarship? With the aim of stimulating thinking, *Making*

1

the Case put forward the argument for a scholarship of service, illustrated by five abbreviated case studies by faculty members who had undertaken professional service activities. But, as institutions began to engage policy changes, many found themselves wishing for explicit guidance and specific examples of documentation.

Making Outreach Visible responds to that paramount need with insights and guidelines for faculty as they document their community work and for institutions as they prepare to review and reward such work. It provides specific guidance in the form of sixteen examples of faculty documentations in a wide range of disciplines. Each was written in a style and format appropriate for submission to peer review on the faculty member's own campus.

This *Guide* is sensitive to the different levels of readiness for change in faculty roles and rewards.

Two major traditions of higher education "make a case" for the protocol suggested by this *Guide,* in that both create a need for documentation of professional service activity and with it a need for guidance and examples. First is the long tradition of the still dominant model of scholarship, that of published research. It is characterized by external evaluation in the form of refereed reviews or the use of external reviewers with expertise in appropriate disciplines. The scholarship of professional service does not fit that paradigm, thus creating a need for guidance and examples so that faculty and administrators in any field can develop the capacity to evaluate individual service contributions. The second tradition is that of service as an individual faculty activity and characterized as "extra" — that is, pursued after meeting responsibilities to teaching and research. Faculty members engaged in professional service typically did so rather quietly and at their own initiative, and certainly didn't consider documenting that aspect of their professional work.

Content and Use of This Guide

Making Outreach Visible is best used in concert with *Making the Case for Professional Service,* because the former builds on the thinking and follows the direction set in the latter. *Making Outreach Visible* is intentionally called a "guide" because it addresses the "how to" issues and needs of faculty and administrators in the context of institutional change.

The major content of this *Guide* comes from the work of faculty and administrators from four campuses: Indiana University Purdue University Indianapolis, Michigan State University, Portland State University, and the University of Memphis. Four provosts (or their representatives) and sixteen faculty members engaged in a three-year project to document the scholarship of service. They debated the issues, explored possible frameworks, and posed pertinent questions about the nature and importance of professional service and its potential for scholarship. The faculty members drafted documentations, which were subjected to repeated review, critique, and revision. For additional feedback, each documentation underwent the peer review process traditional on its author's home campus. In **Chapter Five**, this *Guide* reproduces a major section of those sixteen individual professional service portfolios; other chapters address the principles, guidelines, and insights that emerged from the campuses' documentation struggles. The faculty who participated in the project were truly pioneers, working without a model or tested directions, but as part of a collaborative team comprising other faculty members who shared their strong dedication to service/outreach and supportive administrators. The W.K. Kellogg Foundation funded that intensive and reflective process of developing the faculty documentations and has supported this publication.

The next chapter looks at the process of defining professional service, as a critical starting point for institutional change, and it suggests strategies for individual campuses to arrive at their own definitions of professional service/outreach as a scholarly activity. From there, we provide major "how to" guidance in **Chapter Three**, addressing how to use this *Guide* and its documentation examples; how to prepare a campus for revisioning faculty roles and rewards; the logistics of documentation (content, organization, format), with guidelines for faculty documentation; and how to develop criteria to evaluate such documentation.

Chapter Four provides administrative perspectives on the scholarship of professional service/outreach and insights for the administrative role in the review of that scholarship.

Chapter Five contains the sixteen professional service/outreach portfolio entries.

In **Chapter Six** we reflect briefly on the documentation development process, and what we learned from our work with the faculty and administrators.

This *Guide* is sensitive to the different levels of readiness for change in faculty roles and rewards present across different institutions of higher education. It has been designed to guide the various aspects of the change processes and to support revision of policies and procedures at any stage in those processes. The *Guide* therefore will be helpful for a broad scope of uses:

- A resource in thinking about mission, faculty roles, scholarly agendas, and related institutional decision making.

- Inspiration for a faculty member who expresses interest in undertaking professional service/outreach.

- An orientation aid for new faculty on a campus, offering a broader conception of scholarly activity that includes outreach/service.

- A resource for a faculty member developing a scholarly agenda.

- A guide for development of individual faculty portfolios for review and evaluation.

DEFINING PROFESSIONAL SERVICE/OUTREACH

T o address professional service/outreach as scholarship requires agreement on basic definitions. *Teaching* and *research* are activities universally understood and accepted. By contrast, *service* or *outreach* (usage varies among institutions) is a vague and excessively inclusive term, which has different meanings for different individuals and across different institutional and disciplinary cultures. No widely accepted typology or categorization exists of the kinds of service. To some, service is primarily understood to mean good institutional or professional citizenship. To others, it is active participation in community-based philanthropic activities. We concentrate on service as a professional activity to which professional standards of quality can be applied; such professional service can be a manifestation of scholarship.

What might characterize professional service that qualifies as "scholarly"?

One response was suggested in 1985 by Elman and Smock, who described professional service as work based on the "faculty member's professional expertise" that contributes to the mission of the university (12).

The Elman/Smock definition, with a variety of minor modifications, has become widely accepted. By stressing the individual's professional *expertise,* it excludes a wide range of volunteer work both on and off campus. Insisting that the service contribute to the *mission* similarly excludes faculty activities such as freelance consulting unrelated to the institution's teaching and research.

Many institutions have elaborated on the Elman/Smock definition, most often by making explicit mention of societal needs. For example, under the definition used at the University of Illinois, Urbana-Champaign, professional service activities

- contribute to the public welfare or the common good;
- call upon the faculty member's academic and/or professional expertise; and
- directly address or respond to real-world problems, issues, interests, or concerns. (Farmer and Schomberg 1993: 2)

Typical examples of faculty professional service that meets the criteria include:

- technical assistance and technology transfer;
- policy analysis;
- organizational and community development;
- assistance in program development and evaluation;
- professional development; and
- service-learning activities. (Lynton 1995: 17)

Undertaking a Definition Process

Many in higher education feel a tension associated with the lack of a universally accepted definition of professional service; others prefer the idea of a contextually derived definition, one that fits an institution's individual history, priorities, and circumstances.

Even the best definition leaves grey areas of uncertainty.

We come down on the side of context-specificity, and in the next chapter suggest that an institution address two significant considerations. The first is a definition of professional service that fits the institutional history, priorities, and circumstances. Definitions of professional service generated by others serve as discussion points from which to begin this first process. We urge readers to use **Appendix A** to obtain the materials described there, which contain definitions from other campuses. Those examples will provide a good base for discussion at the departmental, collegiate, or institutional level with the intent of exploring whether any of the examples suit local circumstances or how they might be modified to do so.

The second consideration acknowledges that even the best definition leaves grey areas of uncertainty. Does "professional expertise" mean knowledge of one's formal academic discipline, or can such expertise extend to other fields as well? Are we always talking about *external* activities, or can *on-campus* activities be included; and if they can, under what circumstances? This external/internal issue can be quite thorny, because it raises questions about faculty contributions to their institution or their discipline/profession in serving on campus committees, participating in governance, organizing meetings and other special events, and so on.

Such activities are very important; without them neither academic institutions nor professional associations could function. Yet more and more campuses have come to the realization that such faculty work, however important it might be, typically lacks the intellectual content and other attributes to be "scholarly"; that is, it is good citizenship rather than good scholarship. Of course, there are important exceptions — serving on a task force to revise a core curriculum, for example.

Again, all such matters need to be addressed within the local context. What broad categories of faculty work should be included and what excluded? To what extent do borderline issues need to be resolved in advance, or can they be dealt with ad hoc, as they arise? These questions and others should be part of the process of definition, and decisions about them made according to institutional traditions and culture.

Once an institution reaches initial consensus on definition and nomenclature — subject to review and revision on the basis of the subsequent steps of the process, of course — campus groups can begin to generate and discuss what criteria of excellence they might use to judge this thing they now have defined. **Chapter Three** addresses those next steps in the campus discussions and the processes that must precede and follow the definition decisions.

CHAPTER TWO

Final Comments on Documentation

If professional service/outreach — whatever the details of its definition — is to become an important role for a significant number of faculty members, it must be appropriately recognized and rewarded. In turn, this requires adequate documentation processes so as to make the activity "visible" to academic colleagues and subject to their peer review.

Documentation must mean much more than merely listing an activity or an item in a curriculum vitae. Adequate documentation is a combination of narrative, explanatory, and illustrative material that allows the faculty member's peers to understand his or her purpose and process as well as the outcomes of the professional service activity. Such documentation addresses the whats and hows: It describes the impact the service activity had on the faculty member and the external partner, as well as its impact on colleagues and students.

Making the Case called for a revival of the tradition of professional service, began the definition process, described its potential for scholarship, and suggested criteria for excellence. *Making Outreach Visible* provides the insights, examples, and support that institutions of higher education need in order to follow the direction set by *Making the Case.* Readers are encouraged to use this *Guide* for multiple, campus-appropriate purposes with a commitment to study and reflection on the scholarship of professional service and its documentation.

DOCUMENTATION: GUIDANCE FOR DEVELOPMENT AND REVIEW

This *Guide* is designed to contribute in three ways to the process of reformulating the faculty roles and rewards system to recognize and reward professional service/outreach:

- by providing actual faculty documentation examples, resources, and specific guidance;

- by posing questions and issues for exploration; and

- by encouraging diversity of documentation within a context of common criteria and guidelines.

The *Guide* can serve as a resource early in an institution's reform process, or later when explicit "how to" is needed. Our recommendation is that the institution begin re-visioning its faculty roles and rewards system with a period of intensive study, using specific sections of this *Guide* to spark and guide discussions.

SPECIFIC RECOMMENDATIONS FOR STUDY AND DEVELOPMENT OF DOCUMENTATION

Keeping in mind the three possible applications of the *Guide,* we recommend to institutions a number of processes for studying the issues related to the scholarship of professional service/outreach, revising promotion and tenure guidelines, and restructuring their faculty roles and rewards system. The processes are sensitive to the different levels of readiness for change present across different campuses.

Preparation for Discussion: Building a Knowledge Base

Before a campus engages in a review or revision of its faculty roles and rewards and related policies and procedures, it is important for it to create a shared campus knowledge base — that is, a body of common understandings held by both its faculty and administrators. We suggest that campus representatives (faculty, administrators, members of personnel committees, faculty senators) who will be involved in such a review first become familiar with pertinent literature. Specifically, we recommend three books as starting points:

- *Scholarship Reconsidered,* the seminal Carnegie report by Ernest Boyer, which first drew widespread attention to a broader conception of scholarship.

- *Scholarship Assessed,* Carnegie's follow-up report, which describes common features of all scholarship and suggests a basic set of criteria for judging its quality.

- *Making the Case for Professional Service,* AAHE's companion to the current volume, which lays out our argument for a scholarship of service.

(See **Appendix B** for an annotated list describing these and other useful readings.)

Development of this campus knowledge base will profit from the institution sending teams of faculty and administrators to conferences that offer agendas addressing the kind of changes to which this *Guide* is dedicated. Specifically, the annual conferences of AAHE's Forum on Faculty Roles & Rewards feature many workshops and sessions from which such teams can derive insights and direction. Other valuable conferences and meetings include those of national Campus Compact, the Invisible College, the Association of American Colleges and Universities (AAC&U), and the National Association of State Universities and Land-Grant Colleges (NASULGC). Additional insights and guidance can be gained from materials already developed by other institutions (see **Appendix A**).

Beginning With Inquiry: Defining and Documenting Professional Service

Once a campus has developed this shared knowledge base of service-related issues, we encourage representatives of the pertinent committees, the faculty senate, and the administration to read *Making Outreach Visible* and engage in discussion. Exploratory and reflective, these first discussions begin with the group considering three key questions:

- How do we define professional service at our institution?
- What criteria of scholarly excellence do we expect our faculty's professional service to meet?
- How can professional service be documented such that it is visible and understood by a faculty member's peers?

From there, this *Guide*'s sixteen prototype portfolios can be used sequentially by the group in two different ways. First, the entries can be used as test cases in which the group evaluates the adequacy of the documentation. Second, the portfolios can be used to prompt discussion of how to evaluate the quality of the professional service itself.

Using the Portfolios: Evaluating the Adequacy of the Documentation

The core of this *Guide* consists of sixteen prototype portfolios of professional service by faculty members from a range of fields, from art to veterinary medicine. (See **Chapter Five**.) The service projects described in the portfolios vary widely in external partners, duration, format, and outcomes. Such diversity is to be expected.

For our purposes, that the portfolios are so diverse is highly desirable. It is this very diversity that will prompt readers to analyze and criticize the sixteen examples to arrive at their own conclusions and decisions about the scholarship of professional service and how to document it. We predict discussion of the portfolios will generate a spread of reactions, which can become the grist on the mills of debate in a collegial search for answers to the key questions posed above.

Once the campus representatives have arrived at a tentative definition of quality or a beginning set of criteria, they can test some or all of the portfolios in turn, examining whether each:

- furnishes the information needed to apply the criteria,
- does so in an economical length,
- is organized clearly, and
- is well written.

This "grading" of the prototype portfolios is directed toward the goal of agreement on documentation guidelines to be used at the institution. Here too, the portfolios' diversity of disciplines, type of activity, and style of documentation will lead to lively and fruitful discussion. Different reactions, unexpected issues, and new questions are assets in the process of developing guidelines specific to the institution and suitable to its unique culture.

Using the Portfolios: Evaluating the Quality of the Professional Service

The second use of this *Guide's* sixteen prototype portfolios is a repetition of the process of examining some or all of them, but this time to evaluate the quality of the professional service activity they describe:

- Is the activity outstanding, average, or less than adequate?
- What features make it outstanding, or average, or less than adequate?
- What would improve its quality?
- How could its scholarly nature be strengthened?

Again the group will find that different group members will evaluate differently, and will respond to the questions in a variety of ways. And again, such a spread of reactions is an advantage, as it will trigger substantive and productive discussion of the nature of scholarship and possible measures of its quality. Those discussions can be factored into the campus criteria of excellence, criteria for evaluating the professional service activity, criteria for assessing its scholarship.

Coming to Consensus

Throughout the discussion processes, it is also useful for the group to review examples of materials generated on other campuses (see **Appendix B**). And it is important for group members to stay on task in discussing the portfolios — that is, our observations on various campuses tell us that many group members will automatically focus on evaluating a case, rather than taking it as a prompt for discussions and decisions about the quality of documentation and criteria for scholarship in principle. Finally, their explorations need to be grounded in the particular campus context in order to arrive at decisions and guidelines that reflect the individuality of that institution.

Once there is a campus knowledge base and agreement on definitions, faculty and administrators are ready for the logistics of documentation: appropriate content, format, and organization.

DOCUMENTATION: CONTENT, ORGANIZATION, AND GUIDELINES

Much of the learning captured in this *Guide* comes from the exploratory process of documentation undertaken by the faculty participants whose portfolios appear in **Chapter Five**. Lessons from their repeated revisions and input from multiple reviewers are synthesized below.

Content

One of the major insights the project's faculty members gained from their exploratory process was that to capture the major components of their service activity in a portfolio they needed to provide a substantial personal narrative. For a portfolio's readers and reviewers to understand the nature of the work — appropriateness and clarity of the goals and methods chosen, significance of any impact or outcomes, quality of any collaboration and reflection — requires a familiarity with the faculty member's thinking. That thinking by faculty about choices, decisions, and evaluation is best expressed in a sufficiently detailed narrative.

In a service portfolio, the narrative is accompanied by examples of outcomes, as well as materials illustrating the service methodology, such as a copy of any contract or agreement with the community partner, copies of any survey instruments or questionnaires used, written documentation of meetings, and so on. The project's faculty generated an extensive list of possible support evidence, with attention to alternative forms of scholarship (see **Appendix C**).

Once a set of criteria for faculty professional service at the institution has been formulated, it will become clear what information is needed in order to apply them. Thus, content follows in a fairly direct way from criteria. The other major determinant of content is the project or work itself. That professional service activities vary will naturally lead to varied content categories. Details of criteria also will vary from campus to campus, but we find underlying similarities and consistencies, which point to principal elements of documentation content. Those common content elements or topics clearly emerged in the work of the sixteen faculty in our project:

- A basic description of the activity itself, to include purpose, intended goals, participants, and stakeholders.
- Context for the activity, to include setting, available resources, constraints of resources and/or time, and political considerations.
- The individual faculty member's expertise and prior experience.
- Connection of the current activity to the faculty member's future and past scholarly agendas.
- Choice of goals and methods, with a literature base and working hypothesis directing those choices.
- Evolution of the activity, to include ongoing monitoring, reflection, adaptations, and adjustments.
- Outcomes and impact on various stakeholders, including what the faculty member learned.
- Mode of dissemination to the profession or discipline.

This list is intended to provide an adequate first approximation to be discussed, revised, and refined on each campus according to local preferences.

Organization and Format

The best documentation is one that most effectively communicates and "makes visible" the scholarly activity of professional service. What works "best" will vary depending on the nature of the service activities. The sixteen prototype portfolios in this *Guide* illustrate such diversity of organization and format.

A number of campuses have moved in the direction of asking their faculty to organize documentation according to the institutional criteria to be met. Michigan State University is an example of this approach, suggesting that faculty portfolios be arranged according to four basic points of excellence (see Table 2 on page 19). Other campuses, Portland State University, for example, have suggested that faculty use the criteria found in *Scholarship Assessed,* which the university has reprinted in its promotion and tenure guidelines. In contrast, other institutions provide no guidance to their faculty regarding portfolio organization. Overall, too few higher education institutions have worked out their policies and procedures in adequate detail for us to draw any conclusions about general organizational trends.

As the faculty participants in our project struggled to organize their material into clear and convincing documentation of their professional service, a framework emerged from their discussions and experimentation. As before, we would suggest that framework (see **Figures 1-4** on the next two pages) only as a starting point for campus discussions, as one set of possibilities, not as an intact organizational structure to be applied wholesale. Our faculty participants found that some elements of the framework were very appropriate and helpful to their documentations, and some were able to use it in its entirety. The variation in professional service activities makes it very difficult to have a single, universal framework. What is important instead is that each campus provide guidance to its faculty about institutional expectations of content and that it suggest an organizational scheme.

We make the same recommendation regarding format. In the Kellogg project, we saw two trends emerge from the work of the faculty participants. In one format they used, the examples of evidence were integrated within the narrative (in **Chapter 5** see the Education documentation by Rosaen); another format placed all of the evidence and supporting material at the end of the narrative (see the Engineering portfolio by Rad). That same variation occurred when the faculty struggled to include reflections in their documentation. Some found that it worked well to include mini-reflections after each section (see the Psychology documentation by Ross), while others reflected more broadly at the beginning and/or end of their narrative (see History by Schechter).

The important question is, once again: Which format contributes clarity and convinces the reader? We believe that the choice of format should be left to the faculty member preparing the documentation.

> The best documentation is one that most effectively communicates and "makes visible" the scholarly activity of professional service.

FIGURE 1

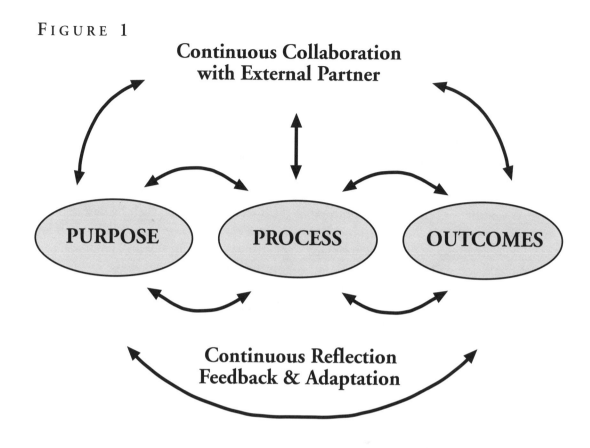

FIGURE 2

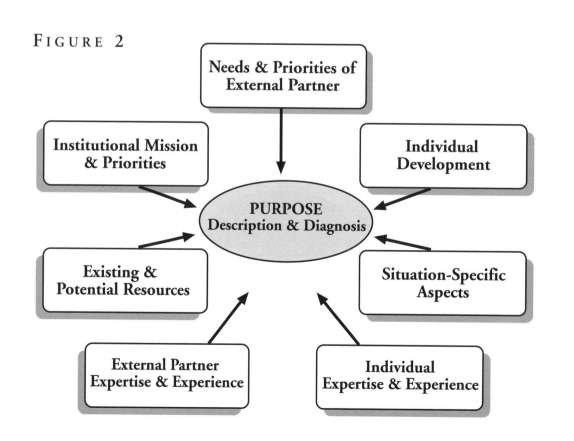

FIGURE 3

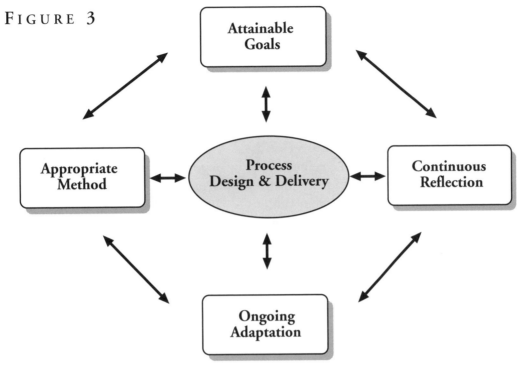

FIGURE 4

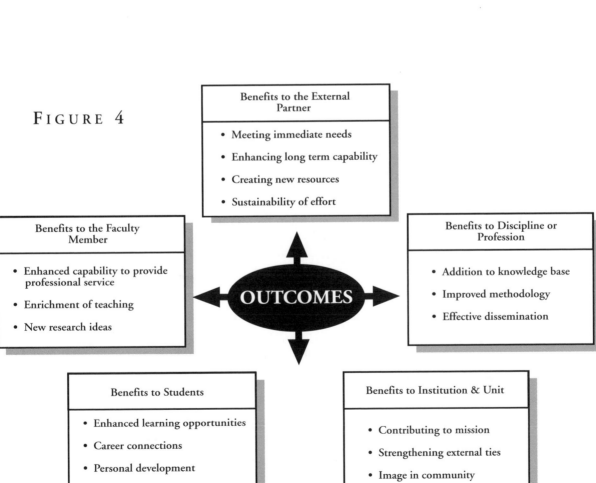

Guidelines

One of the most valuable contributions made by the Kellogg project participants, both faculty and administrators, was the development of a set of **Guidelines for Documenting Professional Service/Outreach.** Those guidelines emerged from the group's struggles, their intense discussions, their repeated revisions, and from their shared decision making. Users of this *Guide* will find them to be of great help in their own documentation efforts. The guidelines are by no means a final set; instead, they are a foundation for the ongoing institutional learning process to which this publication invites readers. We urge you on your campus to contribute any insights you generate from your own discussions and decision making.

GUIDELINES FOR DOCUMENTING PROFESSIONAL SERVICE/OUTREACH

In addition to the ideas presented in this chapter about content, organization, and format . . .

- Consider documentation as an ongoing process, rather than a summary of the outcomes of a service/outreach activity.

- Begin documentation by considering your audience and the purpose of the information.

- Focus on documenting your individual contribution, rather than documenting the project.

- Work to achieve a balance of focus between process and impact.

- Wherever applicable, clarify the intellectual question or working hypothesis that guided your work.

- When presenting community impact, discuss the significance of the impact and how it was evaluated.

- Make a clear distinction between your individual faculty role and that of others in any collaboration.

- Locate the service/outreach activity in a context (campus mission, departmental priorities, national trends).

- Show your individual faculty expertise and experience as inputs.

- Be selective about what information to include; ask yourself whether the information helps make the case for scholarship.

- Show the professional service/outreach activity as a platform for future work.

- Strike a balance between brevity and completeness.

- Keep your reflection and self-assessment focused on process and outcomes.

- When possible, view documentation as an instructive tool or one with which to socialize others about professional service/outreach.

BEYOND THE GUIDELINES: FINAL RECOMMENDATIONS

The faculty participants in our project summarized their final insights in two important recommendations. The first was directed to faculty from the administrator's perspective:

- Develop both a short version of your documentation (almost an abstract) and a longer version including narrative and reflection.

This idea came in response to the dilemma of satisfying different audiences — the initial review committee who insist on detailed documentation versus a final committee or administrator reviewer who cannot realistically work with large numbers of lengthy documentations. (**Chapter Four**, which provides an administrative perspective, further addresses issues of length and detail.)

The second recommendation was from the faculty participants and related to the value of collective critique:

- Make documentation a continuing process, with ongoing feedback from colleagues.

They pointed to the mutual learning that takes place in collaborative or collective critique, and urged institutions to provide such collaborative structures to support faculty documentation efforts.

Before making final decisions about the content of documentation, and even about the format or organization for making the scholarship of service visible, it is essential for an institution and its faculty to know what criteria will be applied to the work. We address this question of standards and criteria next.

CRITERIA FOR SCHOLARSHIP OF PROFESSIONAL SERVICE

In order to decide what the documentation should contain, and what aspects of the faculty member's work that documentation should display and make visible and understandable, it is essential to know what criteria of quality, what standards of excellence, should be applied to the work. What is it that makes professional service a scholarly activity? What are the criteria by which one is able to judge whether a given outreach activity is outstanding or merely routine? creative or merely repetitive?

As always, these questions need to be answered at each institution through inquiry and reflection, with attention to local tradition, circumstances, and goals. We recommend that each department, each school or college, or each promotion and tenure committee formulate its own responses to the question of criteria.

Developing Criteria: How to Begin?

Fortunately, there is no need for each campus to start from scratch. In recent years a substantial consensus has emerged from a great deal of work and discussion as to the nature of scholarship. The annotated bibliography in this *Guide* (see **Appendix B**) lists a number of pertinent publications. Those publications emphasize the inclusive nature of scholarship — scholarship that is not limited to traditional research. They also reflect the thinking that characterizes the sixteen documentation examples in this *Guide*: that scholarship is manifested in the quality of the process of the activity as much as it is in the outcomes. In professional service — as in teaching and research — the documentation must explain the impact of the activity.

A central question in the evaluation of professional service/outreach is the scholarly content of the activity. *Making the Case for Professional Service* identifies creativity as the essential and perhaps even defining characteristic of scholarship. As stated there, scholarship is

> the antithesis of rote and routine. . . . Scholarly work is not carrying out a recurring task according to a prescribed protocol, applying standard methodologies. What unifies the activities of a scholar, whether engaged in teaching, research, or professional service, is an approach to each task as a novel situation, a voyage of exploration into the partially unknown. (Lynton 1995: 25)

This understanding of the nature of scholarship leads directly to the kind of criteria of excellence that can be applied. Once again, we urge each institution to discuss and develop criteria in terms that can be widely accepted throughout the campus. That reflection and discussion can be prompted using examples from other campuses; comparing and contrasting them is a good first step.

Examples of Measures of Quality: Criteria Possibilities

Making the Case for Professional Service suggested the following set of measures to be applied to faculty professional service activity, and indeed to all forms of scholarship:

- depth of the expertise and preparation;
- appropriateness of chosen goals and methods;
- effectiveness of communication;
- quality of reflection;
- impact; and
- originality and innovation. (Lynton 1995: 49)

More recently, *Scholarship Assessed* recommended six criteria that can be applied to the evaluation of all scholarship:

- clear goals;
- adequate preparation;
- appropriate methods;
- significant results;
- effective presentation; and
- reflective critique. (Glassick et al. 1997: 23)

A growing number of universities have addressed the assessment of professional service, and several have completed or are in the process of revising their faculty handbooks and promotion and tenure guidelines to accommodate such evaluation. **Tables 1 and 2** display examples from two institutions with contextually developed criteria.

TABLE 1

Criteria for Scholarship From Indiana University Purdue University Indianapolis

1. IMPACT to include effectiveness, significance to recipients, significance to university, and professional development of faculty;

2. INTELLECTUAL WORK to include command of expertise and innovative, effective, and ethical solutions;

3. SUSTAINING CONTRIBUTION to include work that is developmentally more complex, and that provides leadership in the field;

4. COMMUNICATION including professional, and multiple and diverse modes; and

5. INTEGRATION with teaching and research.

SOURCE: *Report From the IUPUI Task Force on Service,* September 17, 1996. Indianapolis, IN: Indiana University Purdue University Indianapolis.

TABLE 2

"Points of Distinction" Criteria From Michigan State University

1. SIGNIFICANCE
   To what extent does the outreach initiative address issues that are important to the public, specific stakeholders, and the scholarly community?

2. CONTEXT
   To what extent is the outreach effort consistent with the mission of the university and unit, the needs of the stakeholders, and the available and appropriate expertise, methodology, and resources?

3. SCHOLARSHIP
   To what extent is the outreach activity shaped by knowledge that is current, cross-disciplinary, and appropriate to the issues? To what extent does the work promote the generation, transmission, application, and utilization of knowledge?

4. IMPACT (EXTERNAL AND INTERNAL)
   To what extent does the outreach effort benefit and affect the issue, community, or individuals, and the university?

SOURCE: "Points of Distinction: Planning and Evaluating Quality Outreach," 1996. East Lansing, MI: Michigan State University.

Common Features

We could cite a number of other lists of criteria, but the examples above should suffice to draw some general inferences here. At first reading there appear to be substantial differences among the examples; in fact a more careful review reveals considerable similarities and overlap. In some way, all of the criteria sets make reference to the following:

- expertise of the faculty member;
- adequacy of resources;
- appropriateness of goals and methods;
- importance of the process; and
- multiple impacts, including explicit or implicit mention of innovation and the generation of new knowledge.

The criteria in **Tables 1 and 2** reflect the particular priorities and values of their respective institutions. Their differences underscore the importance of individual campuses designing their own criteria with their unique language and priorities. We encourage readers to procure the campus materials described in **Appendix A** and to gather additional examples from nearby or like institutions.

Once again, we urge readers to initiate substantive discussions on their campus to begin the process of generating an appropriate set of criteria with which to evaluate the scholarship of professional service/outreach. Further, we encourage that discussion be informed by a study of examples and the literature, with a focus on questions such as these:

- To what extent should the criteria of excellence our institution applies to professional service be the same as or similar to the criteria it uses to evaluate teaching? research?
- In what ways should the sets of criteria differ?
- What criteria should we consider to be most important when we assess a faculty member's professional service activities?
- In how much detail should we formulate the criteria?

Such a reflective process will yield a set of criteria that are sound and, at the same time, reflect the particular priorities, traditions, and mission of its campus. The process is well worth the time commitment implied by the recommendations described in this chapter. At the University of Memphis, administrators and faculty have dedicated more than three years to the prescribed study and discussion process. We encourage that level of commitment for institutions initiating or contemplating change in their faculty rewards system.

ISSUES FROM AN ADMINISTRATIVE PERSPECTIVE[1]

T he lack of tradition and models for reviewing and evaluating professional service/outreach scholarship leaves administrators on uncertain ground for their role in the decision-making processes of promotion and tenure. At the same time, administrators in higher education have the potential to increase the scope and impact of the service and outreach efforts of their faculty by acknowledging and addressing the issues that currently make their administrative role in those contexts so precarious. In this chapter we intend to begin to identify those issues and concerns, and to make initial recommendations for addressing them.

ISSUES OF REVIEW AND EVALUATION

From an administrative perspective, the major issues to be addressed in the review and evaluation of the scholarship of professional service/outreach are:

1. The need for standards, expectations, and/or criteria with which the documentation portfolios can be assessed.

2. The need for resources to support institutional approaches to the review process.

3. The need for clarity with respect to faculty time commitments to service/outreach.

4. The need for alternative modes of dissemination (publication, presentation, etc.) of the scholarship of professional service/outreach.

5. The need for sophisticated understanding of the nature of service and outreach work and the scholarship that emerges from such efforts.

For some of these issues, what's needed is the same kind of ongoing and intense discussion and experimentation that has been encouraged throughout this *Guide*. The issues only further confirm the importance of institutional study, reflection, and decision making. For other of these issues, the potential exists for resolution on a national level, with supportive implications for individual institutions. Then some of these issues can be easily addressed on the individual faculty or institution level. For most, however, resolution will come only through contextually appropriate responses by individual institutions to their unique cultures.

Issue 1: Standards, Expectations, and/or Criteria at the Institutional Level

A consistent theme of this *Guide* has been a call to describe and establish standards or explicit expectations against which individual outreach/service achievements can be measured. That process begins with a mission or vision statement that not only identi-

---

1. This chapter represents the collaborative thinking of administrators Robert Bringle (IUPUI), Robert Church (Michigan State), Michael Reardon (Portland), Lorilee Sandmann (Michigan State), and Ivan Legg (Memphis).

fies community service/outreach as a priority but also goes on to describe kinds and targets of outreach that are valued. This issue is complicated by the question of locus of control — that is, whether the mission is to reflect the values of the institution, the school or college, the department, or the individual unit. Typically, traditional scholarship (research) is viewed in the context of a discipline and assessed according to departmental criteria, often influenced by standards of that discipline. The scholarships of teaching and service/outreach more often are viewed in the context of an institutional mission, but only occasionally in light of a departmental mission. That the scholarship of service/outreach does not as yet have a tradition means we must consider all levels as we explore the review process for it.

This issue is complicated by the question of locus of control.

Recommendations. The alignment of mission, priorities, and expectations may have to occur at multiple levels, with careful checks for contradictory messages. While that alignment process may be a labor- and time-intensive one, the resulting clarification and consensus will provide consistency for faculty decisions about their scholarly agendas and for a wide range of decisions about resources across campus. From there, it will be possible for institutions to craft a set of criteria to guide individual faculty documentation efforts and to inform the work of reviewers and evaluators of that documentation.

When mission statements are specific and descriptive about the kinds or targets of outreach/service, the development of criteria will be easier. For example, knowing whether a department emphasizes outreach to industrial partners or to K-12 students will inform criteria, but it also will support reviewers in making judgments about a faculty member's service contributions to the departmental mission. When mission statements are vague or ill-defined, the locus of control issue emerges to haunt the review and evaluation process. An individual faculty member who submits her documentation already anxious about how it will be reviewed faces unnecessary stress when the possibility exists for divergent interpretations of how her work fits within the mission of university or department. Promotion and tenure, which is a hybrid of faculty and administrative review, is a practice complicated by diffusion of responsibility — chief academic officers contend that faculty control the process, and faculty counter that administrators set the agenda of what is valued and rewarded.

Thus, a campus that dedicates its resources and time to study and decision making for consistency in mission, priorities, and criteria at all critical levels for the scholarship of service/outreach provides secure footing for the individual documentation process as well as for multiple levels of administrative review and evaluation. Such institutional and departmental clarity and reflection bring with them the additional benefits of the cohesiveness and energy that come with agreement on direction and assignment. For administrators, those payoffs may be well worth the time they might give to discussions that are the precursors of decision making.

Issue 2: Resources and Institutional Approaches

Admittedly, portfolios and the kind of documentation encouraged by this *Guide* can be an expensive form of assessment. But for portfolios to have a significant effect, administrators should not be put off by the apparent high cost of using such documentation as developmental and evaluative tools for faculty.

One factor in the expense is the length and detail of the documentation to be reviewed. The documentation examples provided in this *Guide* are not the kind of evidence that committees are accustomed to reviewing, and their bulk does not allow the review process to work as efficiently as that for the scholarship of research. At the same time, if the scholarship of service is to be reviewed and rewarded, institutions must ensure that a faculty member's departmental colleagues as well as administrators have the resources (and preparation) they need in order to spend the time and energy that thoughtful review requires.

At first glance, the review and evaluation of professional service/outreach scholarship looks much more costly than that of traditional scholarship. However, the referee process through which scholarly manuscripts are reviewed and evaluated, often with multiple levels of critique and revision, carries a high cost too. We just don't often acknowledge the expense of that review system — one that is usually supported by institutions of higher education. So perhaps assessment of professional service is not so different or so expensive. The challenge is how and where to direct resources for the review of professional service scholarship to yield an evaluation system as robust and valid as the one we have traditionally used for research scholarship.

> One factor in the expense is the length and detail of the documentation.

Recommendations. One recommendation here is to establish a national system of peer review for the scholarship of professional service/outreach — a proposal for which is being developed. While such a resource would not absolve individual institutions from their responsibility in the review process, it would offer the potential for excellent guidance and models for campus-based work.

A second recommendation is for workshops and other venues in which to prepare faculty members and administrators for their roles in the review process. Michigan State University has held a series of leadership development meetings targeted to such preparation for department chairs. Sessions also have begun to be available on a national level at conferences such as AAHE's annual Conference on Faculty Roles & Rewards and at individual institutions. The Center for Academic Excellence at Portland State University and the Office of Faculty Development at Indiana University Purdue University Indianapolis have each held mock deliberations of promotion and tenure committees. At these events, faculty and administrators have used cases of the scholarship of service and the documentation examples provided in this *Guide* to explore areas of uncertainty, identify gaps, and affirm the strengths of those examples for the review process. Their deliberations make public the existence of a review process for professional service/outreach, even as they prepare their participants for future responsibilities as actual committee members.

A final recommendation emerges from the possibility of layering the evaluation process. That is, the major review work could be conducted at the departmental level and/or through external review; from there, the department could forward to the next level of review an abstract of the documentation, with the conclusions of the peer and/or external review succinctly represented. Such a layered process already exists at many institutions for the review of other forms of scholarship, so a smooth transition for the review of professional service/outreach scholarship is possible.

Issue 3: Clarity of Faculty Time Commitments

In order for reviewers to make informed judgments about the scholarship of professional service/outreach, they must have an accurate perception of the faculty member's time commitment to the service work or project. Administrators at the unit level must be explicit about their expectations for how faculty members should divide their time between research, teaching, and outreach/service, and so must the individual faculty member be explicit in the description of his outreach work.

This issue at first sounds quite simple to address. However, in many cases it is often difficult to draw a precise division between research and outreach scholarship, or between outreach and teaching. Many of the faculty whose documentations appear in this *Guide* deliberately integrated several aspects of their faculty responsibilities in their service work, but we also urged them to be clear about describing their time investments.

Recommendations. We have begun to address this issue by urging both administrators and individual faculty members to be specific and clear about faculty time commitments to professional service/outreach. When outreach activities have been funded, also providing information about what resources were available assists reviewers of the portfolio by providing more detail to the context description.

Issue 4: Alternative Channels of Dissemination

The long-term tradition of research scholarship being measured by number of publications and quality of journals poses a challenge for review of the scholarship of professional service/outreach. Initially, reviewers of service scholarship quite possibly will do so with a focus on traditional outcomes — number and quality of publications, amount of financial support awarded to the individual faculty member or academic unit for the scholarly work. And as a significant number of the Kellogg project faculty demonstrate in their documentations in **Chapter Five**, those kind of outcomes are appropriate and effective measures for some forms of professional service/outreach.

The challenge for higher education is, however, to create a broad range of accepted dissemination modes. Within that challenge is an agenda for higher education to make its faculty expertise more widely and rapidly available to the society that supports it. Meeting that challenge calls for creativity and initiative on the part of administrators and faculty and their professional disciplines to create and promote alternative forms of scholarship dissemination. We find it encouraging that several discipline-specific professional associations have begun to legitimize the scholarship of service/outreach in both their journals and national conferences.

Recommendations. As noted, a likely direction in the early development of alternative forms of dissemination is through professional associations. AAHE senior associate Edward Zlotkowski (1998) has urged faculty and administrators to lobby their disciplinary associations to make the scholarship of service one of their publishing and conference priorities. His work on AAHE's eighteen-volume *Series on Service-Learning in the Disciplines* provides models of service and outreach scholarship that have already achieved both national visibility and respect. Individual faculty and institutions can provide their support to such projects to advance alternative channels of publication and other dissemination.

Another channel we urge individual faculty members to explore is community dissemination, as have the sixteen faculty members whose documentations appear in this *Guide.* Faculty doing so will need the support and guidance of their peers and administrators. At the institutions in the Kellogg project, insights about appropriate community publication focused on scholarship documentations that went beyond reportage. Participating faculty were urged to seek publication or other dissemination forms that both demonstrated outcomes and provided evaluative commentary about the effectiveness or success of the service/outreach. Such forms need to be developed and demonstrated both locally and nationally.

Issue 5: New Understandings of Service and Its Scholarship

Within this issue is yet another opportunity for leadership by higher education's administrators. Professional service/outreach and related scholarship possess distinctive qualities that differ enormously from the work and documentation of traditional research scholarship. Those differences are only just beginning to be identified and named through the work of the Kellogg project faculty. As those characteristics emerge, however, it will be important for institutions to explore and respect them.

One distinction noticeable in many of the professional service/outreach scholarship examples is the collaborative nature of the work. Evaluation of community-based scholarship is complicated by teamwork. When others are involved in the planning and execution of a faculty member's community activity, it can be difficult to disentangle their respective contributions. Faculty in the Kellogg project struggled to highlight their individual role and contributions while describing the collaborative context in which they worked.

A second distinction of community-based scholarship is that its documentation is heavily process-descriptive, in contrast to the traditional reporting of research. Some of the documentations in this *Guide* are candid about reporting failures, mistakes, and related lessons learned as part of the scholarly process. In research scholarship we seldom hear of failed pilot studies, problems of data analysis, or technical problems of data collection. But the documentation of professional service/outreach relies heavily on process description, because process remains one of the most salient accomplishments of significant community engagement.

A third distinction of the documentation of outreach scholarship is an emphasis on human interactions. Those interactions are integral to and possibly the purpose of outreach scholarship, making such emphasis entirely appropriate. The scholarship of service describes interactions between the academy and the "real world." How effective an individual faculty member's service work is depends greatly on her ability to participate with and empower people with different needs, skills, and values. The documentation examples in this *Guide* highlight scholarly learning and personal growth around issues of diversity, communication, and collaboration.

The administrative challenge here is to understand and reward the distinctiveness of the work and scholarship of professional service/outreach. The next step for administrators is to help further that same understanding and recognition among the faculty and the professions.

Recommendations. One strategy is to use documentations such as those found in this *Guide* for formative evaluation of faculty. An ongoing assessment process would take advantage of the distinctiveness of the scholarship of service/outreach. Its emphasis on collaboration, human interaction, and personal learning has potential for administrative engagement with faculty in an assessment approach that yields guidance and direction.

A second recommendation is for faculty to emphasize and present a clear theoretical rationale for their scholarly documentation. Such a rationale, especially for community work that is ongoing and developmental, can provide administrators and other reviewers a basis for understanding the portfolio's descriptions of decisions, collaborations, adaptations/adjustments, and intended/unanticipated outcomes. Properly placed in a theoretical context, descriptions of process can take on new meanings. Articulating a theoretical base for community work assists faculty in making a case that their efforts transcend the idiosyncratic qualities of an individual project or activities and, in fact, make contributions to the knowledge base.

In Sum

The issues described in this chapter represent a first step in the exploration of administrative perspectives on the scholarship of professional service/outreach. As individual institutions and higher education generally seek a renewed commitment to engagement with community, additional issues, questions, and concerns will emerge. Probing new issues and raising more questions will promote the understanding and acceptance that is sought by those faculty members who blend their expertise with that of communities outside of the academy.

This initial look at issues from an administrative perspective directs academic leaders to create a climate of serious discussion and decision making, as well as to dedicate resources to support and expand the scholarship of professional service/outreach. A critical first step is understanding and communicating the nature and benefits of community outreach. Many of the recommendations made in this chapter will engage institutions of higher education in reflection that can both enhance fulfillment of their missions and enrich professional development of their members.

CHAPTER FIVE

Sixteen Prototype Service/Outreach Portfolios

Anthropology

"Challenges to Community Building in Memphis — Hearing New Voices and Charting New Paths for Urban Development"
Stan Hyland, Anthropology, The University of Memphis

Art

"Creating Identity"
Susan Agre-Kippenhan, Art, Portland State University

Biology

"A Professional Development Workshop for High School Biology Teachers"
Florence Juillerat, Biology, Indiana University Purdue University Indianapolis

Business

"Faculty Development in International Business"
Ben L. Kedia, International Business, The University of Memphis

Education

"The 'Swampy Lowlands' or Academic 'High Grounds': Where Is the Scholarship in New Faculty Roles?"
Dannelle D. Stevens, Education, Portland State University

"Tapping Into Teachers' Dedication: The Tropical Rain Forest Field Experience"
Michael R. Cohen, Education, Indiana University Purdue University Indianapolis

"Enhancing Teacher and Student Learning Through Collaborative Inquiry"
Cheryl L. Rosaen, Teacher Education, Michigan State University

Engineering

"Earthquake Loss Estimation and Mitigation in Portland, Oregon: A Methodology for Estimating Earthquake Losses, and Retrofit Prioritization of Buildings"
Franz Rad, Civil Engineering, Portland State University

History

"Collaborations: The Portland YWCA and Women's History, 1901-2001"
Patricia A. Schechter, History, Portland State University

Landscape Architecture

"Bringing Scholarship to the Public: The Academic Practitioner"
Warren J. Rauhe, Landscape Architecture, Michigan State University

Nursing

"The Broadway Shalom Wellness Center: Reaching Traditionally Difficult-to-Access Inner City Population"
Sandy C. Burgener, Nursing, Indiana University

Political Science

"Free the Children: Testing the Capacity and Methods for Locally Based Efforts to Address Poverty"
David N. Cox, Political Science, The University of Memphis

Psychology/Research

"Evaluation of School Restructuring"
Steven M. Ross, Counseling, Educational Psychology, and Research, The University of Memphis

"Reforming the Process of Change"
Pennie G. Foster-Fishman, Psychology, Michigan State University

Public Affairs

"Delinquent Youths and Their Futures: Can Outreach on the Part of the University Make a Difference?"
G. Roger Jarjoura, Public and Environmental Affairs, Indiana University Purdue University Indianapolis

Veterinary Science

"Professional Development for Michigan Veterinarians"
James W. Lloyd, Large Animal Clinical Science and Agricultural Economics, Michigan State University

Challenges to Community Building in Memphis-Hearing New Voices and Charting New Paths for Urban Development

Stan Hyland
Co-Director, Center for Urban Research and Extension & Associate Professor
Department of Anthropology, The University of Memphis, Memphis, TN 38152
December 26, 1997

I. Statement of The Societal & Intellectual Framework of the Outreach

In the past decade urban scholars have begun to recognize and document that all cities are unique in their blend of history, heritage, demographics, wealth, and way of doing business. The city of Memphis represents a unique blend of a traditional Southern city with contrasting segments of heritage, modernization and urban poverty. Memphis also finds itself in social, political and economic change. Hundreds of community-based groups--e.g. neighborhood associations, block clubs, ethnic groups, and tenants' associations-- have emerged and are struggling to become more engaged in local governance and self-determination. The dominant political tradition in Memphis, Southern Progressivism, has historically viewed grassroots efforts as counterproductive to their attempts at modernization and economic growth.

Many traditional Mid-South institutions and agencies have found themselves frustrated with the delivery of their programs. These agencies operated according to formal, corporate principles, and found their interaction with neighborhood groups problematic. Neighborhood associations, in contrast, were much looser organizations. To the traditionalists the way neighborhood associations conducted business seemed opportunistic and sometimes circular; they would spend inordinate amounts of time on emotional and seemingly personal issues.

1

II. Purpose of the Outreach -- Integrating Discovery, Application, and Teaching

As an urban anthropologist engaged in studying Memphis' social and cultural landscape over a fifteen-year period, I have discussed with former students how we could address the issue of better understanding community-based organizations, and how they perceived themselves as contributing to the quality of life in Memphis.

Since 1976, my students, former students and I have been engaged in a long-term program to document the identity, functions, and goals of the city's community-based organizations. **Our goal was to describe that, in fact, neighborhood associations, like the neighborhoods they represented, were all different, and could best be understood when compared to a family dynamic, rather than a corporate model of behavior**. Each neighborhood association operated according to its own notion of how best to fulfill its unique vision. There was no set standard that governed how the associations were formed or how they conducted business. If agencies understood that concept the friction between the associations and local agencies could be replaced with a partnership approach, and the agencies' outreach programs could possibly become more effective.

In 1993 I secured funding from The United Way of the Mid-South for a pilot project to document the efforts of a number of community-based organizations. **Our goal was to re-orient traditional Mid-South agencies and organizations so that they would be able to redesign their programs, retrain their staff, and engage in collaborative efforts**. Equally important to the goal was to formulate a plan to integrate the documentation efforts into my teaching. In turn this effort would enable university students to more effectively engage in future community building collaborative efforts.

III. An Anthropological Approach to Outreach & Community Building

The hallmark of research for the anthropologist is participant observation, that is-- going into the "field" and living with and observing the customs of the residents. Traditionally the anthropologist felt relatively detached and hence "objective" about field research. The post World War II period saw a challenge to this intellectual tradition through the "action anthropology" of Sol Tax and his students at the University of Chicago. The action anthropologists sought to understand the values and traditions of the Fox and to simultaneously engage in collaborative efforts with the Fox while improving living conditions. Subsequently my mentor, Demitri Shimkin at the University of Illinois, built upon action anthropology in a series of health and economic projects aimed at improving the conditions of African-Americans in the poverty-stricken Mississippi Delta of the 1970's.

That intellectual tradition inspired me to develop an outreach project that would change the way that traditional institutions and agencies did business with marginalized, community-based organizations, through an ongoing process of faculty and student involvement in the Mid-South. My work was directed to four major outcomes:

1. A knowledge base of community-based initiatives that would be useful to ongoing and future efforts;
2. A plan for this knowledge base to be built upon by others committed to to community building in the Mid-South;
3. A plan for dissemination of the writings; and
4. A method of conducting the project that would involve a diverse group of students. (Copy of the Proposal - Appendix A.)

In 1993 The Venture Fund of the United Way of the Mid-South provided $19,930 principally for stipends for graduate students and materials, and challenged The University of Memphis to provide a match showing their level of commitment to the project. The Department of Anthropology responded with a one course reduction in my teaching load (a point that later proved to be irrelevant), as well as matching monies for graduate assistants and space.

IV. The Design Process - Linking Research, Teaching and Community Building

The first step in executing the program was to integrate the project into the teaching mission of the Department of Anthropology. Therefore I created a new special topics course called Neighborhood Development and Poverty. (See Appendix B - Course Syllabus.) The introduction of the new course generated a series of discussions at the department and college level about the kind of research and outreach we were proposing, and the implicit commitments we would be making to sustain these efforts.

The design of the course provided a theoretical framework that placed the students' documentation projects of community-based organizations within a national context of historic and current political and economic policies. The course provided an opportunity to invite academic scholars and community leaders to present and discuss their perspectives about the nature of community building with the students. Finally, the course enabled me to integrate my own past research, expand my theoretical and methodological interests, and involve students in a new learning venue.

A second step involved my compilation of previous local efforts at the documentation of community-based initiatives. I found that most of the materials were in what some urban scholars call "the gray area" - non scholarly journals and books. (Appendix C - List of References). In addition to the "gray" material, I found that local historians, novelists, and journalists had provided a rich description of the history of local struggles related to race, class, and gender.

Unfortunately the localized struggles at the neighborhood level were largely ignored or described as trivial in significance. (Appendix D - List of References.) I also reviewed the literature on community-based initiatives in other cities and their linkage to national policy. This search revealed a wealth of information from a variety of other disciplines including urban and regional planning, social work, public administration, political science, sociology, economics, and community psychology. (Appendix E - List.)

IV B. Early Reflections on Critical Issues in the Project Design

The major theoretical issues that emerged from the literature focused on two major questions. The first was access to power by community-based groups and the nature of empowerment at the grassroots. The second question dealt with how best to capture the voice of community activists.

Equally important was the discussion of an appropriate methodology to collect/document the stories of community-based initiatives. These issues centered around the following concerns:

1. Using an approach that would capture the language of the community-based organizations in a holistic fashion that would examine the complex social, political, economic, and heritage interrlationships;
2. Providing the interviewed leaders with an opportunity to review the writeup of the case studies.

IV C. The Design Process Continued - Recruitment and Outreach

Recruitment of Students

A third step in the process was the recruitment of students for the program/course. Instead of relying solely on open enrollment, I targeted a portion of the project's budget to provide four course scholarships for students outside of The University of Memphis. I contacted

5

the faculty at LeMoyne Owen College (a historically black college in South Memphis) and Shelby State Community College to each recruit two students who were interested in neighborhood development and poverty to participate in the course. I also recruited three graduate students with extensive experience in neighborhood development to assist in the course. One of the students was from the College of Education, the others were from anthropology. The course was designed to enable advanced undergraduate as well as graduate students to enroll.

Students who enrolled in the course were asked to identify those neighborhoods where they had active connections. They were then organized into teams of two with one of the three graduate assistants assigned to mentor their work. Each team developed materials related to data collection and dissemination.

Recruitment of Stakeholders and Developing Linkages

A fourth step was to get the involvement and ongoing feedback from major stakeholders in the project/course design. Thus, I approached three members of the Venture Fund Committee of the staff members to give presentations on their organization's activities. One of the three committee members agreed to jointly teach the course.

With respect to neighborhood involvement, I approached the director of the Center for Neighborhoods about the project and was subsequently invited to make a presentation of the project-- as well as to solicit input on how it should be conducted and who would be interested in participating. Neighborhood leaders were invited to give talks to the class on a variety of issues that they felt were significant to them.

IV D. Reflections on the Design Process - A New Role for Anthropologists

While I had done previous work on documenting the role of neighborhood associations in

6

Memphis, I had not attempted to build this work into an intellectual framework that was easily comprehensible to policy makers nor had I involved students in a classroom setting that discussed, and collected, this type of information. The role that I was beginning extended the traditional participant observer role to include that of research analyst and facilitator. This role involved assisting in the training of students to collect new information about community initiatives, and building bridges among the three major stakeholders who did not understand nor trust each other. In addition, the course design effectively integrated the material collected to an ongoing curricula that could be built upon by myself, other students, and the faculty in future semesters.

.V. Monitoring of the Project

The program/course developed a series of methods that were used to monitor and reflect on the progress of the project. These methods included the following:

- ☐ The Neighborhood Development and Poverty course met on a weekly basis and followed the syllabus;
- ☐ The graduate students met with me on a weekly basis to review each student's field work;
- ☐ Quarterly reports were submitted to the Venture Fund Committee;
- ☐ Weekly verbal discussions were held with members of the Venture Fund Committee and leaders of community-based organizations.

VI. Mid-Stream Reflections on The Project & Changes

The feedback methods provided a series of insights into the project/course that led to a series of minor adjustments and major adaptations. The major adaptations fell into four areas.

- ☐ The extension of time deadlines for completion of data collection, rapport building, understanding, writing, analysis, reflection, feedback from key leaders, and rewriting. The students found that neighborhood leaders were busy people with demanding schedules. In short, collecting field data proved to be much more demanding than doing library research.

- ☐   The student stories of neighborhood-based initiatives varied greatly in length, quality of content, quality of writing, and format. Having the students submit three drafts did not resolve the wide variation in the write-ups. The graduate assistants and I worked an additional six months on these write-ups.

- ☐   The rewrite process resulted in the identification of recurrent themes in the community initiative process, and in the writing of a research paper constructing a new conceptual framework for community development in Memphis. (Appendix F)

- ☐   The class discussions and student papers also led to the development of a new product-- "Time-line On Community Building Initiatives In Memphis." A time-line was determined to be absolutely critical for students and policymakers to understand the historic context of the transformation that is occurring at the grassroots in Memphis. (Appendix G)

In reflection I believe the optimal method to produce the case studies would have been for students to spend extensive periods of time observing and participating in the daily routine of community leaders, and possibly even living in the neighborhood. Secondly, it would be desirable to have had examples of case studies so that students would have a framework to guide their writing. Finally, in retrospect it would have been important to have the students and myself use our own voice in the writing of the stories. Many of the students had ongoing relationships in the neighborhood that they wrote about. The identification of their first person voice would have helped to better understand what they had learned. These improvements require time and commitment which often go beyond the life of a semester.

VII. Impact, Benefits, Significance

Immediate Project Outcomes/Impacts

Table 1 shows how the project/course attained the objectives agreed upon by the Venture

Fund Committee and myself.

Table 1 Outcomes of the Community-based Initiatives Project

Objective 1 A knowledge base of community-based initiatives	Product 1a	A set of case studies on community-based initiatives in Memphis	Appendix H
	Product 1b	Memphis Neighborhood Timeline	**Appendix F**
Objective 2 A plan to expand and sustain the knowledge base	**Product 2a**	Institutionalization of the Neighborhood Development and Poverty course into the University of Memphis curriculum	**Appendix B**
	Product 2b	Funding by other agencies/foundations to continue similar programs of documentation of community-building initiatives	**Appendix I** Evaluation of the Mott Foundation's Neighborhood Small Grants Program
Objective 3 A plan for dissemination of the materials	**Product 3**	The dissemination of the case study material to policymakers and agencies such as the Memphis Public Library and Public School	**Appendix L** Letters
Objective 4 A method for conducting the project that would involve a diverse group of students in the project	**Product 4a**	Student evaluation of the Neighborhood Development and Poverty course	**Appendix M**
	Product 4b	Expansion of the course to provide scholarships to 10 teachers and community activists in an inner-city neighborhood	**Appendix I** Project funded by the Community Foundation of Greater Memphis

9

Reflective Critique

Beyond the documentation of the initiatives, the project led to an understanding and articulation of community development in Memphis that involved identity, vision, networking, and connectedness (Appendix F). Equally important to me, the writings raise a series of new questions about how neighborhood activists sustain commitment to revitalization efforts and attempt to broaden levels of participation in action.

The project also led to the development of a Memphis Neighborhood Timeline that traces the styles of decision-making that have been used by policymakers and community activists. It also notes key national policies that affected the course of events in Memphis. The Timeline represents a perspective that can be enlarged and tailored to meet the needs and intents of the user, whether that is an elementary school teacher or public housing resident leader.

By developing the project within the context of a new course, it also accomplished its objective of being sustainable and expandable-- i.e., the course is offered every other year and builds upon previous community-building initiatives. New participants are brought in each time the course is taught in order to expand its knowledge base. For example teachers and community activists from a targeted inner-city neighborhood were given scholarships to participate in the course and develop a curriculum related to their neighborhood. (This project was funded in 1995 through the Community Foundation of Greater Memphis Appendix I).

Equally important, the course (see syllabus) provided a mechanism for a dialogue that links local grassroots initiative to national issues, as well as to local business, governmental, and non-profit leaders. Speakers present their perspectives on development and collaboration, and have the opportunity to engage the diverse student groups in clarifying neighborhood

10

revitalization issues. Thus the content as well as the process contributes to the building of a knowledge base about community-based action.

Student-agency interaction in the context of the course/project has also led to the development of internship programs (Appendix J- List of Internships) with local agencies that were the focus of some of the community-based initiatives discussed in the course. Specifically the original funder, United Way of Greater Memphis, has employed several of the students who participated in the course as interns. The question of how their experiences can be written-up and integrated in the future publication of the Community Initiative is critical to the overall goal of the project.

The United Way of Greater Memphis has also sponsored seminars on the lessons learned from "The Community Building Initiatives" and "Memphis Neighborhood Timeline" for their service organizations. This seminar has been modified to look at community initiatives and its relevance to community education efforts. Twelve public schools (Appendix K) have participated in this seminar. The efforts of teachers and agency leaders in neighborhood outreach needs to be documented, examined and added to our knowledge base.

VIII.   Other Outcomes & New Questions

What emerged after the project/course is equally important to document and understand. The members of the United Way Venture Committee had knowledge and networks that could be translated into new programs. The activists had validation of their efforts and new networks with students and agencies. The students developed research that led them to new theoretical and methodological issues. Like the students, I had increased my understanding applications in the setting of the urban Mid-South, but two major questions arose for me. One question centered on

11

how this knowledge could be linked to colleagues outside of my discipline within the University who were addressing serious outreach issues in the city. The second was whether the knowledge base about community-based initiatives was sufficient to redirect citizens' ability to affect urban critical policy areas such as affordable housing, job creation, or school reform, through their own empowerment.

To respond to the first question, future efforts on my part would have to engage colleagues on significant urban issues and bring the community-based knowledge to bear in the course of the conceptualization, design, and execution of a future project. A later example of this was the joint project with Dr. David Cox of the Political Science Department to collaborate on development of the enterprise communities, and later the planning of future public housing in Memphis.

Concerning the second it seemed to me that the "Community Building Initiatives" Project would have to be re-thought through the eyes of those people who empowered themselves to change how things got done in their neighborhood. The stories could be presented as narratives of inquiry, discovery, and reflection, using the authors own voice and those of other participants. The stories of empowerment could focus not so much on the events of the neighborhood but rather the opportunities and challenges that he/she experienced in his/her role. The stories should be written by various stakeholders--residents, neighborhood activists, faculty members, students, and program directors who share an intimacy of involvement with their work.

Appendices

A   "Mid-South Community Building" - Proposal to The Venture Fund Committee of United Way of the Mid-South
B   "Neighborhood Development and Poverty" syllabus
C   List of Non-scholarly References on Neighborhood Development in the Mid-South
D   List of Scholarly References on Local Struggles Related to Race, Gender and Class
E   List of References on Community-based Initiatives in U.S. Cities
F   Paper on Community Development in Memphis
G   Monograph "Memphis Neighborhood Time-line: An Anthropological Perspective"
H   Monograph " Community Building: A New Way of Doing Business in Memphis"
I   Proposal to The Community Foundation of Greater Memphis "Evaluation of the Neighborhood Small Grants Program"
J   List of Student Internships with Memphis Community Institutions and Agencies
K   List of Community Building Workshops at Memphis Public Schools
L   Mid-South Agency Letters of Support
M   Student Course Evaluations

References Cited

Beifuss, Joan. (1985). *At The River I Stand*. Memphis: B & W Books.

Biles, Roger. (1986). *Memphis in the Great Depression*. Knoxville: University of Tennessee Press.

Center for Neighborhoods. (1985, 1987, 1990, 1992). *Directory of Neighborhood Associations*. 701 N. Looney, Memphis, TN, 38103.

Foote, Shelby. (1977). *September, September*. New York: Random House.

Shimkin, Demitri. *Black Social Institutions in the Mid-South: a dialogue between Demitri Shimkin and Nkosi Ajanaku*. Memphis: Memphis State University, Anthropological Research Center's Occasional Papers Series.

Shimkin, Demitri, Edith Shimkin and Dennis Frate editors. *(1976). The Extended Black Family*. The Hague: Mouton Press.

Tax, Sol. (1960). Action Anthropology. *Documentary History of the Fox Project*, F. Gearing et al., eds. Chicago: University of Chicago, Department of Anthropology.

The Metropolitan InterFaith Association. 1974-77. Oral Histories of Eight Memphis Neighborhoods.

Tucker, David. (1980). *Memphis Since Crump*. Knoxville: University of Tennessee Press.

Documentation of a Professional Service Project

Professional service is the engagement of state of the art knowledge to address community - relevant problems critically and reflectively in collaborative settings in a manner that builds capacity and informs both practitioners and scholars.
- definition by the participants in the project to document professional service 1996

Creating Identity

Purpose - Description, Origins, Shareholders and their Expectations

Process - Preparation, Delivery, Resources

Outcomes - Results, Goals Met, Unforeseen Impact, Dissemination

Reflection - Issues and Strategies, Unresolved Issues

Appendix

Susan Agre-Kippenhan
Associate Professor
Department of Art , Portland State University
March 1998

Purpose

In the winter of 1996 I offered the first community based learning course offered through the Portland State University Department of Art. I engaged graphic design students in a project that I had developed with a community partner that utilized a process of inquiry and design leading to the generation of a new visual identity for the partner's organization. Working with a community partner gave students real world experience in the design profession -- while they developed their design ability they provided a valued service to the community.

Description:

This partnership between a community organization, Friends of the Children, myself and my Portland State University undergraduate graphic design class, took about one academic year (three quarters). It began with my work to develop the partnership and define the student involvement and the working process (1 quarter). The actual duration of the class and the majority of student involvement was 10 weeks (2nd quarter). Follow up and finalization stretched through the last quarter of the academic year.

Origins: The community need - Friends of the Children, in need of a new graphic identity system, is a non-profit organization that provides continuous adult mentors for "at risk" children, second grade through high school. The organization was undertaking a concerted fund raising effort, creating a need for a strong visual identity.

Stakeholders and their Expectations: Participants in the project were

Client -Friends of The Children with Kristin Linden, director, serving as the contact.

Expectation- To find a new visual representation for their organization reflecting the characteristics that sets the organization apart from others, and in particular represents a caring relationship that is sustained consistently over a long period of time.

Class - Thirty graphic design students,the majority juniors, all graphic design majors, all prepared through a solid foundation of courses and one full year of study in graphic design but with no previous experience with a real client

Expectations - To gain a real life perspective on problems that are more typically simulated in a class setting, by creating a graphic design solution that fills a genuine need; gain a command of the working design process; work on their graphic skills and learn both design and client interaction techniques.

Faculty - Susan Agre-Kippenhan

I came to teaching after ten years as a design practitioner and my scholarly agenda has always been devoted to using my expertise to connect the University to the community. I have carried forth my work in a variety of ways, serving as vice president of the board of the Portland Chapter of the American Institute of Graphic Art, maintaining an active design practice, doing pro bono work for community causes, and actively bringing a variety of design opportunities to students.

My strong background in professional practice has driven my decisions to engage students in learning experiences that are centered in the community. Friends of the Children offer an exciting prospect since their work is rare in that the relationships they develop last for a minimum of ten years.

Expectation - To facilitate the partnership and create a positive learning experience that benefits both class and client. I expected to gain personally by connecting my beliefs that design is a community resource and that designers are excellent problem solvers. I viewed the partnership as a chance to show the power of design, and believe that the experience of working in a partnership to create design is a relationship of personal importance and satisfaction.

Academic Community - The Portland State University mission statement, "Let knowledge serve the city" indicates an institutional commitment and support for community involvement.

Expectation - The needs of the community and the needs of the students were to be met in a mutually beneficially partnership. This class was observed as a case study by the Portland State University Center for Academic Excellence and the specific study of this partnering will add to the knowledge base about community based or service learning .

Design Community - Portland is situated in a vital and energetic internationally recognized design community.

Expectations - That a viable design program in an urban University will take on real world design problems and that students graduating from such a program will not only have the design abilities needed to be a professional designer, but the poise and confidence born of real client interaction.

Summary - The need of the community partner provided opportunities for all the shareholders involved with the project. The faculty's area of inquiry, the student's need for stimulating learning experience, and the University's relationship to the community.

Process

The act of defining an organization's identity is a visioning process. In the most ideal circumstances it involves a partnership between the organization and the designer. The designer listens, observes, deciphers information and mirrors back to the client as together they refine an identity that matches the goals of the organization.

Logo - A symbol designed for easy and definite recognition.

Identity System - Employs a logo as the center of a functionally related group of design pieces that aid in the consistent and strong message of an organization's communication.

Preparation : Foundation needed to achieve expectations

Client - The client's needs and my interest and expertise are connected by the University community partnership director. My initial work with the client is to define expectations, the working process, and to address the interaction of client and student.

Theoretical principles
The client has not previously worked with designers - So, on one hand, there is an opportunity to create a relationship or partnership without predetermined characteristics on the other hand, the client has not had experience with visualization and is not familiar with the process that designers use to produce work. We worked to view design as a collaborative process where by the results are something neither party (client or designer) could arrive at alone, a result that will utilize the best of what each party can contribute.

Methodological principles

Parameters that client must agree with in order to involve the students are: direct involvement with students; feedback (the form for the feedback was determined as we worked); and provisions of some manner of closure.

Class -The students had previously worked on logo development as class assignments and so the concept of creating visual representation for an organization was familiar, although previously their experience has been exercises without real clients. I work with the class to provide a foundation for:

Theoretical principles

The class and client will form a working relationship. Students must educate the client about the working process and assist the client with visualizing finished results. This project creates challenges that are richer and more interesting than the typical professional sales driven projects, or class exercise. For many students, taking on a non-profit organization enlarges their perception of the design discipline.

Methodological principles

Through reading and discussion I prepare the class by teaching them: to identify the problem -- not just symptoms that they need to solve; and to dig deeply and research the client and other similar organizations; to redefine the problem in a written guide that addresses all the perameters. Through the project I help students keep a clear understanding of the idea that the process transcends the subject matter.

Faculty - My role in this project is complex and varied. With the client I work to address their need and translate it into a project that will be workable for 30 students. As faculty I manage the project. As a liason between client and student I guide and facilitate input.

Theoretical principles

We are working to create a common ground, a visual and verbal language that involves both the class and the client, so that both parties feel comfortable.

Methodological principles

Concentration on helping students to see the project as one example of a working process. This includes the ability to redefine problems, to see process vs. content, and to connect visual decisions with justification founded in facts.

Delivery: Process of delivering to the client

What is the difference between the classroom and the boardroom? There are concerns addressed by designers in a discipline specific language that does not translate directly to the client's world. I teach students to accompany design decisions with verbal and written justifications -- a visual/written language common to both class and client. By preparing and making client presentations, students learn some behaviors are useful in the classroom while others are useful in the boardroom.

Involvement : The three main shareholders

Client involvement

Initial meetings with client and faculty were held to discuss process. The client presents materials to the class and provides input to students in a variety of forms: written comments, written group summary, letter to the class, verbal comments, and selecting specific work to continue in the process. This process helps provide a closing experience for the class. [See appendix Phase I, Letter on completion]

Student Involvement

Student involvement is balanced to address both the needs of the client and the needs of the students. Work is viewed as responding to client needs while being an example of the process students will need to apply to future clients. I work with the class to develop a problem statement that, approved by the client, is the first step in the process. This results in a lively and constant exchange of ideas, design strategies, and constructive criticism. All students participate by developing individual design solutions and a written justification. All students refine their designs based on the input, and selected logos are then presented to the client one-on-one. Choices are further narrowed and the identity system is expanded to include letterhead, envelope, business card, and a T-shirt. [See appendix Phase I, II, III, Final Logo, Video taped interaction]

Faculty Involvement

Initial client contact - Our goal is to define a loose course of action and set dates for initial activities. I work with the class on developing the interviewing and inquiry skills needed to gain useful information from the client. I provide a feedback loop that addresses design issues as well as the content issues specific to our client, and constantly monitor the experience so that all students, not just those whose work has been selected, stay involved. I provide scheduling, act as design critic, provide resources for students, facilitate the experience, and cheer lead, as needed. [See appendix Faculty Reflective Journal].

Students present over 40 initial logo designs to the clients. Initial selection is narrowed through several phases to 5 finalists and then one ultimate solution. [See appendix Phase I, II, III, Final Logo]

Resources: Needs that arose during investigation and delivery-

Student creativity provides the service, the primary activity takes place in the classroom, and students mobilize to form transportation carpools and volunteer time after class.

Summary - The shareholders agree on visually avoiding cliché images while representing the loving (but not to be confused with sexual) relationship that exists in the client program. The imagery cannot be gender or racially specific and phase-oriented delivery process must allow for input and refining. The focus stays on both the development of the logo and the development of the student's working process.

Outcomes

In the final week of class, the community partner selects a final design.

After the course ends I work with client to prepare the artwork for production and oversee production of letterhead, envelopes, business cards, T-shirts, labels, and thank you notes.

Goals meet:

Client - The new identity system captures the qualities that makes the organization unique- a caring relationship over time. The system reflects elements of interaction, growth, achievement, pride, aspiration, and confidence. Purple and gold color scheme is stable yet interesting and rich. [See appendix Final Logo]

Class - The class gained experience working with a client, and learned there are a variety of perspectives that effect design. They learned critical thinking -- problem identification and problem re-definition. They also investigated differences in perception and in communicating emotion. [See appendix Center for Academic Excellence Case Study Documentation]

Faculty - Tbis experience served as a direct opportunity to bring what I have learned in professional design practice to the classroom. The project joined academia with the community and turned the university into a learning community by creating a place for the forum. [See appendix Faculty Reflective Journal]

Institution - The institution has design as a valuable commodity, and the design student as a valuable participant in the community. [See appendix Thank you from the president, University Partnership Brochure]

Design community - The student work appeared in their portfolio and is ultimately viewed by other designers, and became documentation of the University'sconnection to the community.

Unforeseen Impact

Client - Client comments on the affirmation provided by the class as they listened and translated to the visual. It was a positive collaborative process that exceeded client expectations.

Class -Students expanded the definition of design and they gained confidence as individual designers. They experienced the role of the student as a teacher as they helped to educate the client while the client educated them. The Students' approach now is more confident and with fewer preconceptions. [See appendix Center for Academic Excellence Case Study Documentation]

Students also learned the distinction between a good visual design and one that is a good visual solution. [See appendix Student Reflections One Year Later]

Faculty - The value of the experience was articulated by students. It also included beneits ofcollaborative learning, peer review, peer support, and a sense of the classroom community that grew during this experience. The roles of teacher and learner are blurred as students teach each other and the client while I become a colleague and a facilitator. As a result, I have offered this section again as a Community Based Learning class and I am integrating community learning experiences into more classes. [See appendix Faculty Reflective Journal]

Design Community - In the final stage of design the client brings in an outside designer to evaluate the choice of design. They support the decisions made by the class and the client.

Dissemination of Knowledge

Client- There is a high visibility of the solution, including use of materials for national presentations by the client.

Students - The process has contributed to enhanced expectations and affected subsequent student graphic design work. One year after completion of this project the students still see this as one of their most outstanding learning experiences. When given the opportunity many have continued with community design problems, and have taken on the planning and implementation of work as independent groups using the faculty as a consultant. These projects include a new brochure for the Portland Bureau of Maintenance (in addition to design, the students researched a new distribution method that saved the city thousands of dollars.) and a brochure for Parking Enforcement Office. Other projects were done for Portland State Athletic Gear, the State of Oregon Sport's Hall of Fame, and Poetry in Motion, an arts literacy program.[See appendix Student Reflections One Year Later]

Faculty - Contributions to the knowledge base involved both national and internal presentations on the Community Based Learning component of the experience, and it's effect on student learning, andproposals for discipline specific conferences and papers. [See appendix Outline of AAHE Presentation]

I was the first faculty to receive the Judith Ramaley Community Scholar Award (spring 1997) as a result of this program I was nominated by Community Partner Kris Linden.

I was also appointed to chair the University Capstone Committee -- the committee that reviews proposals for the senior level of the University's general studies program -- an experience that focuses on a community based learning experience.

Institution - Our case study information contributes to high profile in the national dialogue on Community Based Learning.

The project was included in a profile of Portland State University community involvement at Portland International Airport in 1997

The faculty and project were also included in the University partnership brochure.

Design Community-Through my involvement in the American Institute of Graphic Arts I have engaged area designers in assisting with community learning experiences.

Summary - Several months after the completion of this project students reported that they had seen a group of children wearing "their" logo. While none these "reporters" had been finalist in the logo selection process, all took ownership.

Reflection

The process of delivering a Community Based Learning experience relies on reflection and assessment. The flow of the experience is at times unpredictable and requires mid-course adjustments and constant accommodations. It begs contemplation of the day-to-day issues as well as the long range implications on student learning and faculty activity. [See appendix Reflective Faculty Journal]

General Strategies - Lessons learned

Flexibility is key in the faculty role. The ability to keep the project moving by assisting both the class and the client with their roles in the partnership is of the utmost importance, as is creating a learning environment that exists between the University and the community. Acknowledging the contrast between the atmosphere of the classroom and the decorum of the workplace, understanding that the vocabulary and expectations differ in each, and helping all shareholders to develop a mutual respect and understanding of one another's perspective is important as well.

It is vital to communicate the idea that not knowing is a resource, one that allows students to investigate freely. Students need to be reassured that there is no predetermined solution to this problem - only an honest process of inquiry. We invent the classroom as a safe haven and a place to experiment and sometimes fail.

There is great importance in working with "the right" partner in this collaborative endeavor. the partnership requires steady contact and a community organizations willing to give the class the attention the class is giving to their need.

The value of student reflection on the project and the process is is tremendous. Both while the project is proceeding and after its completion. These assist in making the experience meaningful in the short term, providing miscourse adjustments and in the long term where the day to day incidents fade and the students can actually articulate the lasting effects of their experience.[See appendix Center for Academic Excellence Case Study Documentation]

Unresolved Issues

There is a constant tension produced between logistics of the University and the community. The length of student involvement is controlled by the quarter system, and vacations, and finals weeks break up the work flow. Client obligations elsewhere may also delay timely responses to the class.

How does one define success for this expereince when class activity is tied into a client project? How does the success or failure of the project effect the student experience? How do learning objectives enter into the perception of a successfull experience?

Closure is an important issue, as is determining realistic perameters for the involvement and a graceful ending to the project. Friends of the Children continued to come back with more requests related to their identity system for one year. While this demonstrates the strength of the relationship, the design class had disbanded and there were no mechanisms in place to provide the assistance required. I continued to work with the organization to develop resources to meet their needs.

Summary - The classroom atmosphere changed in the course of this Community Based Learning class. The students became a strong working unit, faculty became a facilitator, and the project became a group effort. The scope of the effect of the project is far greater than a traditional classroom experience. It changed the very definition of the field for some students, created fresh opportunities for students and faculty, and created ripples in the department that encourage more student and faculty participation.

Appendices

Phase I Friends of the Children Logo Design
   Spiral bound book- Logo Designs
   Contents:
      - Class letter to the Friends
      - Individual pages : 40 student logo designs. Each design is presented in a small and a large size. In black and white and color. Each with written justification, bulleted points that give explanation of visual decisions.

   Letter from Kris Linden to the class in response to the designs

   Video Tape - Friends interacting with student ambassadors as they give input on the designs for Phase I

Phase II Friends of the Children Logo Design
   -Slides of 10 Logos selected to go to Phase II

Phase III Friends of the Children Logo Design
   -Slides of 5 Logos, Letterhead, envelope, business cards, T-shirt designs selected to go to Phase III

Final Logo Friends of the Children
   -Samples of completed pieces - Letterhead, Envelope, Business cards, notecards, stickers, T-shirt

Letter from Friends of the Children to the class on completion of the project

Thank you from Portland State University President - Judith Ramaley

Reflective Faculty Journal

Center for Academic Excellence Case Study Documentation
   -Interview Transcripts
   -Focus Group Transcripts
   -Student Impact Study

Student Reflections
   - One year after completion of The Friends of the Children Logo Design Project

Outline of American Association of Higher Education Presentation on Faculty Roles and Rewards - January 1997
   -Portland State University Case Study Story

University Community Partnership Brochure

A Professional Development Workshop for High School Biology Teachers

Dr. Florence Juillerat
Biology Department
Indiana University Purdue University at Indianapolis
723 W. Michigan Street
Indianapolis, IN 46202-5132

I. Introduction

This paper describes an in-service workshop on Building Foundations in Human Genetics offered by Indiana University Purdue University at Indianapolis (IUPUI) for forty-three high school biology teachers. The workshop featured collaborations with school districts, science teacher organizations, professional genetics educators, and university faculty. The Indiana Higher Education Commission (IHEC) provided seventy percent of the program's support through its Eisenhower Professional Development Program fund. At the completion of the project participants were incorporating human genetics concepts into their existing curricula with constructivist pedagogy, and sharing their successes with other teachers.

II. The Project

In-service workshops for pre-college biology teachers employ a strategy familiar to university faculty who seek effective links with secondary school teachers-- collegial collaboration. Although faculty and high school teachers work in separate institutional worlds, they share common interests in student success. In-service workshops provide opportunities for universities and external partners to form temporary synergistic learning communities based on outreach/in-reach principles.

From 1996-1997 I served as project director (principal investigator) for a professional development program in human genetics for high school biology teachers at IUPUI. Forty-three teachers from school districts throughout Indiana participated in a two week intensive workshop in the summer of 1996. The instructional staff featured a renowned genetics educator and four award-winning teachers and faculty with national reputations in science teaching. Sessions included content updates, constructivist teaching strategies, curriculum explorations, and practical laboratory activities. During the following year teachers established a computer network for discussion, resource retrieval, and information dissemination. They implemented projects of their own design to infuse human genetics into course curricula at their schools, and shared in-service ideas in local workshops to multiply the project's impact.

Midway through the year teachers returned to IUPUI for follow-up seminars with twenty-nine new recruits. This conference featured more current research in genetics and constructivist teaching by summer workshop staff, reports on classroom infusion projects by summer participants, and consulting sessions on computer networking and resource acquisition. Participants in the year-long program and new recruits provided the in-reach for planning a subsequent workshop scheduled for 1998-99. Attachments I, II, and III describe the workshop's course of study, the participants' school districts, and the qualifications of the in-service staff.

Guiding a pre-college professional development workshop was consistent with my preparation and expertise, as I had cultivated a user-friendly reputation for the IUPUI Biology Department by organizing monthly evening seminars for area teachers and faculty. The loosely knit group, known as the Central Indiana Biology Teachers Focus Group (CIBTF), provided the in-reach by selecting its own seminar topics. I published the group's monthly teaching newsletter (whose circulation grew to over 400), and supported the project through internal university grants and the goodwill of colleagues in the science education community.

With a planning committee of CIBTF colleagues, university faculty, high school administrators and professional genetics educators, I then coordinated the development of the successful grant proposal for the genetics workshop described here. The proposal was submitted to the Indiana Higher Education Commission for funding through the Eisenhower Professional Development Program. With leverage funds from other sources, the grant award grew to $100,000. Two-thirds of the funds supported participants through stipends, living expenses, and class materials. One-third covered staff salaries, supplies, and institutional costs.

As project director, I guided the workshop's instructional design and learning activities through formative feedback from participants and staff. I provided day-to-day grant administration to assure a smooth integration of goals, staff, participants and facilities. Although my primary instructional role during the workshop was ongoing formative evaluation, I also conducted course sessions on needs of underserved and underrepresented students. My knowledge of research in science education, national curricular reform movements, and teaching resources; networking ability with state biology teachers; expertise in instructional design; and faculty role within the IUPUI Biology Department provided the leadership required to establish this productive university-K-12 partnership.

III. Outcomes and Impact

For Community Partners

As external partners, Indiana schools, participants, and the IHEC realized substantial gains from this in-service program. Higher Education Commission funding guidelines required workshops to economically address issues of impact, duration, systemic connections, and assessment. The genetics workshop offered twelve days of quality in-service for biology teachers for $2,000 per participant which is less than half of a National Research Council estimate of $4,500 (adjusted to 1996-97 dollars). One seventh of the state's school districts were represented in the project. (Attachment IV is a summary of the workshop's final report filed with the IHEC.) The complete narrative addressed such grant concerns as collaborative planning; recruitment; plan of operation; project fulfillment of the needs of underserved, underrepresented, private school, rural, minority, low income and gifted students; evaluation of participants; dissemination of workshop content; and lessons learned.

An evaluator, with research expertise in in-service workshops, helped me collect formative feedback. He prepared the summative assessments. Together we constructed a picture of the complex needs of the people and institutions participating in the grant, and of the interactions that seemed to bring about positive changes in what and how to teach. Participants provided information on the program's impact as it unfolded through satisfaction questionnaires, workshop implementation plans and reports, staff interviews, and computer network discussions. They gave excellent ratings to the program's organization, content, and teaching/learning strategies.

The best evaluations of in-service accomplishments and classroom impact were the participants' implementation plans for incorporating workshop ideas into their class lessons on genetics. Teachers have disseminated their projects at second tier in-services in nearby schools and at professional meetings. For example, one-fourth of the biology sessions featured at the 1997 Annual Meeting of the Hoosier Association of Science Teachers were given to the 2400 attendees by genetics workshop participants. Some workshop creative products merit publication in state and national science teacher journals and publications are in process. Attachment V provides more information on the assessment process and results.

For The University

Professional development programs for pre-college teachers are important outreach services of universities. Indiana University's new Strategic Directions Charter calls on faculty to develop programs based on the "in-reach principle" where community clients suggest needs and participate in planning. The charter specifically recognizes the university's expertise in the design and delivery of instruction to meet the growing needs of K-12 education with expanded summer workshops and in-service programs. The mission statements of IUPUI and its School of Science also include providing professional service and continuing education to the community.

The contribution of the genetics workshop to the service mission of IUPUI, the School of Science, and the Department of Biology is positive and substantial when seen in the context of university strategic directions. Although the Indiana University School of Education has a distinguished history of external partnerships with K-12 teachers, maintained by strong infrastructures and ongoing alumni support, IUPUI's School of Science has few outreach programs. My project established the School of Science as a visible leader in the biology education community of the state. It provided incentive to continue and expand university linkages with pre-college science teachers. Some school departments, for example, now encourage their faculty to join professional science teaching organizations. Others have created discipline-based faculty positions for individuals with expertise in science education.

My work in the Biology Department focuses on service and teaching. I have been recognized for both distinguished service and teaching by the University and by state and national education organizations. I have held leadership positions in local, state, and national science teacher organizations serving both college and pre-college teachers, and received grants at all three levels for science teacher workshops. The Eisenhower grant, described here, represents peer recognition of my competency in outreach and instructional design. Although the IHEC competition invites proposals in all areas of science, mathematics, and technology, the human genetics workshop was the only grant addressing specific needs of high school biology teachers awarded within the last several years. The commission funds an average of 12 grants per year. The number and type of proposals submitted varies with yearly guidelines; the funding available changes with congressional allocations. Attachment VI lists grants awarded by the IHEC in the last four years and describes the agency's peer review process.

For My Professional Development

Personally I have been enriched by the service in this project. Developing a statewide in-service program was an amoeba-like process, requiring a long lead time for establishing collegial credibility and nurturing links with diverse pre-college teaching stakeholders. Reaching out to K-12 communities-- by consulting, speaking, and judging science fairs in schools; acting as a liaison to university resources; serving as President of the Hoosier Association of Science Teachers and member of the Board of Directors and Chair of Publications of the National Science Teachers Association-- helped me identify potential external partners with needs and resources. The workshop's design then became a dynamic experiment in applying knowledge about how students (and teachers) learn. The process required using people skills to help teachers from diverse school districts not only link national and state science standards and proficiencies to their own particular curricula, but also to agree on common training goals. I had to be conversant in science education research, current science teaching reform movements, and the literature of my own discipline.

My teaching of undergraduate non-majors courses in contemporary biology and the biology of women has been improved by the intense workshop exposure to recent advances in medical genetics, and the opportunity to again feel the pulse of the high school biology environment. In-service colleagues have convinced me that students who will arrive in my classes in coming years will have very different attitudes and expectations. They will bring to class an appetite for inquiry-based learning, an interest in collaborative problem-solving, and a knowledge base distinctly different from what I possessed as an undergraduate. The project also renewed my appreciation of team teaching.

Building Foundations in Human Genetics was a cost effective opportunity by the state of Indiana to address new national biology teaching goals in <u>Benchmarks in Science Literacy</u> and the <u>National Science Standards</u>, issued by the American Association for the Advancement of Science and the National Research Council. Extensive reform movements, however, require decades to demonstrate significant impacts on student learning as in-service staff, teachers, students, administrators, parents, and public and private funding agencies struggle to respond to change. Although new systemic models of continuing education are being developed, university K-12 partnerships for teacher workshops will remain the predominant form of professional development for some time to come. The workshop described here reached biology teachers statewide, established IUPUI's School of Science as teacher friendly, employed national experts in genetics who know issues in biology teaching, and featured outstanding peer instructors as role models. Hopefully, the foundations of collegiality and knowledge built will help teachers take ownership of current reform efforts in science teaching and gradually replace inefficient practices with successful ones to improve student learning.

IV. Reflections

At first glance, in-service programs seem to be relatively straightforward projects, with hundreds of previous workshops to use as models. Yet each new in-service has its own scholarly challenge in project design, implementation and assessment. Professional development programs associated with universities evolve in non-linear fashion over many years through complex interactions of institutional goals and people. Successful implementation requires satisfying the separate needs of many stakeholders: teachers and their administrators, local and national curricular goals, university faculty and departments, project staff, funding agencies, professional organizations, and companies producing educational materials.

While faculty, as project directors, do action research on embedded scholarly questions as in-service programs unfold, the primary focus is on client satisfaction. Workshops are by nature limited interventions. Participants use them to construct new knowledge through the concepts they already possess and to share ideas with peers. The assumption is that continuing education and energizing of teachers throughout their careers translates into more active learning by several generations of students. Project outcomes are usually reported in grant agency summaries of applied work rather than as investigative journal articles. More often than not, unique ideas and products that emerge in workshops (lab experiments, problem scenarios, pedagogical techniques, etc.) are incorporated into the large, diffused initiatives of school districts, university departments, and state educational agencies. They lose their origin and identity as teachers adapt products and processes to fit local needs.

The major issues of stakeholders conducting and experiencing effective professional development in science teaching have changed little over the past 40 years. Leaders and participants still lament the relatively small number of teachers reached by in-service activities, the lack of coordination among various professional development programs, and the limited duration of projects or participant-staff connections. Within the last decade another concern has been added to the list-- meaningful assessment of program effectiveness and student achievement. These four issues received renewed public attention with the recent federal Goals 2000 mandate that "the nation's teaching force will have access to programs for continued improvement of their professional skills" and "US students will be first in the world in math and science achievement."

The day-to-day facilitation of Human Genetics workshop activities provided an environment for reflective thought on what practices contributed to its success and what issues of concern require attention in future proposals. Given the parameters above, the area of action research that should receive more exploration is workshop format. Several client recommendations about what professional development should look like in coming years emerged through informal discussions with participants. All have support in research literature. In-service programs of the future need to (1) retain some face-to-face interaction. Meaningful learning in science is constructed through interchange -- i.e. hands-on, minds-on group problem solving. Training must also (2) preserve the concept of periodic reinforcement, of reunions where participants revisit ideas with others and gain inspiration. Workshops should (3) use appropriate instructional technology. That technology must be a blend of cutting edge (for teacher vision, and practicality) for use in high school classrooms. In-service programming must (4) offer more options and modes for learning. Delivery strategies should accommodate the narrowing windows of opportunity for continuing education in the lives of teachers. Flexibility and timing are the keys. Finally, workshops need to (5) provide usable products and instructional aids in compatible formats. The management of information and resources is a major problem in contemporary classrooms.

Aspects of these five concerns have been included in a second grant I recently received from the IHEC for 1998-99 (Building Foundations in Human Genetics - II). While workshop content will address the exponential growth in new knowledge about human genetics, the format will shift to the preparation of teams from five large Indiana school districts. To multiply the effect of group training, school teams will host second tier regional workshops and serve as resource agents in their area of the state.

Scientists, science educators and citizens agree that university faculty can best meet two fundamental needs of pre-college biology teachers: (1) leadership in defining the kinds of in-service programs that foster inquiry-based teaching and are attractive enough to entice teachers, scientists, and science educators to participate and (2) mechanisms for disseminating new information on what and how to teach throughout school districts. Universities, therefore, have the obligation to provide quality in-service training that promotes ongoing professionalism. By integrating pre-college and college science communities, workshops--and the networks for continuing education that grow from them-- challenge both participants and faculty to cultivate instructional strategies that encourage meaningful learning by students.

Attachment I - Workshop Advertising Brochure

Attachment II - Description of Participants' School Districts

Attachment III - Workshop Staff Qualifications

Attachment IV - Indiana Higher Education Agency Report Summary

Attachment V - Participant Assessment Results

Attachment VI - IHEC Peer Review Process and Grants Awarded (1993-1996)

Professional Service and Outreach Project
FACULTY DEVELOPMENT IN INTERNATIONAL BUSINESS
Ben L. Kedia

Objective and Context of Project:

This project grew out of a grant (Center for International Business Education and Research) awarded to The University of Memphis by the U.S. Department of Education. The Center for International Business Education and Research (CIBER) program was established for universities to provide international education, research and training activities that help U.S. businesses prosper in a global marketplace. The CIBER program enables universities to marshall their internationally-oriented educational, research and outreach resources in a manner that serves to strengthen the international competitiveness of the United States.

The world's markets for goods, services, labor, and capital are becoming much more integrated, and the future economic welfare of the U.S. will depend substantially on increasing international skills in the business community. In spite of the need for internationally oriented personnel, business schools in the United States have been slow to internationalize their curriculum. This is largely attributed to the lack of faculty trained in international business. A global survey conducted by The Academy of International Business (1993) reported:

> ". . . On average, 68% of the faculty had minimal international business education/training, or none at all, with some 22% having only moderate education/training." *(International Business Education in the 1990s: A Global Survey, p. 18)*

Given the lack of prior international business education/training on the part of business school faculty, "retooling" of the faculty in the international domain is highly desirable. However, the internationalization process often requires faculty to give up some of what they do well in their functional areas of accounting, economics, finance, marketing, and management in order to reallocate time and energy for the acquisition of new international skills and knowledge. At most universities, faculty rewards such as tenure, promotion, pay raises, travel, honor (status), and other benefits are tied closely to research and publications in functional disciplines. Because it represents a newer emerging area in our discipline, international business has a more limited body of existing research and fewer publication outlets; hence, faculty members may be reluctant to dilute their professional efforts in an area that might be viewed as less rewarding. In addition, faculty also may perceive a lack of need for international skills and knowledge.

Background, Experience and Expertise for the Project:

The 1993 global survey confirmed my own experiences in the academic world. Having taught business courses in both general and international business at five universities I came to know, first hand, the lack of international focus in business schools. My observations were echoed by those business firms with whom I served in a consulting capacity. The indifference of business schools to international business orientations seemed remarkable to me in light of the new geo-politics and I resolved to try to do something about it.

My initial efforts in this regard were made at Louisiana State University. From 1983 to 1985 I secured a grant from the Louisiana Board of Regents to examine the barriers to international business for Louisiana firms. Based on the results of this study, I received a subsequent grant for 1985-87 from the U.S. Department of Education. The grant was used to develop a program that would bring business managers and business students together to conduct feasibility studies regarding the expansion of business firms in the international domain. As I attempted to get other faculty involved in the process I came to recognize that the knowledge, skills, and interests of faculty in this regard were rather limited.

2

Toward the end of 1987 I learned that The University of Memphis intended to strengthen the international focus of its business school. Through the Fogelman College of Business and Economics, the University established the Robert Wang Center for International Business with a vision and mission to internationalize the business school and the University. A position of endowed chair and director was established. I was honored to be selected for this position and joined the University in 1989.

As director my immediate task was to translate the center's mission into an identifiable program and to procure funds to support the program's activities. Fortunately for us, the Wang Center's start-up efforts coincided with strategic initiatives in the U.S. Congress to increase international skills in the business community. The CIBER Program (Centers for International Business Education and Research) was established by Congress and administered through the U.S. Department of Education. The intent of the CIBER legislation was to help universities strengthen their international education, research, and training activities in order to increase international competence and strengthen this country's competitive position.

In 1990 I submitted a grant to the U.S. Department of Education proposing to establish a Center for International Business Education and Research (CIBER) at The University of Memphis. Our proposal emphasized the Wang Center's potential for leadership in the Lower Mississippi Delta, a relatively poor region of the U.S. where international education is underfunded and often ignored. The U.S. Department of Education looked favorably on our proposal and the University of Memphis was awarded a three-year CIBER grant. We have been designated a CIBER institution for nine consecutive years (1990-1999), receiving nearly $3 million in grant funds to engage in a broad range of internationally-oriented teaching, research, and outreach activities. At present there are 26 CIBERs in the United States representing public and private universities around the nation, including Columbia, Duke, Michigan State, Illinois, Purdue, Texas, UCLA, and Washington. Competition for the CIBER grant is always strong and designated CIBERs are expected to produce measurable results.

As director of a CIBER I have tried to take a holistic approach, mapping a strategy that could lead to ever-widening circles of CIBER activity both inside and outside the academic institution. Congress' mandate requires that CIBERs become innovators and facilitators, catalysts and entrepreneurs — but always in a team context. The goals and purposes of the CIBER program are to promote and foster collaboration among disciplines and institutions. As a CIBER director, I have worked hard to achieve this goal at The University of Memphis and regard these experiences to be among the most satisfying aspects of our work on campus. The same goal/value (i.e. collaboration) applies to our relationships with other educational institutions.

In accordance with the mandates of the CIBER legislation, CIBER institutions are expected to help other academic institutions enhance their capacity for teaching international content. In our role as a CIBER, the challenge to The University of Memphis was to create an outreach program that would sufficiently equip business faculty (in other colleges and universities, as well as our own) to teach their functional field and incorporate an international focus. Therefore, the Faculty Development in International Business (FDIB) program was designed at The University of Memphis *to help college and university faculty teach courses in a global context by infusing international material into existing courses.* The program develops not only professional knowledge about the field of international business, but also the pedagogical skills that facilitate the teaching of international business. The FDIB learning environment also benefits faculty who simply seek a larger understanding of the international aspects of business.

This infusion approach (i.e. adding the international context to existing functional courses) is the most practical. It is consistent with most business schools' *functionally-based* department structure. It is also consistent with the goal of developing student awareness of the international dimension of business. However, the infusion approach may not impart an in-depth understanding of international business.

The overall design of the program has proven to be successful and has been well received by program participants. Each year for the past six years the FDIB program has offered four concurrent seminars (e.g. International Business, International Finance, International Management, and International Marketing). During this period approximately 220 faculty members from academic institutions across the country have participated in the program. Given that seminar attendees are all Ph.D.s and experts in their basic disciplines, we believe that fifteen hours of exposure to the international dimension of their disciplines provides participants sufficient knowledge (i.e. a solid working base) to be able to teach and/or infuse their courses with an international flavor. Seminar content includes theory, pedagogy, materials, case studies, etc. The program enables faculty to obtain a grasp of international material and to identify effective ways for incorporating it into their future teaching.

Successful partnerships with the CIBERs at Duke University, The Georgia Institute of Technology, Michigan State University, and the University of Connecticut add new dimensions to the FDIB program. This collaborative arrangement has allowed us to expand the number of expert seminar leaders for the program. The seminar leaders are nationally known scholars in the international dimensions of their respective functional disciplines, with particularly strong teaching skills. For example, in the International Management course I teach with Professor Arie Lewin of Duke University. Attendees are able to compare and contrast two styles, approaches, and philosophies of teaching that generally complement each other, and to learn from the expertise of two leaders. While Dr. Lewin and I maintain our own style we work very hard to provide a unified body of knowledge.

FDIB seminars foster a unique teaching and learning environment. My experiences as a seminar leader challenge me to conceptualize, and to articulate more clearly, the theoretical foundations and pedagogical processes by which knowledge is transferred (i.e.

knowledge about the international field and its implications for business education). Latent spillover effects from the FDIB training program become transparent in the doctoral seminars and Executive MBA classes I normally teach at The University of Memphis. These same spillover effects also help guide and shape the International MBA degree program, which I direct at the University.

Monitoring of the FDIB program is done largely through a written survey and evaluation conducted at the conclusion of the seminars. All participants are required to complete the evaluation. The results so far have been highly positive. The second step of the process occurs two weeks after the faculty have returned to their respective campuses. A letter and short survey form is mailed to each FDIB faculty participant asking them to summarize their experience in the program and to inform us about its impact on their teaching and research. The return rate for this type of open-ended evaluation is much lower than the initial survey, however, again the comments attest to the quality and effectiveness of the program:

> "The program was the best conference (organization, faculty presenters, site, etc.) that I have attended in my 14 years as a university faculty member. The program has also caused me to begin to re-think the direction of teaching."

> "The conference provided me with some great tools, references, and overviews for increasing the international integration of the courses I teach. This was particularly helpful to someone like myself who is in the early stages of international study."

> "I enjoyed the sessions, but more importantly, I learned things that I can use to enhance the international module of my Business Strategy classes."

Outcomes and Impacts:

The evaluation and feedback process has confirmed the success of the program in achieving its objectives. The seminars tend to generate considerable interest among faculty participants with respect to international business -- an interest not previously felt, or perhaps ignored. For example, the following is a typical comment from participants: "The scholars

6

in attendance and the ideas that were discussed have broadened my understanding of the teaching and research needs of the international management domain." Participating faculty become enthused about the international field, recognize its importance, and acknowledge the need to incorporate this dimension in their future teaching and research.

The Wang Center does not have the resources for conducting a longitudinal study to examine the impact of the FDIB experience on individual institutions (i.e. how many faculty apply/implement what they learned in the FDIB program). However, the fact that many institutions repeatedly send faculty participants each year to The University of Memphis, suggests that the FDIB program is helping to bring positive change to their campuses.

A reciprocal benefit is the impact on seminar leaders who are constantly challenged by the solid thinking and strong conceptual skills of the participants. In the dialogue and discussion seminar leaders may have their ideas questioned or refuted, or their concepts reaffirmed and strengthened. As a result, the seminar experience can actually influence their future teaching and research. Furthermore, the leadership capacity of our seminar leaders — and participants — suggests that the FDIB program may leave an imprint on both the profession and a related knowledge base.

The FDIB program has enhanced the visibility of The University of Memphis as a leading institution in the field of international business in the Mid-South region. Participating faculty acknowledge the quality of our facilities, organizational skills, and above all, the expertise of the seminar leaders. Through the FDIB program faculty from around the nation have received an excellent, first-hand experience at The University of Memphis. This national exposure helps our University to recruit students for our international business program (International MBA). It is also an excellent vehicle for developing future placements for our doctoral graduates from the Fogelman College of Business and Economics.

Reflection:

The University of Memphis CIBER initiative illustrates the importance of basic principles that should guide any project that seeks to evoke change. The first is that proposed goals and actions must fit the defined problem. The second is that leaders, organizers, or presenters are influential resources, so seek to involve the best. The third principle is to adopt a strategy of collaboration and cooperation for mutual gains from the endeavor. The presence and enthusiasm of FDIB faculty participants is a reminder that in every institution there exists a cadre of enlightened faculty who are open to change — ready to share with others, ready to learn from others. The true spirit of the institution is not ego driven. It draws its motivation and inspiration from the joys of learning, the challenge of teaching, and the belief that such endeavors can shape the future. The FDIB seminars (Faculty Development in International Business) are no more — and no less.

Appendices (not included here):

- Program Announcement
- List of Participants
- Course and Pedagogical Materials
- End of Seminar Evaluations
- Subsequent Overall Evaluations

The "swampy lowlands" or academic "high grounds":

Where is the scholarship in new faculty roles?

Dannelle D. Stevens, Ph.D.

Portland State University

School of Education

The successful applicant will coordinate field-based programs; work with local school districts on advanced and ongoing staff development and school improvement; develop and supervise research projects on school reform and the improvement of teaching and learning; and assist academic departments across the university as they begin preparing for high school students (<u>Chronicle of Higher Education</u>, Winter, 1994).

Four years ago I was hired to fill the tenure-track position described above. My official title is Coordinator of the Professional Development Partnerships (PDP) for the School of Education. The job description emphasized the need for the new faculty member to work in the field on issues central to school improvement and to bring those issues to the academic community. Working on public school reform, partnering with area schools and carrying the school reform message to academic departments all require a radical change in the definition of faculty role.

Donald Schon (1995) defends the need for this new type of academic position when he asserts that professors should abandon the technical-rational model, the "academic high grounds," where "manageable problems lend themselves to solution through the use of research-based theory and technique". Instead, professors should focus on the "swampy lowlands where problems are messy and confusing and incapable of technical solution." These swampy lowlands are where the problems of the greatest "human significance lie," he continues. The purpose of this paper is to describe the scholarship in my new faculty role as I work across both public schools and the academic community.

My job is to build bridges from the academic "high grounds" to the school-community "lowlands". By building this bridge, my hope is to foster change at both sites. School reform does not lend itself to easy, technical solutions and, as many have noted, higher education and public schools are separate cultures unto themselves (Sirtonik & Goodlad, 1988; Watson & Fullan, 1992). To be successful as PDP Coordinator, I must bring about

> changes not only in the *cultures* of these two traditional types of institutions, but also in their *cultural relationships*. The latter raises acute and complex problems for change and improvement because the cultures of schools and the cultures of universities differ from each other in basic and profound ways. (p, 214, Watson & Fullan, 1992)

How does one affect the separate and different cultures of universities and schools? How does one alter the relationships between these distinct institutions? Further, how can this work, called "community outreach" at Portland State University, be called "scholarship"?

All scholarship including the scholarship of community outreach is the result of two-way communication. Scholarship does not result from a series of isolated events and activities. It depends on building relationships among people, processes, projects and even ideas. High quality communication will cement relationships and foster cultural change.

My immediate community outreach task has been to build new types of school-university partnerships between the School of Education and the broad educational communities we serve. At the same time, my role as a scholar has been to study the processes by which these partnerships came into being, and then, as a teacher, to share this knowledge and experience with my students and colleagues. This is obviously a work in progress. Endpoints are difficult to identify. Yet my community outreach, my scholarship, and my teaching all interrelate. My work embodies the motto of the Graduate School of Education, "Meeting our communities lifelong educational needs" which is an extension of our university motto, "Let knowledge serve the city."

Let me describe several examples of my new faculty role where the work interrelates. Over the past three years in community outreach I have led the creation of Professional Development Partnerships (PDPs) between Portland State University and four public schools: Beach, Lent and Kelly Elementary in Portland Public Schools and Wichita School in the North Clackamas School District. In my own research I have used experiences gathered in creating the PDPs in an article, "The ideal, real and surreal in school-university partnerships: Reflections of a boundary-spanner." Together with Dean Robert Everhart, Principal Paul Steger of Lent Elementary, Principal Karen Lachman of Wichita Elementary and two of her teachers, I organized and directed a symposium, "What IS the value of school-university partnerships?" for the Northern Rocky Mountain Educational Research Association Conference. I have invited the teachers to describe their project to my action research class. and I have involved my students and cooperating teachers in action research projects at these PDP sites, several of which have been presented at a Portland Regional Goals 2000 Conference where 500 attendees shared their action research projects in their classrooms.

From a variety of arenas, I bring powerful resources to bear on the issues facing schools and universities. I have formed and monitored the development of two consecutive 16-member PDP Advisory Councils which have included School of Education faculty, school-based educators from PDP sites and representatives from: PSU Continuing Education, Portland Association of

Teachers, Portland Educational Network, the Portland Public Schools Environmental Middle School, the Portland City Bureau of Environmental Services and PSU's Center for Academic Excellence. This advisory board has become a conduit for university and school resources where PSU Seniors do projects at school sites, public school principals team teach classes with university professors. I have presented two keynote addresses on action research at state education conferences and conducted over twenty professional development workshops for schools to facilitate the development of teacher action research projects. I have invited speakers to share school reform issues with PSU faculty in the noontime Faculty Forum which I initiated.

In another arena, I have shared my expertise on professional development and school-university partnerships with international audiences. As a member of a three-person team selected by the Dean, I am an active participant in studying high school reform in Japan and the United States. My emphasis is the professional development opportunities related to school reform in both countries. I co-presented at School of Education, regional, national and international symposia on Japanese-American high school reform. I now have a former American English teacher in Japan as a graduate student who is working toward her Masters degree studying high school reform. In the future I hope to continue this practice of combining my work on school-university partnerships, research and teaching in an interactive way.

In this paper I intend not only to show the interactive nature of my work but also to demonstrate the scholarship in community outreach. In the PSU Promotion and Tenure guidelines a scholar, "engages at the highest levels of life-long learning and inquiry". Informed by the seminal work of Boyer (1990), PSU Promotion and Tenure Guidelines defined the "highest levels of learning and inquiry" through a list of criteria, which must be present for the work to be considered scholarship. In addition the guidelines apply the general criteria to all three traditional areas of academic work-- teaching, research and community outreach. These are the criteria for scholarship:

1. Clarity and relevance of goals

2. Mastery of existing knowledge

3. Appropriate use of methodology and resources

4. Effectiveness of communication

5. Significance of results

6. Consistently ethical behavior

To demonstrate my scholarship in community outreach I will answer the central question embedded in each of the above criteria.

1. How clear and relevant are my goals?

My goal in community outreach is to foster the development of new "cultural relationships" between the university and public schools. As suggested by Watson and Fullan (1992), school-university partnerships are the "sine qua non" of school reform. One fundamental question guides my work: What role does the university play in facilitating school reform? In answering this question, I bear in mind that objectives are evolving as a result of the collaborative process across the institutions. That does not mean, however, that my knowledge of educational theory such as action research is unimportant. It simply means that I must avoid the temptation to try to mold the results into a tightly controlled plan, while at the same time providing enough structure to build trust. Of all the activities listed in Table 1, 21 out of 22 are collaborative projects. I provided the leadership and brought people together. The collaborative "we"-- principals, teachers, university faculty, graduate students-designed the activities. I feel most confident about the outcomes of such projects when they are collaborative.

2. What is the evidence that I have mastered existing knowledge?

Because school-university partnerships are a collaborative effort, each participant brings something different to a shared process. I bring the more theoretical side of educational research, as well as the experience of working across area school districts. Teachers and principals bring their real-life classroom experiences. As a former public school teacher turned university academic, I feel I am in an excellent position to oversee and understand the interaction between the two. Schools look to me for advice and collaborative expertise. I look to them for an authenticity check.

In particular, school reforms are usually mandated by state and federal agencies (in this case, the state of Oregon), a situation that often leaves educators feeling powerless and sometimes hostile to implementing reforms. The collaborative action research strategies that I have outlined in my article, "The ideal, real and surreal in school-university partnerships" are an outgrowth of my work in public schools on school reform. By applying, teaching, and modeling collaborative action research strategies in our partnership efforts, I am able to study the process and to develop new theories about what works in school reform and what builds school-university partnerships. I have been asked in 1995, 1996, 1997 and 1998 to contribute to the development of the Goals 2000 grants with area school districts. Every year the number of our requests increases and results in more and more faculty involvement in these grants.

3. How have I demonstrated appropriate use of methodology and resources?

I consider community outreach to be both a scholarly endeavor and a professional service, and my methods reflect that dual concern. My "methods", for example, may seem like a flurry of unrelated activities: attending numerous meetings (during 1996-97 alone- 5 meetings at Oregon Department of Education, 85 at school sites), writing in field journals, making public presentations, giving keynote addresses, and helping districts create surveys to assess impacts of reforms. Yet all of these community outreach methods are resources for schools, their faculties and the state school reform agenda.

For example, I keep a professional journal with field notes from every meeting I attend. This not only ensures my own reflection but also models reflective practice for my partners. After a meeting people often ask for copies of my journal pages. My journal has also proven useful for documenting insights from interactions in the field. This has led to the creation of a symposium with school-based educators for the Northern Rocky Mountain Educational Research Association Annual Conference this year and to an American Educational Research Association paper on structuring school-university partnerships.

Another example of this dual approach of scholarship and service in community outreach is the work I have done to assist districts in evaluating existing programs. Together we have developed surveys to analyze the results of Goals 2000 collaborative action research projects over the last three years. For example, to measure the value of a collaboratively-designed Portland Metro Goals 2000 Conference, I conducted a survey of the participants (500 attended) and the results were published in the Professional Development Network Newsletter which is sent to over 350 area educators.

4. How effective is my communication?

Collaborative school-university partnerships require constant, ongoing communication. Because of this, I maintain detailed records of ways to contact key field-based educators throughout the Portland Metro area. I communicate with this network through both oral and written methods.

My oral communication methods are more numerous and more difficult to define. These involve anything from formal, keynote addresses to timely workshops in field settings, to simply having a cup of coffee in the teachers' lounge in any school of the over 50 schools in which I have worked.

5. What is the significance of this work?

Watson and Fullan (1992) note that "basic change in the relationship between schools and universities is a *sine qua non* of educational reform." Over the last year and a half, Curriculum and Instruction faculty have been placing student teachers at each of our elementary partnership sites. Eight teachers at the PDP sites have participated in action research projects. We call these Professional Development Partnerships (PDPs); others call them Professional Development Schools (PDSs).

My PDP goal is to blur the boundaries between the university and the public schools so that schools inform university curriculum, the university influences schools, and what we finally do together facilitates student learning. This is an ambitious goal. The centerpiece of this goal is collaboration. Table 1 shows that all of my activities except one have been collaborative. What strengthens the collaborative aspect of these activities is setting goals, sharing knowledge, fostering communication and encouraging reflection. This becomes my scholarship. On the horizontal axis on Table 1, therefore, I have shown how each activity represents one or more of the attributes of scholarship. Examples of collaborations with the field include designing the "Call for Participation" which invited area schools to become PDP sites, working for agreement on "Letters of Commitment" between the PDP Schools and PSU, and creating the Portland Metro Goals 2000 Conference with an ad hoc board of district administrators.

I have become the main contact person for school districts seeking a higher education partner in the Goals 2000 grants. Over the last three years our contacts with districts have grown: from five partnerships in 1995 (the first year) to 11 in 1996, 9 in 1997 and 12 in 1998. From these projects, teachers have presented what they learned to others at the Portland Metro Goals 2000 Conference. In 1996, 21 out of the 37 projects presented were from our school-district partners; in 1997, 34 out of 80 projects presented were from PSU faculty partnerships. This means teachers have the opportunity to share what they have studied in their action research projects. In the survey of Goals 2000 conference participants teachers noted that presenting at the conference helped them learn more about their projects and they valued the collaborative nature of the action research process. Teachers are their own best resources in making significant changes in classroom practices. Doing action research helps them to be systematic in the study of classroom changes. Beyond the number of conference presentations, an increasing number of area school districts collaborated with us to design and implement the Portland Metro Goals 2000 conference (In 1996, 140 attended with 4 school district partners; in 1997, 500 attended with 10 school district partners). There are an increased number of faculty involved in district collaborations on Goals 2000 projects (1996- 3 faculty; 1997- 5 faculty).

Even outside the framework of the PDP, I have promoted university faculty collaboration with the public schools. This is significant because school district partners work with University faculty in new ways, and university faculty have an opportunity to hear and work with a variety of school districts on problems and issues. Our newly designed district-based teacher certification program in North Clackamas School District is an example of school district-university collaboration. One principal and I collaborated on an article on our PDP work for the University faculty magazine, the PSU Faculty Focus. The PSU Center for Academic Excellence has a representative on the PDP Advisory. She will be bringing teams of PSU Seniors to PDP Schools to do their Senior Capstone experience, a project designed to complete their undergraduate major.

During my first two years at PSU, in response to a faculty need for more communication and conversation across the departments, I initiated a Faculty Forum, a model from Whitman College where I was for three years. This Forum is designed to facilitate communication, even collaboration, among the faculty about a variety of topics- sharing a book review, showing slides from a trip, providing information about new state assessment guidelines, or hearing about school reform issues from our colleagues in the field. We meet once a week at noon; light lunch is provided. This has been instrumental in facilitating communication across the departments as well as keeping faculty informed about activities and interests in the field. School-based educators have participated in ten of the School of Education forums over 1995, 1996, and 1997. There have been 47 forums so far with attendance varying from 4 to 60 people, even though I stepped down from leadership a year and half ago, other faculty have stepped forward to continue this new "tradition". This is a significant change in the isolationist culture of university faculty.

6. How have I demonstrated consistently ethical behavior?

My goal has been to foster school-university partnerships. Schools do not have time for people who are not trustworthy and contributing to their overall development. In my experience, schools will not come back to the same source if they feel that their trust has been violated. If the area educators, my colleagues and my students trust me, I believe that I have been acting in an ethical manner. One demonstration of that trust is an increase in participation rates. In every instance of my work-- Professional Development Partnerships, Goals 2000 projects, Faculty Forums, PDN Newsletter and, even among my advisees, there has been an increase in participation over the years. I believe that this shows that our partners, my students, and my colleagues trust me and respect the work that I do.

Conclusion

As Donald Schon's aptly describes, the "swampy lowlands" and the "academic high grounds" are the traditional academic views of the landscape between schools and higher education. Yet, where the most perplexing and pressing problems exist is in the field, the swampy lowlands, not in the bound and dusty library serials. By bridging the two distinct cultures in these landscapes-- public schools and the University-, I have been able to illuminate problems for us and our field-based educators to study and solve. Work in the swampy lowlands can engage the scholar in the "highest levels of lifelong learning," and, thereby, be considered scholarship, the scholarship of community outreach.

Table 1: Professional Development Partnership activities by Essential Attributes of Community Outreach Scholarship.

		Essential Attributes of Community Outreach Scholarship*				
Dates	Activity	1. COLLABORATE Participate in collaborative activities	2. SET GOALS Define, structure and document goals & expectations	3. SHARE KNOWLEDGE Share faculty expertise	4. COMMUNICATE Celebrate changes publicly	5. REFLECT Build in opportunities for reflection
1995 1996 1997	School of Education Faculty Forum organized	X	X	X	X	X
1995-98	Teach Action Research class	X	X	X	X	X
1995-96	Formed PDP Advisory, meets to plan "Call" to seek new PDPs	X	X	X		X
1995, Dec.	"Call" sent to all area school district. superintendents	X	X			
1995 1996 1997 1998	Goals 2000- Round 1- 5 Sch. Districts Round 2- 9 SDs Round 3-12 SDs Round 4- 12 SDs	X	X	X		
1996, June	4 PDP schools selected by Advisory	X				
1996 1997	PDP Letter of Commitments 1996-1 1997-3	XX	XX	XX		X
1996-98	New PDP Advisory formed & meets	X	X	X		X
1996 1997	Portland Metro Goals 2000 Conference. 1996- 34 presentations 1997-80	XX		XX	XX	X
1996 1997	PDN Newsletter launched	X		X	X	
1997	New models of School-University. partnerships- North Clackamas District-based cohort	X		X		
1997	Presented at NRMERA Conf. with school-based educators	X		X	X	
1997	Sent in article on my work			X	X	X
1997-98	PSU Undergrad Senior Capstones in PDP sites	X		X		
1997	Article in PSU Faculty Focus with school principal	X	X	X	X	X
1998	National Conference. Presentation on structuring school-university partnerships	X		X	X	

* Derived from PSU Criteria for Scholarship in the Promotion and Tenure Guidelines: #2-Clarity of Goals; #3- Mastery of knowledge; #4- Effective Communication.

Support material.

1. List of Faculty Forum presentations: 1994, 1995, 1996, 1997.

2. "Call for Participation" inviting schools to become partners: 1995.

3. Portland Metro Goals 2000 Conference Programs: 1996, 1997

4. List of partners for Goals 2000 grants: 1995, 1996, 1997, 1998

5. PSU <u>Faculty Focus</u> article on PDP work written with principal from an elementary school: 1997.

6. <u>Professional Development Network Newsletters</u>: , 1996, 1997, 1998

7. Article to be published in <u>Teaching and teacher education</u>: "The ideal, real and surreal in school-university partnerships: Reflections of a boundary-spanner"

References

Schon, D. (Nov/Dec., 1995). Toward a new definition of scholarship. Change, 27-34.

Sirotnik, K. A. & Goodlad, J. I. (1988). The meaning and conduct of inquiry in school-university partnerships. In Sirotnik, K. A. & Goodlad, J. I. (Eds.) School-university partnerships: Concepts, cases and concerns (pp. 169-190). New York: Teachers College Press.

Watson, N. & Fullan, M. G. (1992). Beyond school-university partnerships. In M. Fullan & A. Hargreaves (Eds.), Teacher development and educational change. London: Falmer.

Tapping Into Teachers' Dedication: The Tropical Rain Forest Field Experience
Michael R. Cohen
School of Education
Indiana University - Purdue University Indianapolis

PURPOSE AND RATIONALE

"The natural world is by far the most diverse and evocative intellectual stimulation known to humans." (Jansen, 1988).

I have been involved with in-service education since 1966 when I worked with teachers outside Syracuse, N.Y., implementing a new process skills program in elementary science. Most in-service education for teachers involves a period of study on a specific topic. Many include follow-up meetings during the academic year. Teachers are often grouped by grade level and discipline and committed to changing. However, few in-service "experiences are truly energizing," (Udall & Rugen, 1997). Teachers return to their students and are shortly back to their usual content and methods. The university faculty who conduct the program also return to their university responsibilities little changed.

I have not been deterred by the seeming ineffectiveness of in-service education for teachers. My understanding of the limits of in-service education and my expectations for change among the teachers provided a foundation upon which I thought I could develop a potentially effective program; (Posner & Gertzog, 1982; Posner, Strike, Hewson & Gertzog, 1982; Osborne & Freyberg, 1985). The Tropical Rain Forest Experience, a cooperative program between our School of Education and the Indianapolis Zoo, began as a simple, straightforward in-service program. I felt this program's first goal of increasing teachers' scientific knowledge about tropical rain forests would be *enhanced through a field experience* in Costa Rican rain forests. First hand experiences would help the teachers understand the content at a deeper and more meaningful level. This would lead to the second program goal of helping the teachers integrate rain forest science concepts into their curriculum. I was intrigued by Jansen's statement about "intellectual stimulation" for the human mind. I felt we had a chance of overcoming the limits of traditional in-service education because the "stimulation" would insure cognitive change.

Returning from the first field experience in the rain forest I began to realize we had more than an approach to improve teachers' content knowledge. What began as a straightforward in-service program turned into its own source of "stimulation" for my teaching and research. The first group of twenty teachers who participated in the 1989-90 program surprised me when they presented rain forest programs to more than 12,000 students *outside* their own schools in the eight months following their field experience. This confirmed my perception that there was something special about the program. These teachers seemed to have changed, at least in the short run. In 1997, these teachers still talk about the way the program changed their perceptions of themselves as teachers.

1

In our second program, during the summer of 1991, I observed the risks the teachers endured to become better informed about the science found in tropical rain forests. The teachers ended one busy day transferring from a small runabout to a large boat in four- to five-foot swells. I watched in awe and fear and was filled with respect for the courage of these teachers. This represented a turning point in my perception of the program and in-service education. What had started with a focus on "content" had evolved into an adventure education/outward bound experience. I realized that the dedication of the teachers would be the defining aspect of cognitive change. I learned "that adventure programs have a major impact on the lives of participants, and this impact is lasting," (Hattie, Marsh, Neill, & Richards, 1997). The following is a description of the program's history, activities, and lessons learned.

PROCESS

"Quviannikumut. An Eskimo word used to describe the exhilaration and deeply happy feeling you have as you appreciate the climate and observe wild animals." (Lopez, 1986).

The Tropical Rain Forest Experience was a yearlong science education program involving workshops in Indiana and a two-week field experience in the rain forests of Costa Rica. Four different groups of twenty experienced kindergarten through twelfth grade teachers from the State of Indiana participated in each program during the years 1989-90, 1991-92, 1992-93 and 1993-94. The program was partially funded by a grant from the Indiana Higher Education Commission under the Federal Government's Eisenhower Science and Mathematics program. Each successive program changed as we learned more about the science content of the rain forests, the needs of the teachers, the range of activities available in Indiana and Costa Rica, and the importance of adventure and challenge to the program. The following description is a composite of all four programs.

History: The basis for the Tropical Rain Forest Experience began about 1979 when faculty from the School of Education coordinated an Informal Learning Network with the Indianapolis Zoo and sixteen other informal institutions around Indianapolis. As the most senior faculty member I was the leader of the Network. Our major activities were devoted to integrating formal and informal science education.

When the Indianapolis Zoo was contacted about conducting teacher education workshops in Costa Rica their first step was to contact me. In December 1988, I joined two persons from the Zoo for a five-day visit to Costa Rica to view a potential site for in-service teacher education programs. Upon returning to Indiana I worked with Davis Fishel from the Zoo and wrote several program outlines and proposals for potential teacher education programs. These proposals were the basis of the first Eisenhower Science and Mathematics grant during the 1989 - 90 school year.

It is important to emphasize the cooperative nature of the initial steps of this program. Prior to the program, a trusting relationship was developed between our School of Education faculty and the staff at the Indianapolis Zoo. This cooperation was critical to initiating the program and a continuing factor in the long term effectiveness of this program. This experience shows that universities and schools must be patient when supporting the efforts of faculty developing relationships with outside organizations.

In looking at the relationship between service and scholarship each of the following activities added to my understanding of science curriculum, instruction, and in-service education. These activities also helped me see the relationships between the goals of teacher in-service education and the format and venue of the program. The teacher education community needs to understand that teachers require more than additional information to change their instruction. We need to help teachers see that they can face and overcome challenges, become knowledgeable through experience and interactions with others, and be respected as teachers for pursuing additional study.

Publicity and recruitment: In most in-service programs recruitment is not seen as related to program development. Our publicity and recruitment worked like the science research program studied by Fleck (1979/1935). Ideas in the general community reflected how we advertised our program and people's perception of our advertisements affected perceptions of our program. The local Public television station assisted with recruitment by running advertisements. Initially, these were announcements at the end of various natural history programs. During the last year of this rain forest program they prepared a longer announcement, to accompany a video with scenes from tropical rain forests. Several newspapers around the state also ran articles on the teachers and the program prior to and following each field trip.

We continually worried that we would not have enough new applicants. However, each year, as more teachers learned about the program, we had a stronger set of applicants. Part of the lesson is how long it takes to get the word out and encourage some teachers to take a chance and apply. The exposure provided by the Public television station helped increase the image of the teachers and the IUPUI School of Education. The perception among the general public and our colleagues provided another source of recruitment and affected how we perceived our own program. Our most interesting recruitment was a teacher in the 1992 program encouraging the supervisor from her student teaching experience to apply for 1993. The younger teacher said she wanted to show her appreciation for her mentor. As Fleck (1979/1953) found, our project was becoming interdependent with the community of teachers in Indiana.

The initial five workshops: Saturday workshops ran from April to July. The participants learned about the science behind tropical rain forests, worked on team building, began to think about turning the experience into classroom instruction, and planned for the two week field experience. The team building experiences proved to be critical to our program. These activities included trust walks, guided imagery, and cooperative activities. They helped break down the false distinction between elementary, middle, and high school teachers, common among many in-service programs, and showed how each participant is important to the team.

The two week field experience: No amount of reading, lectures, slides, or videos could have prepared the teachers for the experience of seeing sloths, poison arrow frogs, exotic birds, plants on plants so that each tree was described as its own garden, and watching sea turtles lay eggs. There was no way for the project staff to know that the teachers would experience *quviannikumut* (satisfaction, exhilaration, and deeply moving experiences) as they were drenched by rain, sloshed through mud, or bounced along in a bus on a rough dirt road. The challenge of visiting a foreign country, walking through strange and scary forests, and taking part in adventurous activities added a unique dimension to the value of the experience.

The experience also demonstrated the importance of social, cultural, and economic information when trying to understand science and especially environmental issues. Prior to leaving Indiana we were all experts on the problems of tropical rain forests. Saving tropical rain forests was a simple matter. Many of the teachers had their students collect money through recycling drives to bring to the Monteverde Children's Rain Forest. But our views changed after seeing not only examples of destruction, but the fact that many of those closest to the destruction gained little financially. The problem became much more complex, created cognitive dissonance and the need to reevaluate the science content we teach about tropical rain forests.

Most of these teachers never thought others would be interested in hearing about their adventures. One of the exciting parts of the program is the response the teachers hear when they meet other people during the trip to and from Costa Rica or interact with tourists in Costa Rica. This recognition has come from airline crews who announce the program over the intercom, and from tourists who mirror the teachers' excitement about the opportunity to share firsthand experiences with students. It was important for me to see that others recognized the dedication of the teachers.

Follow-up sessions: After the field experience, we had at least four additional formal Saturday workshops, and several informal gatherings. The first post-trip meeting was officially to review slides and videos and to share how each person had spent the last few weeks readjusting to a "normal" environment. The first year I missed being aware of the reverse culture shock the participants would have returning home. Having had overseas sabbaticals, I should have been aware that coming home has its own culture shock. But I never realized it would happen in just two weeks. For subsequent programs the project staff was better prepared for this problem.

Each year we have learned new ways to conduct these post-trip meetings. The last group included one teacher who has a large number of reptiles and amphibians in his high school classroom. He suggested we meet there and arranged for the school to provide lunch. This was very successful since many of the teachers not only had questions about animals in the classroom, but needed to see how they were kept. They seemed to understand the importance of firsthand observations. This meeting led other teachers to invite the group to their school for a meeting. The 1992-93 and 1993-94 groups are still meeting *on their own*.

Informal, participant-initiated meetings: Various groups of participants met to prepare instructional material for their classes, develop a video, or plan for presentations at professional meetings. These are all signs of the empowerment felt by the teachers. It is at this point when the program staff has to be willing to only provide support and encouragement. As with many educational programs this is our ultimate goal to have the participants continue on their own. If they could trudge through a "wild" jungle in a downpour with water flowing over the tops of their boots, surely they could plan their own meetings.

OUTCOMES

"A wilderness environment is challenging and unpredictable, and thus any person who is interacting with that environment, to be effective, must actively modify his or her behavior," (Hattie, Marsh, Neill,& Richards, 1997).

Cooperative activities: The history of this program provides the first important concept we learned. Cooperative ventures that evolve from long-term associations have the potential to benefit all parties in ways unanticipated when the venture began. The local public television station's cooperation with our program went from providing advertisements to a relationship with workshops on filming, photography, and documentary techniques. When nationally televised programs on rain forests were available the local station arranged for a live statewide discussion that included the "stars" of the PBS special, and teachers from our TRF program. This opportunity enhanced the teachers' self-image.

Insight into in-service: One modification of our view of in-service education was having one program for K-12 teachers from a variety of areas of specialization. The multi-grade, multi-subject, teacher-teacher interactions that resulted from this diverse group of teachers were critical to the success of the program. The interactions among elementary school, Special Education, and high school biology, chemistry, physics, and earth science teachers provided us with a broader base of background information and an enhanced set of observations about the rain forests. This clearly differed from most in-service programs where subject matter and grade level create isolated groups.

Experiential learning: The real learning did not begin until we stepped off the plane in Costa Rica. The sights, sounds, and smells quickly let the teachers know they were in a foreign country. Meeting the faculty from the University of Costa Rica, and the naturalists, quickly calmed and excited them at the same time. The idea of experiential learning began to sink in. The teachers could finally "experience" and internalize what they had learned from the workshops. Experiential learning was probably as important as the challenge/adventure experiences. It was now seen as more than a laboratory exercise or a hands-on activity.

From experiential learning to challenge: After conducting this program with four different groups of teachers we understand that the "challenge" of the trip is its key feature. It

5

provides the confidence the teachers need to take risks back home in Indiana. They understand *quviannikumut*.

Changes in teachers: The confidence teachers gained surviving the rain forests led them to believe they can face any challenge. We met one of the teachers from our 1991 program tagging turtles in Costa Rica in 1992. She said our program gave her the confidence to apply for this new challenge. Several teacher (about ten percent) have taken their own students on field trips to Costa Rica, Peru and its Amazon area, Belize, and the rain forests of the west coast. In addition, prior to this program most teachers had no idea they could obtain outside funds for projects and programs. This program created the need for several teachers to find outside sources of funding to travel long distances to the meetings in Indianapolis.

Another lesson on confidence comes from the publicity experiences. Positive publicity helped our educational program and the status of all teachers. The newspaper articles published after each trip helped enhance the image of the teachers involved in the program while publicity by the Public television station did the same for the School of Education. This small part of the Tropical Rain Forest program, in its own way, supported the School of Education.

Curriculum development: Several teachers have built tropical rain forests in their classrooms. Some of these simulated rain forests have been shared with other teachers. Many of the teachers have moved to implement experience based projects such as river study programs. Again, our tropical rain forest program provided the confidence needed to join other programs.

Unfortunately, only a few of the eighty participants created innovative approaches to instruction in the area of rain forests. While we expanded the teachers use of experiential learning -- and the teachers leading their own students on extensive field experience programs are excellent examples -- true curricular innovation will require additional time, effort, and approaches. We have not overcome all the pitfalls of in-service education and have areas to improve for future programs.

Traditional Outcomes: In addition to the anecdotal examples provided in this paper, there were several traditional outcome measures. The project staff and participants have developed and presented papers at national and international meetings (see appendix). Since 1991 participants' work has been presented at state and national meetings and some of the participants' activities have been published. A television documentary, *Classroom Under the Canopy*, was developed during the 1992-93 program and shown on public television, WTIU in Bloomington, Indiana, in 1996. A contract for national distribution was concluded in July 1997. We received four Eisenhower grants.

REFLECTION

"Sweet are the uses of adversary,
Which, like the toad, ugly and venomous,
Wears yet a precious jewel in his head:"

Shakespeare, W., *As You Like It*

The Tropical Rain Forest Program was successful because the challenge and adventure of the program created positive and long-lasting experiences in the professional lives of the participants (McGuire, 1994) , the project staff, and me. The Tropical Rain Forest program served as a catalyst for my thinking about the problems of curriculum, instruction, experiential learning, and in-service education. Without the "dangerous and unknown" challenges I would have missed the opportunity to tap into teachers' dedication. I would have continued to develop in-service programs for specific groups of teachers, on specific topics, and concentrate on a limited view of *"intellectual stimulation."*

In the eight years since the first field experience I have met many of the participants at professional meetings, in their classrooms, and when they visited, taught, or took classes at the University. In every case they comment on the continuing affects of the program. Frequently they say it was their most significant professional experience. In thirty years of in-service teacher education experiences this is the only project where the "*the exhilaration and deeply happy feeling*," as the teachers have put it, continues to be felt for years. I believe the teachers' idea of "a happy feeling" refers to the pleasure of successfully completing this challenging task.

Appendix

Presentations at professional meetings show our evolution from a description of our activities, to a recognition of its adventure nature, and finally to its affective power on the participating teachers and program staff.

Cohen, M., Furuness, L. & Fishel, D., 1990. What's the tropical rain forest really like? The results of twenty teachers' field experiences. North American Association for Environmental Education, San Antonio, Texas.

Cohen, M., Furuness, L. & Buehler, D., 1992. Teachers trek the tropics. World Congress for Education & Communication on Environment and Development, Toronto, Ontario, Canada.

Cohen, M.R., Furuness, L.B., Buehler, D., McGuire, J.A., & Calvo, C.A. 1994. Fostering teacher growth and curriculum development: The tropical rain forest experience. International Symposium on World Trends in Science and Technology Education, Veldhoven, The Netherlands.

Acknowledgment

This chapter was written in the first person, since it refers to the service component of a faculty member in a university setting. But I could not have accomplished any of this without the help of colleagues and participants. The key players, many of whom helped with the papers presented at professional meetings, were:

David Fishel, Indianapolis Zoo (1988 - 90.)
Linda B. Furuness, IUPUI (1989 - 94. Director 1992 - 93.)
Deborah Buehler, Indianapolis Zoo, (1991 - 94.)
Carlos A. Calvo, University of Costa Rica, (1990 - 93.)
Judith A. McGuire, Indianapolis Public Schools, (Participant 1991. Researcher 1992.)

References cited

Fleck, L. 1979, (Originally published in German in 1935). *Genesis and Development of a Scientific Fact.* Chicago, IL.: University of Chicago Press

Hattie, J., Marsh, H.W., Neill, J.T., & Richards, G.E. 1997. Adventure education and outward bound: Out-of-class experiences that make a lasting difference. *Review of Educational Research,* 67:43-87.

Jansen, D.H. 1988. Tropical ecology and biocultural restoration. *Science,* 239:243-244.

Lopez, B. 1986. *Arctic Dreams.* Toronto: Bantam Books.

McGuire, J.A. 1994. *Learning Science in the Mud: How a Tropical Rain forest Experience Affected Teachers.* Unpublished Master's thesis. Indiana University - Purdue University Indianapolis.

Osborne, R. & Freyberg, P. 1985. *Learning in Science.* Auckland, N.Z.: Heinemann.

Posner, G.J. & Gertzog, W.A. 1982. The clinical interview and measurement of conceptual change. *Science Education,* 66:195-209.

Posner, G.W., Strike, K.A., Hewson, P.W. & Gertzog, W.A. 1982. Accommodation of a scientific conception: Toward a theory of conceptual change. *Science Education,* 66:211-227.

Shakespeare, W. 1988. *As You Like It.* New York: Bantam Books.

Udall, D., & Rugen, L. 1997. From the inside out: The expeditionary learning process of teacher change. *Kappan,* 78:404-408.

Enhancing Teacher and Student Learning Through Collaborative Inquiry

Cheryl L. Rosaen, Ph.D.
Associate Professor, Teacher Education
Michigan State University
March 1998

A Portfolio of Outreach Scholarship
Developed as part of the W.K. Kellogg Foundation Funded
Project on the Peer Review of Professional Service

The Problem

A central goal across my career as an educator has been to improve the quality of teaching and learning for all students. If all students are not experiencing education that sparks curiosity and enthusiasm, prepares them to engage competently in meaningful work, helps them become contributing members of society, or initiates a lifetime of learning, then I must continue to search for ways to accomplish these goals. These beliefs are in keeping those expressed in national dialogue among educators, policy makers, and the public at large. Drawing upon my own experience as a teacher educator and a growing knowledge base, I committed my professional work to one key aspect of school reform: initial and continuing professional development for teachers. It is the quality of the learning opportunities that teachers are able to offer K-12 students that will ultimately determine whether our schools will prepare youngsters adequately for their participation in today's society.

Ambitious goals for schooling create challenges for teachers and teacher educators. Experienced teachers face the challenge of rethinking and reimagining what they want to accomplish in their classrooms, and how they want to go about working toward newly defined goals for their teaching. Teachers entering the profession are expected to embrace new visions of teaching and learning that require reforming--not just fitting into--existing teaching practices. But traditional ways of preparing beginning and experienced teachers through courses and workshops that offer simplified answers to complex problems have proven to be inadequate preparation. Just as teachers need to rethink and reimagine what teaching and learning can look like, teacher educators need to improve professional development opportunities for teachers. My professional work was directed to that improvement.

Investigating the Potential of Collaborative Inquiry as a Form of Professional Development

The outreach scholarship described in this narrative was developed over seven years as I engaged in collaborative inquiry as a form of professional development with various groups of teachers. I define collaborative inquiry as researchers and teachers engaging together in systematic inquiry to explore and address mutually defined local problems of practice and develop insights that are shared with the larger educational community. This work took place at Elliott Professional Development School in Holt, Michigan. Compared to the district as a whole, there are higher numbers of students at Elliott who are eligible for a free lunch program, referred for special education services, and living in homes with other than their two biological parents. Several Elliott teachers were interested in exploring ways to enhance their students' learning.

Michigan State University's professional development schools (PDSs) were conceptualized initially to create contexts where teachers, administrators, teacher educators, researchers and community members could work together toward three interrelated goals: (a) improved education of prospective and experienced teachers; (b) improved teaching and learning for K-12 students, and (c) generation of knowledge that can be used to enhance teaching and the teaching profession. In keeping with this broad agenda, I reflected on the possibility of this PDS site becoming a shared context where teachers, professors, graduate students, and students could live, inquire and learn together, not just for the duration of one outreach project, but as an ongoing, sustainable approach to professional development intended to enhance student learning.

While addressing the PDS goals, my work investigates the following central question: **What role can collaborative inquiry play in improving the education of prospective and experienced teachers, improving teaching and learning for students, and generating knowledge to enhance teaching and the teaching profession?** I pursued this broad question over seven years in the context of three projects with three different sets of teachers. In each context, the focus of the collaborative inquiry was developed jointly by myself and classroom teachers and evolved in response to the needs of the situation and the participants. Graduate students also participated in a variety of roles in each project, thus expanding the professional learning community to include novice researchers and teacher educators.

In the Literacy in Science and Social Studies Project (1990-94), a fifth-grade teacher and I investigated the teaching effectiveness of a writers' workshop model. In the Home-School Connections Project (1994- present), a first-grade teacher was interested initially in revising her literacy instruction to make sure all students, even those who struggle, were learning to read. Over time, a second teacher joined the collaboration, as we pursued specific questions related to children's writing. In a third project, the Teacher Education Inquiry Project (1993-95), a colleague and I supported two first-year teachers in collaborative inquiry into issues of establishing their own sense of authority, autonomy and control in the classroom. At the same time we investigated the role their inquiry played in supporting their professional learning. In each project the questions we pursued grew out of the teachers' immediate concerns. Approaches to the inquiry were adapted to the particular situation. Each new project's design benefited from prior experience and learning from preceding projects so that they became increasingly responsive to the teachers' needs.

I brought to this work some initial assumptions, working hypotheses, and many questions. Like those who advocate action research, I viewed the inquiry process as an opportunity to improve teaching and learning through systematic investigation into real problems identified by classroom teachers. I believed that reflecting in and on one's actions is a critical aspect of professional practice. Moreover, the best available knowledge does not just come from traditional research but also emerges from one's professional experience. I hypothesized that while pursuing and addressing specific problems through action research, teachers and teacher educators could enhance their understanding of children, learning processes, curriculum development, assessment, and approaches to teaching. In that way, action research would become a powerful form of professional development for both teachers and teacher educators. In turn, professional development would lead to enhanced teaching and learning for children.

As I approached my PDS work, I rejected traditional roles university faculty have played in school settings such as "staff developer" or "consultant" or "researcher." I embraced the projects with the intent of joining teachers, graduate students, and children in living, inquiring, and learning together over time. I wanted to see how, through a relationship of reciprocity and interdependence, we could learn more together than we might learn separately. I wondered how our work together could draw upon our respective areas of expertise, enhance each person's professional development (including my own), lead to improved student learning, and generate insights we could share with the larger educational community, including preservice teachers.

In a PDS setting there are two sets of stakeholders. I view the several persons whose learning is at stake as the primary stakeholders: elementary students, classroom teachers, the principal, teacher candidates, MSU faculty and graduate students. Elliott was one of several PDSs that were funded initially by three institutional stakeholders who each brought different expectations to the effort. The Michigan Legislature was interested primarily in fostering improved student achievement. The Michigan Partnership for New Education, a non-profit organization, was interested in exploring ways to restructure schools. Third, Michigan State University's land grant mission supported outreach activities as a form of scholarship.

Developing and Adapting the Collaborative Inquiry Process

As I described briefly above, collaborative inquiry took place within three projects whose time periods overlapped. My colleagues and I reflected on what we accomplished and learned from one project and these reflections informed the goals and questions asked and approaches used to pursue questions in subsequent projects. A pattern emerged of continual collaboration, reflection, feedback and adaptation which generated project-specific impacts. One type of impact was local knowledge that was useful to the classroom teacher in her practice. Knowledge gained from one inquiry cycle informed the planning and design of the next cycle. These inquiry cycles also produced another type of project impact: public knowledge shared in the form of conference presentations, research reports, and published chapters and journal articles. These activities can inform the larger educational community about the specific issues related to teaching and learning, and the role inquiry might play in professional development. Figure 1 also indicates that these activities and what I learned from each successive cycle resulted in broader impacts that enhanced my teaching, additional research and further outreach work.

Each project's participants, particular inquiry questions (developed jointly with project participants) and project activities (adapted to the local situation) are summarized in Table 1. Adaptations in the collaborative inquiry processes are discussed below. Insights gained (local knowledge) about the collaborative process are summarized in Table 2 and also discussed below.

In the **Literacy in Science and Social Studies Project** (LISSS, 1990-94), I joined with a fifth-grade teacher in collaborative teaching and research for the establishment of a writers' workshop (see Table 1). The teacher took an active part in the process. The project responded to time demands during the second and third years by providing the teacher with additional reallocated time, however, the daily demands of her work were not reduced. We learned that creating the enabling conditions for effective professional development outlined by current research (time, collegiality, and explicit support) cannot be accomplished by simply funding reallocated time (Table 2). A second challenge was in developing research questions that arose out of the teacher's daily practice, not solely out of the research center's agenda. We began to co-teach during her writing classes which enabled us to ask questions about "our" changing practice rather than about "her" practice (see Table 2). This brought about a greater parity in our collaboration for making curriculum changes and asking meaningful questions about the practice.

While the LISSS Project work was coming to a close, I focused my attention on another aspect of our professional learning community at Elliott. In the **Teacher Education Inquiry Project** (TEI, 1993-95), a colleague and I studied two beginning teachers' professional learning as they engaged in practical inquiry (reflective dialogue, reflective writing and action research). Our approach reflected what I had learned from the LISSS project work. The content of the inquiry was completely open and there were no timelines imposed by outside funding sources. As each teacher collaborated with one of us to develop and pursue her own inquiry questions (see Table 1), we documented the inquiry processes and inquiry group conversations. In this way the novices were "research subjects," but also participated as "co-investigators" in data analysis and reflective writing about their participation and learning. The four conference papers which resulted in one published article developed out of close collaboration where we shared writing responsibilities, exchanged drafts, revised, and so on (Table 2).

In 1994 while finishing the TEI Project writing, I joined the **Home School Connections Project** (HSC, 1994-present). I have been collaborating with a first-grade teacher to improve her literacy curriculum and instruction. We engaged in several cycles of action research: framing problems of practice, working toward practical and specific solutions, and studying the results of decisions and actions (Table 1, 1994-5). Subsequently, we generated a broader question to pursue that has the potential to inform daily practice as well as public knowledge that can inform the larger educational community (Table 2). This process of engaging in multiple cycles of inquiry is more integrated and recursive than the approach taken in the LISSS Project and even the TEI Project, and reflects my ongoing learning about how to make the inquiry process responsive to teachers' local needs and our intellectual questions.

Table 1: Summary of PDS Projects

	Literacy in Science and Social Studies Project 1990-94	Teacher Education Inquiry Project 1993-95	Home-School Connections Project 1994-present
Project Participants	• 3 experienced classroom teachers • 2 MSU faculty • 3 research assistants	• 2 beginning teachers • 2 MSU faculty • 2 research assistants	• 3 experienced teachers • 2 MSU faculty • 1 research assistant
Joint Inquiry Question(s)	• What is the impact of a writers' workshop and conceptual change instructional model on fifth grade student's learning? • How can goals for writing be connected to other content area goals? • To what extent can or should content area writing allow for the full range of decisions published authors make? • What topics, forms, and writing purposes are most beneficial and why? • Who should be the primary audience for students' content area writing? • What should be the focus of the teacher's response to student writing? • To what extent is a writers' workshop model appropriate for supporting students in using writing to learn in other content areas?	<u>Beginning Teachers' Questions</u>: • How can I support 4 students in collaborating more actively and appropriately in the classroom? • How do the various roles I play influence learning opportunities for children? <u>MSU Faculty's Questions</u>: • How can novices be supported in using practical inquiry to inform their practice? • What might it look like during the first year of teaching? • What does (or doesn't) it help novices learn from teaching?	<u>1994-5 Questions</u> • How can the literacy curriculum be revised to enhance learning for all children, especially those who are struggling? • What more could be done in my reading program to support the learning of all children? • To what extent/how are reading teams helping children become better readers? • How can response to literature become an integral part of a program that is also focused on learning to read? • As parents increase their involvement in the curriculum, how will they learn to recognize signs of their children's participation and learning? <u>1995-6 Questions</u> • What does "reflectiveness" look like in first graders? • What kind of development in reflectiveness is appropriate to expect in first graders? • How can reflectiveness be fostered? <u>1996-7 Questions</u> • How can student learning be assessed in language based inquiry projects in a multi-age classroom?

Project Activities	Collaborative Inquiry • joint curriculum development • regular team teaching • assessment and evaluation • data collection and analysis • collaborative writing • conference presentations	Collaborative Inquiry • data collection and analysis • collaborative writing • conference presentations	Collaborative inquiry • joint curriculum development • occasional team teaching • assessment and evaluation • data collection and analysis • collaborative writing • conference presentations

Table 2: Examples of Local and Public Knowledge

PROJECT	EXAMPLES OF LOCAL KNOWLEDGE	EXAMPLES OF PUBLIC KNOWLEDGE

Literacy in Science and Social Studies Project (1990-4)	Insights about the collaborative process:
	
	• reallocated time does not solve fully the problem of time for teachers to engage in sustained analysis and writing, especially with externally driven time tables
	• co-teaching enables joint inquiry into mutually identified problems
	• collaboration enables reciprocity and interdependence in teaching and research
	
	Insights about teaching and learning:
	• specific strategies and resources for implementing a writers' workshop model
	• specific strategies for assessment of students' participation and learning
		• **14 Conference Papers and Presentations**
		
		• **9 Research Reports**
		  (See Appendices A-1; B-1; B-2)
		
		• **5 Published Articles and Chapters**
		  (See Appendices A-2; B-3; B-4)

Teacher Education Inquiry Project (1993-5)	Insights about the collaborative process: • open-ended content for inquiry enables ownership of inquiry question • open-ended time table for inquiry helps address time problem for teachers engaging in analysis and writing • cross-conversations and reflective writing about specific questions help novices gain insights into their own questions and teaching practice Insights about teaching and learning: • beginning teachers play a central role in constructing their own "problems" of practice • planning decisions influence classroom management problems	• **4 Conference Papers and Presentations** • **1 Published Article** (See Appendix A-3)
Home-School Connections **Project** **(1994-present)**	Insights about the collaborative process: • successive cycles of inquiry enable teachers and university faculty to identify questions that have the potential to generate local knowledge to inform daily practice and public knowledge for the educational community • preparation for conferences and writing for publication generate ideas for classroom curriculum and teaching Insights about teaching and learning: • parent involvement in their children's learning enhances students' literacy learning opportunities • increasing interaction among children of all abilities around children's literature and their writing enhances children's learning opportunities	• **4 Conference Papers and Presentations** (See Appendices A-4; B-5) • **1 Article (Under review)**

Immediate Impact: Meeting PDS Goals, Building Capacity and Developing School-University Relationships

PDS Goal: Improved education of prospective and experienced teachers. One working hypothesis was that collaborative inquiry would become a powerful form of professional learning for myself and the participating teachers. There is evidence that this occurred in all three projects.

The LISSS Project teacher increased her knowledge of children, resources, and specific strategies for implementing a writers' workshop (Table 2). We created ways to assess students' learning (Appendix B-1) from which we developed case materials for use in teacher education courses (Appendix B-2). Most important, we engaged regularly in reading, thinking, discussing and reflecting about our practice as a form of ongoing learning, as documented in a co-authored case describing our professional learning (Appendix A-1). By the end of the second year, this teacher became an advocate for all her students as learners and was eager to explore additional areas of the curriculum to revise and improve. She became an active participant and presenter at numerous professional events. She agreed to co-teach a two-semester language arts methods course with me. She also provided in-school support for student teachers in their curriculum development and unit planning and supported the learning of seniors and student teachers who taught in her classroom. These multiple and sustained ways of choosing to continue and share her learning over time are further evidence that she valued her experiences.

In the TEI Project, the two beginning teachers' views of their own learning are captured fully in a published case of their professional learning (Appendix A-3). One teacher now understands the part she played in creating some of the "problems" she perceived in her practice and understands better the choices she can make as a beginning teacher. The other teacher came to understand the connection between her own planning and discipline problems in the classroom. Both articulated ways in which the inquiry process contributed to their growing insights over time (Table 2). These teachers participated voluntarily in writing about their experience and responding to drafts for publication. Through our own inquiry process, my colleague and I gained insights into ways in which inquiry can be structured to support novices' learning.

During a recent interview, my collaborators in the Home-School Connections Project reported that they consider their PDS involvement to be a critical factor in their professional development. During four conference presentations the first-grade teacher reported on insights about children's learning and on ways to organize and implement her curriculum to address the learning needs of all children (Table 2). Working alongside practicing teachers in the teaching and inquiry process enhances my own understanding of the issues we investigate, curriculum choices, and student learning. I share these insights in my teacher education courses. We are currently writing an article out of our work which is another opportunity to articulate our newly developing understandings.

PDS Goal: Improved Teaching and Learning for K-12 students. Another working hypothesis was that collaborative inquiry could become a tool for improving teaching and learning for children at Elliott. To be worth the investment of time, energy and resources, a teacher's professional learning must lead ultimately to improved curriculum and teaching practices and enhanced student learning.

When I began working with the LISSS Project teacher, students were doing grammar exercises out of a text book and very little writing. By the end of the second year, students were writing in a variety of forms for sustained periods of time on a daily basis. We documented students' increased knowledge of and skill in creating certain forms of writing and their more active participation in the writing community. Students showed increased skill and propensity for collaboration and viewed themselves as authors (Appendix B-1, 2,3,4). Many students even wrote pieces voluntarily at home.

In the TEI Project, because our focus was on the classroom teachers' concerns and on their own learning, we did not gather direct evidence that student learning was enhanced as a result of our project.

In the HSC Project, several cycles of inquiry focused directly on understanding children's learning. Regular classroom assessment strategies (e.g., reading aloud with children) and standardized measures administered during the beginning and end of the year showed significant improvements in students' reading abilities. Our work on reflectiveness in first-graders was largely descriptive, with the aim of understanding more fully what it is that children reflect upon (Appendix B-5). Analysis of new data on student learning in a multi-age classroom is still in progress.

PDS Goal: Generation of knowledge that can be used to enhance teaching and the teaching profession. Table 2 provides a summary of ways in which many of our local learnings have become public knowledge in that they have been shared with a variety of audiences, both interactively and through refereed publications (Appendices A-1-3; B-1-5). We shared insights about student learning, teaching methods, curriculum, assessment, and the inquiry process as a form of professional development. The audiences included classroom teachers, administrators, researchers and teacher educators.

Capacity Building and Developing School-University Relationships. There has been increased interest in and commitment to teacher education issues at Elliott. I feel comfortable in having teacher candidates participate in classrooms of teachers with whom I have collaborated because I know first-hand that these teachers model professional learning. In course evaluations, teacher candidates report positive experiences consistently. HSC Project teachers open their classrooms to my students for "group field visits" where the entire class observes and discusses literacy practices.

During 1995-6, MSU also commissioned an independent evaluation of PDS activities across the several sites. Providing high quality sites for teacher education was found to be the overwhelming strength of the PDS efforts since 1990. The Michigan Department of Education's 1995-6 review of MSU's teacher education program included extremely positive feedback for our extensive collaborative teacher education arrangements with Professional Development Schools.

Through its modeling of effective teaching practices, its active teacher education work, and its generation of knowledge, Elliott is also a resource for the state and the nation. Knowledge is shared with the larger educational community through publications. Educators from other schools, colleges and universities visit Elliott frequently. Professional activities at

Elliott illustrate for other teachers who work with teacher candidates how inquiry is a form of professional learning.

Impact on Teaching, Research Agendas and Outreach Scholarship

Impact on Teaching. Outreach activities strengthen my teaching of undergraduate and graduate courses in a number of ways. Participating in classroom activities on a regular basis helps me to stay in touch with the practical aspects of teaching and expands my knowledge of curriculum and instructional practices. Classroom teachers' participation in these courses on campus and in their school enhances our program offerings.

My own published work and that of my colleagues provide cases of professional learning for study in doctoral seminars on teacher education. My course syllabi (Appendix C-1, 2) illustrate how PDS work helps me to demonstrate how reflection and collaborative inquiry can become critical forms of professional development. Quotes from student course evaluations (Appendix C-3) indicate positive responses to the course connections to school-based practices. Elliott teachers are guest speakers and discuss their ongoing inquiry. My published writing from the LISSS project (Appendix B-4) is used by other instructors as a teaching case in TE 301, an introduction to learners and learning in classroom contexts.

My experience with teaching as research has caused me to change my own approaches to teaching. I now frame my courses as investigations into central questions about teaching, learning, and professional learning, and provide tasks that engage undergraduate and graduate students in their own inquiry. I model and illustrate for students how learning to teach includes cycles of inquiry into teaching and learning. I co-authored an article about how I use practical inquiry to make improvements in my own teaching.

Impact on Professional Development Knowledge Base . In a chapter on collaboration in professional development (Appendix A-2) I described professional development activities across several professional development schools and identified seven critical practices in professional learning, three of which grew out of my own and others' collaborative work in PDS settings. In addition, I drew upon my growing expertise in ways to support professional learning as I co-chaired the Michigan English Language Arts Frameworks Project's Teacher Education Task Force (1993-6). I provided leadership in developing Guidelines for the Professional Development of Teachers of English Language Arts (September, 1996) (see Appendix A-5). Numerous ideas and examples in this resource document stem from my PDS work. As part the dissemination of these Guidelines, along with content standards in English language arts in Michigan, I helped plan and implement a three-day conference attended by representatives (six-person teams) from 40 Michigan school districts. The conference emphasized shared planning and teaching, and collaborative inquiry.

Impact on Research. Following what we learned from the Teacher Education Inquiry Project, my colleague and I initiated an inquiry group for teacher interns and studied how the inquiry process supported their learning. A journal article reporting the findings has been accepted for publication in an international journal. Finally, my past work documents well a co-occurrence of professional learning and student learning, but it does not illuminate fully the connection between the two forms of learning. I am working with colleagues to obtain funding to pursue this new research agenda.

<u>Accountability of the Department and College to Institutional Stakeholders</u>. Participation in outreach activities that generate scholarship and teacher education opportunities are valued highly in the teacher education department. Still, the College of Education is under increased scrutiny by the university administration and the Michigan Legislature regarding whether or not PDS work has been evaluated adequately in terms of productivity, cost-effectiveness, and student achievement outcomes. More organized efforts at developing school wide documentation of improved learning outcomes for teachers and students are currently underway at Elliott through my leadership.

Reflecting on the Documentation Process: An Epilogue

In my Professional Development School work, I have encountered what Donald Schon would call the "swampy low lands" of professional practice--the undefined and messy work of collaborating with classroom teachers toward the broad goal of improving teaching and learning. In meeting day-to-day demands, it is easy to lose sight of my real purpose for spending time in schools on a regular basis: to engage in collaborative inquiry as a form of professional development that will lead to better teaching and learning. Documenting my outreach scholarship has been an important opportunity to reflect upon and articulate goals, processes and outcomes. I want to get better at communicating with colleagues about what I am doing, how I go about it, the problems and issues I encounter, and what the work contributes to teaching and learning. This type of work is rich, complicated and diverse. It makes important contributions to solving practical problems while it also contributes significant knowledge. We need to develop better ways to communicate the potential of outreach scholarship.

Now that I have been through several cycles of the writing process, I recognize that the documentation of my work will never feel complete, since the work itself and my ability to communicate about it are still evolving. More important, I recognize that my narrative is shared not as a model that others are to follow, but rather as an example or "case" of what one person's outreach scholarship looks like and the issues and problems associated with documenting that work.

This project has helped me articulate the intellectual framework and significant question of inquiry that underlie my work. Reflecting on the processes and outcomes is assisting me in identifying strengths, weaknesses and accomplishments. I am thinking more deeply about what I want to accomplish in future projects. Finally, looking at how collaborative inquiry cuts across my PDS projects and other areas of my work (teaching, research, other outreach scholarship) enables me to appreciate its value and its potential. I have many insights about this work that I did not have before the project began.

This progress would not have happened without the various interactions with my colleagues in. Initially, our conversations about what outreach scholarship is and what to include in a narrative were a helpful beginning. It was intriguing to learn that colleagues in vastly different fields with projects that looked very different from mine on the surface were experiencing similar challenges and dilemmas in representing their work to others. Thoughtful and constructive feedback from MSU colleagues and those from other institutions helped me identify some major areas that were not addressed clearly or adequately. This feedback helped me "re-see" my initial draft and feel encouraged to tackle some major restructuring and rewriting that I might not have been inspired to do otherwise. The documentation process is not one that should be tackled alone. The conversation, the insights and the learning about outreach scholarship in general and my own work in particular are ample rewards for the time invested.

ANNOTATED LIST OF ITEMS TO INCLUDE IN APPENDICES

APPENDIX A:
EXAMPLES OF IMPACT ON PROFESSIONAL DEVELOPMENT

APPENDIX A-1: Rosaen, C. L. & Lindquist, B. (1992). *Collaborative teaching and research: Asking "What does it mean?"* (Elementary Subjects Center Series Report No. 73).   East Lansing: Michigan State University, Center for the Teaching and Learning of Elementary Subjects.

> Research Report on role of collaborative inquiry in professional learning (LISSS Project). Includes numerous quotes from fifth-grade teacher regarding her own professional development in this project. This report was included as a sample case in doctoral seminar, TE 970: The Curriculum and Pedagogy of Teacher Education.

APPENDIX A-2: Rosaen, C. L. (1995). Collaboration in a professional culture: Renegotiating barriers to improve practice. In J. Brophy (Ed.), *Advances in research on teaching, Volume 5.* Greenwich, Conn: JAI Press, 355-385.

> Published chapter on the role of collaborative inquiry in professional development.   This chapter was developed out of an analysis of my own and others' efforts at participating in various types of collaborative research. It identifies seven critical practices in professional learning. This chapter is included in the reading list for TE 971: Teacher Learning in School Settings (LISSS Project).

APPENDIX A-3: Rosaen, C. L. & Schram, P. (1997). Professional development for beginning teachers through practical inquiry. *Educational Action Research, 5,* 255-281.

> Journal article which describes the role of collaborative inquiry in supporting the learning of beginning teachers (TEI Project). It was written collaboratively with the beginning teachers and contains numerous quotes that describe their views on and the content of their professional learning. These teachers also discuss how the inquiry process supported their learning.

APPENDIX A-4: Rosaen, C. L. & Zietlow, K. (1994). *Professional growth through teacher research.* Presentation at the Annual Meeting of the Michigan Council of Teachers of English, Lansing, MI.

> Handouts from a conference presentation focused on the role collaborative inquiry plays in professional learning and improving curriculum and instruction (HSC Project). It illustrates the research cycles we engaged in and how the questions from one cycle grew out of what was learned in the previous cycle.

APPENDIX A-5: *Guidelines for the Professional Development of Teachers of English Language Arts* (September, 1996).

> Resource developed under my co-leadership for the Michigan English Language Arts Frameworks Project (MELAF) Teacher Education Task Force. Many of the ideas and examples in the document stem from my PDS work.

APPENDIX B:
EXAMPLES OF IMPACT ON CLASSROOM TEACHING AND LEARNING

APPENDIX B-1 Rosaen, C. L. & Lindquist, B. (1992). *Literacy curriculum-in-the-making: A case study of Billy's learning* (Elementary Subjects Center Series Report No. 58).   East Lansing: Michigan State University, Center for the Teaching and Learning of Elementary Subjects.

> This report (LISSS Project) contains a detailed description of one student's experience in learning to write. It chronicles his changing attitudes, knowledge and participation across the year, showing how Billy gradually went from dutifully completing writing to 'get it done' to becoming engrossed in creating a detailed short story.

APPENDIX B-2: Rosaen, C. L. & Lindquist, B. (1992). *Understanding one writer's growth: Case study materials* (Elementary Subjects Center Series Report No. 66). East Lansing: Michigan State University, Center for the Teaching and Learning of Elementary Subjects.

    Research Report on student learning (LISSS Project) that were developed out of a case study on one student's learning (see Appendix B-1 above), in which ways of assessing Billy's learning are investigated. It is written in a format that allows for group discussion of major issues of assessment. These materials were used in preservice teacher education courses (TE 310: Methods of Instruction in Reading and Writing; TE 311: Practicum in Teaching Reading and Writing). They have also been used in numerous presentations with preservice and practicing teachers.

APPENDIX B-3: Rosaen, C.L. (1994). Voice and empowerment in the classroom: Learning about integration from a fifth-grade student. *Holistic Education Review, 7*, 32-42.

    Published article on student learning (LISSS Project) that describes Brenda's development as a writer across her fifth-grade year. It shows how Brenda made connections between what she was studying in social studies and writing, and learned to draw upon multiple sources to influence her writing.

APPENDIX B-4: Rosaen, C. L. & Roth, K. (1995). Similarities & contrasts between writing during writers' workshop and writing in science: Examining the teacher's role. In J. Brophy (Ed.), *Advances in Research on Teaching, Volume 5*. Greenwich, Conn: JAI Press, 291-354.

    Published chapter highlighting questions about writers' workshop and conceptual change models of instruction (LISSS Project). Included in the chapter are detailed descriptions of Sarah's and Maria's participation and learning in the writers' workshop. This chapter is used in a preservice teacher education course taught by my colleagues (TE 301: Learners and Learning in Classroom Contexts).

APPENDIX B-5: Rosaen, C. L. & Zietlow, K. (1996). *What is reflectiveness in first-grade writers?* Presentation at the Annual meeting of the National Council of Teachers of English, Chicago, IL.

    Handouts from an interactive conference presentation for a teacher and teacher educator audience focused on exploring what reflectiveness looks like in first-grade writers (HSC Project). It includes an emerging model of reflectiveness that considers four aspects: content, processes, attitudes, context. Included were specific examples of student's discussions of their writing journals.

APPENDIX C:
EXAMPLES OF IMPACT ON UNIVERSITY TEACHING

APPENDIX C-1: Course Syllabus from doctoral seminar, TE 970: Curriculum and Pedagogy of Teacher Education, Spring 1996.

    One segment of the course (weeks 9-11) draws upon my developing understandings of the role of collaborative inquiry in professional development to examine "Teacher Reflection and Teacher Research as Professional Development."

APPENDIX C-2: Course Syllabus from doctoral seminar, TE 971: Teacher Learning in School Settings, Spring, 1997.

    One segment of the course (weeks 8-9) draws upon my developing understandings of the role of collaborative inquiry in professional development to examine "Guiding the Learning of Preservice Teachers in School Settings: Collaborative Inquiry." Another session is devoted to exploring "The School Setting and Professional Learning."

APPENDIX C-3 Quotes from doctoral student course evaluations (TE 970; TE 971) that indicate a positive response to the use of examples of school-university connections.

PROJECT TITLE:

EARTHQUAKE LOSS ESTIMATION AND MITIGATION IN PORTLAND,

OREGON: A METHODOLOGY FOR ESTIMATING EARTHQUAKE LOSSES, AND

RETROFIT PRIORITIZATION OF BUILDINGS

PROJECT FACULTY:

FRANZ RAD, PROFESSOR, DEPARTMENT OF CIVIL ENGINEERING

PORTLAND STATE UNIVERSITY

I. PURPOSE AND DESCRIPTION

Applied Earthquake Engineering is a complex network of technical, professional,

educational, societal, economic, and political interests and issues. It is multidisciplinary and

interdisciplinary, encompassing civil-structural engineering, geology, seismology, construction,

planning, and economics. As a professor of Civil Engineering, I have had continuous involvement

in the utilization of my expertise in earthquake engineering for earthquake hazard mitigation in the

Portland metropolitan area and in the state of Oregon. My work to provide technical expertise to

solve community problems is consistent with the mission of the Civil Engineering Department

and with the mission of the University. With all of my community-based projects, my overall goal

has been to help provide the following:

Assessment of earthquake vulnerability

Upgraded building codes

Education and research capability

Economic retrofit prioritization

The areas of earthquake vulnerability and economic retrofit prioritization have been at the

forefront of important goals set by local governmental agencies in recent years. I have been involved in the education aspects of those agendas and in the dissemination of related changes in building codes. As President of the Structural Engineers Association of Oregon (1985-86), I led efforts that resulted in significant movement toward upgrading the seismic code for Oregon. I have continued my service to the city of Portland, and to the state, in research and seismic upgrade efforts. I have worked on related projects with the following agencies and task forces:

City of Portland, Bureau of Buildings

Task Force on the Seismic Strengthening of Existing Buildings (City of Portland)

Seismic Rehabilitation Task Force (State of Oregon)

Oregon Department of Geology and Mineral Industries

My most current work originated because of the potential earthquake hazards in Portland. In my most current work, that is in earthquake loss estimation and mitigation, the stakeholders were Portland's public and governmental agencies. Their needs were for high quality research and modeling of estimation and mitigation, as well as a field inventory of commercial buildings. I worked closely with the agencies to seek reasonable and economical solutions for seismic upgrading issues.

II. PROCESS

To achieve the goals of this current project, I have developed and accessed significant resources:

1. Faculty and student participation

Over the past five years, about fifty students (graduate and undergraduate) along with several faculty and staff members have been engaged in the seismic assessment of commercial buildings. These students represented Portland State University, Oregon State University, and the University of Oregon, and in varied majors including civil engineering, architecture, computer science, and geology.

2. Financial support

The project has used grants and contracts totaling approximately one-half million dollars.

3. Knowledge base

The foundation for planning and carrying out the described project has been the knowledge base of research and practice in geology, seismology, geotechnical engineering, computer programming, and mathematical modelling.

The theoretical and methodological principles used to define the issues of this work included those of structural analysis and design, and GIS mapping. In addition, the "best practices" in team building, communication, training, and cost analysis informed the process of preparation, planning, and implementation.

The design for this particular earthquake assessment project has some situation-specific elements that make this current activity significantly different from any in my prior experience, and from descriptions in the literature. First, no other project has applied the "visual assessment" methodology to a large metropolitan community. Second, no mathematical models were available to be based on field results. Third, previous models had worked with only a sample of buildings and drawn a general conclusion. We decided to survey all buildings for greater confidence in the conclusions. Thus, the magnitude of the project, and the number of participants and activities to be coordinated, comprised a significantly unique context.

To prepare for the initiation of assessment methodology, students and faculty/staff were trained for two weeks. The community stakeholders provided needed preliminary information such as tax data and GIS maps. Weekly review meetings were held with community agency partners; daily meetings were held with students and colleagues. Each of the participants played a major role in the process of implementation:

Students engaged in the field work and provided daily feedback on the process.

Staff/faculty reviewed results and provided evaluative feedback.

Community partners reviewed results, fine-tuned the process, and provided leadership for

related research.

The project objectives were: 1) to utilize the seismic hazards data for about 45,,000 non-

residential buildings in Portland in developing an earthquake damage and loss estimation model;

and 2) to develop a retrofit prioritization methodology for maximum system efficiency. To

conduct the buildings survey, a special Rapid Screening Procedure (developed by the Applied

Technology Council) was used. For each building, the data set contained 16 descriptors including

information such as the number of stories, non-structural falling hazards, estimated average

number of people, building use, etc. The modeling methodology incorporated these data, and the

effects of soil conditions from earthquake hazard maps. The modeling methodology also included

provisions for estimating loss of life and serious injuries in the event of a earthquake. In the

retrofit portion of the project, a building classification system was formulated, and cost-benefit

analysis was utilized, to establish retrofit prioritization.

The results of the loss estimation modeling has been expressed in terms of percent (or

dollar) damage to buildings, and number of expected casualties. The damage for the Portland

metropolitan area was analyzed and compiled based on type of structure, age, number of stories, a

defined area within the region and a variety of other characteristics. The retrofit prioritization

methodology provided a list of high benefit-to-cost ratio buildings that should be targeted for

possible seismic retrofit.

III. OUTCOMES

The major conclusion of the project is that it appears possible to obtain more accurate estimates of damage due to earthquakes of various magnitude, and to plan retrofit programs in an urban area, based on more refined building stock data, earthquake hazard geologic maps, and cost-benefit analysis. To measure the quality of outcomes and effectiveness of the project's methodology I engaged national and Portland area professional peers in a review process. Related papers, presentations, and seminars were subject to peer review by refereed journals, conference committees, and expert task forces.

This work has had significant impact on the research and educational capacity of the Department of Civil Engineering; on teaching, learning and program development in the department; on my research focus and scholarly contributions to the profession; and on the community of Portland.

Impact on the Department of Civil Engineering. The course offerings in civil-structural earthquake engineering have expanded significantly. New courses in Advanced Masonry Design, Seismic Site Evaluation, and Current Issues in Earthquake Engineering are just a few of the curricular areas influenced by this project's accomplishments. In 1995 an innovative approach to instruction and program development was recently undertaken through a series of videotaped distinguished lectures in earthquake engineering. The series was later aired on public television.

Approximately one-fourth of all upper division and graduate students were involved directly or indirectly in the project in fieldwork activities. These students gained a working knowledge of seismic issues, structural engineering, mapping, field work, computer data entry, and other related computer work. Those same students also benefited from the insights gained from teamwork, community interactions, and relationships with engineering faculty.

The project has enhanced the research capacity of the Department of Civil Engineering.

Related to the project has been the addition of a seismic simulator to the department's technology resources. The simulator is the only one in existence in the state.

Individual Research and Scholarship. This community experience has significantly affected my own disciplinary understanding, my research activities, and my teaching. The work has strengthened my understanding of theory and practice specifically in earthquake engineering. At the same time, I developed sensitivities to and knowledge of the workings of various public agencies, and of the complexity of collaborating with a multiplicity of stakeholders. In the area of seismic issues, my knowledge base and insights have been expanded and my teaching in those areas improved. My own personal research thrust has been modified, and I now have a cohort of colleagues who are interested in earthquake hazard mitigation research.

In the area of research scholarship, I have been successful in the dissemination of insights and results through publications and presentations (Appendix). Those scholarly pieces have successfully described the modeling process, community impact, and student learning.

Community impact. This work on seismic assessment, determination of vulnerability of commercial structures to earthquakes, and information on avoiding large losses by economical prioritization of buildings for retrofit action have had an enormous impact on the community of Portland. Both city and state agencies have been engaged in the process and have collaboratively studied the issues for new insights and for data to impact engineering processes. I have personally addressed numerous community gatherings (Appendix) to share the insights and conclusions.

In the broad sense, the target audience for this project has been the general public. Over the five years of this work, the public has had significant exposure to earthquake hazard issues. Public awareness has been targeted through the news media, TV shows, and personal appearances at meetings organized for that purpose. In the future, other cities may follow Portland's lead in the performance of seismic hazards modeling and information dissemination.

IV. REFLECTION

As I reflect back, the value of my involvement in this project over the past 5 years has continually increased. I appreciate the fact that I now know more about earthquake engineering and that this knowledge is being disseminated to many others: students, engineers, policymakers, and the general community. This project has afforded me the opportunity to work with varied groups in different settings--groups that have different value systems and agendas. Finally, this community-based project has made me a better-informed faculty member and, more important, a wiser man.

V. APPENDIX (SAMPLE SUPPORT MATERIAL)

1. <u>Scholarly Publications</u>

Rad, F. N., & McCormack, T. C. (1997). Earthquake loss estimation using earthquake hazard maps and building data. *Proceedings of the 1997 American Society of Civil Engineers Structures Congress.*

McCormack, T. C., & Rad, F. N. (1997). An earthquake loss estimation methodology for buildings based on ATC-13 and ATC-21. *Earthquake Spectra*, November.

Rad, F. N. (1995). An overview of seismic analysis and retrofit recommendations for Portland Public School buildings. *Oregon Geology, 57* (3), 67-69.

2. <u>Technical Reports</u>

Rad, F. N., & McCormack, T. C. (1996) Development of a model to estimate potential earthquake damage for buildings. Submitted to Metro.

Hasenberg, C., McCormack, T. C., Rad, F. N., & Gorji, M. (1995). Seismic analysis and retrofit recommendations for four Portland public schools buildings. Submitted to DOGAMI.

3. <u>Professional Presentations</u>

"Earthquake Risk and Seismic Rehabilitation of Existing Buildings" for the Oregon Seismic Safety Policy Council, Portland, Oregon, September, 1996 and for the Oregon Department of Geology and Mineral Industries, November 1996.

"Teaching Reinforced Concrete Design in a Laboratory" for the American Concrete Institute Spring Convention, Vancouver, BC, March 1993.

Community-Based Learning Project Documentation

Collaborations:
The Portland YWCA and Women's History, 1901-2001

Patricia A. Schechter
Department of History
Portland State University
1998

Collaborations:
The Portland YWCA and Women's History, 1901-2001

Opening Reflection

This document provides an overview of the Collaborations history project for the purpose of promotion and tenure review. The documentation emphasizes my role as a teacher in the classroom, an historian in the community, and my personal intellectual journey as a scholar. I selected materials to assist in evaluating the quality and substance of teaching, service, and scholarship. I hope this sample can guide faculty who need to document multi-year service-learning projects at an early or middle point.

Ideally, any such documentation should distinguish and articulate a project's elements, theorize the relationships among the elements, and describe the dynamics, changes, and impacts of these elements over time. Yet at the early or middle stages of multi-year projects, these documentation goals cannot be fully met. The results simply are not in yet. What follows distinguishes the parts fairly well, suggests but does not fully define their relationships, and only sketches out possible directions of change and final impacts. I present the material in outline form for clarity in the midst of a our own messy midpoint. As a final goal, I hope to later produce a more integrated narrative that incorporates more varied materials like articles and photographs and thereby give a richer sense of our work.

I. Introduction

Our purpose is to research, write, and present the history of the Portland Young Women's Christian Association (YWCA) through a series of University Studies Capstone courses beginning in 1996 and ending in 2001, the year of the YWCA's centennial celebration. We plan to accomplish this purpose with a book of articles, a series of student forums, and a final mounted exhibit open to the general public in downtown Portland, Oregon.

The YWCA's archivist, Rebecca Shoemaker, approached Portland State University with the idea of having an institutional history written in celebration of the organization's centennial in 2001. Working with the Women's Studies program, the YWCA history project has been framed as collaborative in form, structure, and content. It is about students, faculty, and community partners working together to explore how women in Portland in and around the YWCA worked together over the past 100 years. With this in mind, faculty facilitators have been breaking the YWCA's century of history (1901-2001) into course-sized pieces. This report documents our first two courses. In the spring of 1996, a "pilot" capstone focused on the Northeast Center branch of the YWCA in the 1960s and 1970s and involved oral history. The second capstone in the spring of 1997 explored the archives at the downtown center and focused on the World War II era (1940-1950).

Collaborations is thus an institutional history research project situated in an innovative teaching venue that is linked to the service missions of both Portland State University and the Portland YWCA. The project's service-learning framework is distinctive because Collaborations makes the meaning and history of "service, "community," and even "citizenship" central to our approach and outcomes. Integrity demands this since the missions of the YWCA--"the advancement of women and the elimination of racism and other forms of discrimination"--and of PSU--"Let Knowledge Serve the City"--raise as many questions as they answer about what these institutions--and, indeed, we ourselves--are about. Students are well aware that these missions themselves are in flux and potentially conflict. We have found that most of the history we grapple with is a record of multisided struggle over constituting and making concrete the concepts of citizenship, service, and community in institutional life and in the city at large. I hope that the lively sense of engagement with these questions generated by the capstone courses is conveyed in the following pages.

II. Framework

The framework for Collaborations relies on the academic practice of history and sociology. We proceed from the premise that history is not just something that "was" in the past but something we also "do" in the present. In this spirit, participants in Collaborations investigate, analyze, and present their findings about the YWCA's one-hundred year career in the Portland community.

Through scholarly papers and articles, public forums featuring student research, and exhibits, we hope to contribute significantly to the burgeoning field of Western women's history.[1] The fine-grained community study we have in mind also touches on a number of pressing questions in twentieth-century American history and sociology, among them the movement of social service provision from religious and community-based institutions to government and the roles women played in this transformation at the grass-roots level.[2] Other key historical themes include feminism, religion, and politics among organized women as well as the issues of race, class, and ethnicity in female religious life and social action. Sociology helps us conceptualize the process of community formation and patterns of social activism, especially in the contemporary period.

III. Resources and Stakeholders

A. Portland State University

1. University Studies: Through an ACME grant, PSU has been the primary source of funding for this project. The University Studies curriculum shapes our general learning objectives to foster critical thinking, written and oral communication, group projects, and social responsibility.

---

[1] See, most recently, Writing the Range: Race, Class, and Culture in the Women's West, eds. Elizabeth Jameson and Susan Armitage (Norman: University of Oklahoma, 1997) in which work on Oregon women is extremely sparse. See also Karen J. Blair, ed., Women in Pacific Northwest History: An Anthology (Seattle: University of Washington Press, 1988).

[2] See, briefly, Robin Muncy, Creating a Female Dominion in American Reform, 1889-1935 (New York: Oxford University Press, 1990). Linda Gordon, Women, The State and Welfare (Madison: University of Wisconsin, 1990).

2. Women's Studies Program: Women's Studies is the primary administrative center for this project and manages our funding, accounting, and staffing needs. The program actively supports the documentation of women's history in the Portland community and encourages the critical use of feminist theory and pedagogy in WSC courses in the University Studies curriculum. Melissa Gilbert, a sociologist and Program faculty member, has been a co-facilitator of Collaborations.

3. Department of History: The Department of History cross-lists The YWCA capstone courses among its own offerings. Former Chair David Johnson and current Chair Gordon Dodds have been extremely supportive of the project, committed as they are to the University Studies curriculum as a whole. Collaborations supports the Department's stated mission by providing students with the opportunity to "integrate knowledge" and "engage in critical thought and research."

4. Students: Each capstone student is an active and significant stakeholder in this project. Their work is passed along to the next cohort of student researchers. The findings, field notes, transcripts, and essays of capstone participants will be made available through the use of a computer data base management system which is currently in the planning stages. Students also identify their learning needs through a written self-assessment at the capstone's beginning and complete a course evaluation at the end of their work.

B. The YWCA: The YWCA is an organization with roots in nineteenth century Anglo-American Protestantism. During the twentieth century, the YWCA changed from a primarily evangelical organization to a social service organization. Throughout its history, the YWCA has embodied a commitment of religious women to working in the interest of women and girls in local, national, and international contexts.

1. Local context: The downtown center has an archive with holdings that include board minutes, an extensive photography collection, financial records, and numerous files of clippings, correspondence, and ephemera. In addition, Portland women throughout the organization and community play a central role in recovering and retelling the story of the YWCA through oral history. These women are active participants and major stakeholders in this undertaking. The Portland YWCA is very pleased and excited about this project. However, the official posture of the Board of Directors and the general relationship between the YWCA and PSU will shift as the project proceeds and funding requirements change.

2. YWCA/USA: Rebecca Shoemaker and I have had conversations with the staff at the national headquarters of the YWCA/USA in New York City. They are extremely excited about the Portland project and shares our hope that this work might be a model for other local YWCA histories. Dorothy Wick, their new archivist, is more than willing to support our work through, for example, letters of recommendation for grant applications. We plan on developing this relationship more fully in the coming years. The microfilm collection at national will be useful in documenting the Portland story.

C. Patricia A. Schechter: My expertise and training is in nineteenth century U.S. history with concentrations in women's studies and African-American studies. My experience in interdisciplinary work stems from my co-editing of <u>Critical Matrix</u>, a scholarly journal published by Princeton University's Program in Women's Studies in 1989-90. Collaborations is my first endeavor in community-based research and teaching. My dedication to this project derives from both PSU's and my department's commitment to University Studies and my own enthusiasm for socially engaged research.

D. Other Community Members: The project draws on the expertise and interests of a number of additional individuals and institutions. These include Chris White, head of manuscripts at Oregon Historical Society, for her guidance in reorganizing the YWCA's archives; Professor Susan Lynn, Professor of History at Portland Community College, Slyvania Campus, who is an expert on the history of the YWCA in the USA in the twentieth century; and Dr. Doug Erickson of Lewis and Clark College, who teaches archival management and methods at PSU. His students have been the interns who have organized and catalogued the downtown archives.

IV. Process

Collaborations actively involves students, faculty, and the community partner. Together we create meaning in dialogue, not just retrieve it from the archives. Intellectual exchange among students and between students and YWCA community members is central to this process of creating meaning. Of course, intellectual struggle has emerged and will continue. This struggle testifies to the vital engagement of the participants and their critical understanding of what it means to do and make history. Powerful consensus also operates to hold us together. We share a belief in the importance of exploring the lives of women--people who often lack institutional, political, and economic power--in order to fully understand and appreciate the past. Such explorations require redefining what constitutes "power," thinking critically about historical agency and social change, and examining that much over-used word "community" in the context of female networks and friendships that often remain outside the official records of institutions.

A. Scholarship: Collaborations has introduced me to new areas of historical inquiry and offers new opportunities for scholarship. First, I have begun to assimilate several historiographies with which I had limited experience in the past, specifically on women in American religion, Western women's history, and post-World War II U.S. history. In addition, I have done new work in oral history theory and technique as well as reading in the practice of local history and public history. Finally, collaborative historical research and writing is a new field for me and I feel extremely fortunate to have such excellent colleagues in Women's Studies and in the city at large to work with. As I complete my current (first) book on journalist and reformer Ida B. Wells-Barnett, I look forward to the YWCA project as the next focus of my scholarly career.

B. Student learning: Collaborations places PSU faculty, the YWCA, students, and community members in a shifting and dynamic relationship. Faculty work self-consciously as facilitators of student inquiry rather than as final authorities on the Portland YWCA. Faculty stress student responsibility for the approach, execution, and completion of the work. Because of the experimental nature of the project and its innovative pedagogy, the roles of teacher/student, service provider/client can move around with sometimes exciting, sometimes unnerving, and often productive results.

1. Oral History Pilot: This capstone was co-facilitated by Melissa Gilbert and myself in the Spring of 1996. Faculty tried to respond to student-identified learning objectives to "do something different," to use their academic skills and knowledge in a practical way, and to connect the classroom with "real life." To these ends, we planned for each student to generate one oral history interview and write a series of analytical papers on their work. With Rebecca Shoemaker's help, we identified a group of YWCA women who had been active in the late 1960s and 1970s in Northeast Portland--a group that still keeps in touch and socializes. Each of nine students contacted women from this group and a total of ten women were interviewed (one interview was done jointly). Time constraints permitted only the writing of one final paper on one of a series of themes identified by the students (friendship, activism, family, religion, etc.). A public forum concluded the pilot.

The main process issue for this course concerned identity politics and prejudice in oral history interviewing. Students struggled with the significance of race, religion, age, and gender in the ethics and methodology of interviewing. Faculty created a context for students to read and think about how social relations shape the creation of knowledge. The class came to a consensus to use multiple interviewing approaches, though this aspect of the research was not well integrated into the final presentation of material to the public.

2. World War II Team: In the Spring of 1997, I facilitated the YWCA capstone on archival research focused on the 1940s (Appendix). This group of seven students had a bit more in common than the pilot group; all but one knew each other previously and had been students of mine. They were eager for more "hands on" experience with history though they ranged broadly in experience from one who is bound for a Ph.D. program in history, to a biology student, to an individual who had never been to PSU's library. After preliminary readings and lectures, these seven students and I dug through boxes at the YWCA archives together. Students each wrote a final research paper and for the public forum, teamed up and integrated their findings around the themes of organizational life, community, and politics.

The signal process issue for this capstone was the team approach and its success. Extensive collaboration throughout--literally sharing work space and materials in the archives--made for rich and informative interactions. Students circulated, read, and commented on each other's written work at every stage as well as received comments from me. They also met in groups outside of class on weekends and explored other libraries and archives in Portland on their own initiative.

V. Outcomes

Outcomes at this early stage of the project (year two of six) are strongly tilted toward student learning and teaching. Scholarly outcomes--i.e. academic papers--have also been generated but as yet are unpublished. Service outcomes are perhaps the most exciting outcome and remain the most difficult to evaluate. The final articles and exhibit will not even exist before 2001 and indeed, the precise form and content of the final products themselves is still under discussion. We are only learning what we have to work with as we go along. The very diversity and uncertainty of the products raises still more challenges regarding quality and evaluation. What follows is a discussion of our accomplishments and outcomes with necessarily the most preliminary of evaluations. The various responses of the YWCA, community members, students, and professional scholars provides a beginning index for where the project is heading as well as thoughts for other possible directions and emphases.

A. Impact

1. Curriculum: Our approach has been multidisciplinary, incorporating methods from sociology and history (oral history and traditional archival research, for example) to achieve its goals. Given the diversity of research materials (texts, photographs, video) and the diversity of possible final products (articles, an exhibit, perhaps even a documentary film), there is plenty of opportunity for students with skills outside the traditional humanities to participate. Yet historical research and argumentation is our fundamental framework. Through recruitment and publicity, faculty have been able to inform and advise students of these features before registering for the YWCA capstone. Thus a major impact on teaching has been to refine in practice the difference between "interdisciplinary" versus "multidisciplinary" work, with Collaborations tending toward the latter.

B. Results

1. Community: YWCA administrators, staff, project participants, and community members are very enthusiastic about Collaborations. YWCA women's willingness to be interviewed, to share information and personal materials, and to attend and contribute to public forums has been extremely rewarding for both students and faculty. Students and faculty have been welcomed and embraced by the YWCA community. After each of our public forums students have been invited to volunteer on YWCA committees; faculty have been offered honorary membership in the organization. Certainly we have a role to play in the world's oldest and largest women's membership movement still extant, one of 400 YWCA associations in the U.S. and in 90 countries abroad. The precise nature of that role is an on-going part of critical reflection as we proceed.

In general, dialogue between PSU and the YWCA about the project has been consistent and positive. I addressed the YWCA's 95th and 97th Annual Membership meetings in 1996 and 1998, and in this way have kept the organization broadly apprised of our progress. The YWCA has received copies of student papers, interviews, and exhibit inventories in order to make our findings available to interested members. Grant applications to the National Endowment for the Humanities and other institutions are planned for the fall of 1999.

Our most significant results to date are our public forums. The first was in June of 1996 in which YWCA and PSU administrators listened to student presentations, including visuals, based on the oral history interviews with women from the Northeast Center. The second, entitled "The YWCA in World War II-Portland," was held on June 10, 1997 at the downtown center. The forum included three student panels that synthesized our research and was followed by discussion with the audience. We also mounted an exhibit of photographs, documents, and ephemera on the 1940s from the YWCA archives, most of which had not seen the light of day for decades. The exhibit was on display and open to the public for one week following the program.

2. Students: Student impact has been varied and presents both challenges and hopes for the enrichment of learning. Collaborations provides a setting in which students evaluate the meaning and implications of "service" and "citizenship" as they figure in our research, their education, and their lives. They quickly discover that their own sense of "citizenship" is multiple and fractured. Searching questions consistently appear. What exactly do the students "owe" the community partner? Who can "own" knowledge" Do professional ethical guidelines clarify or cloud the matter? Such reflection can be destabilizing but we feel it has enhanced the quality of the questions being asked of the team and of the material. The significance of the capstone approach is in the opportunity to build multiple layers of conflict into the intellectual framework of our work.

On a more mundane level, Collaborations has generated opportunities for students to do new kinds of intellectual work outside of the classroom, mainly through independent study and through archival management internships. The capstones also provide students with a chance to "publish"--that is, every student participant is a co-author of the final capstone products and will be listed as such. In addition, a few of the students' individual research papers are of such high quality that they may well find publication outlets on their own. Finally, in just about any field or job, producing a report or piece of research involves variables similar to this capstone: time constraints, difficult sources, uneven levels prior expertise, and team work. In Collaborations, students learn these valuable skills by doing.

3. *Scholarship:* The YWCA project as academic scholarship is perhaps easiest to document. Our project has joined the on-line and newsletter networks of YWCA/YMCA researchers and investigators across the country which will enhance our visibility and our access to scholarly resources and support. I have given academic papers on the Portland YWCA for the Pacific Northwest History Group at Oregon Historical Society and at the Pacific Coast Branch meeting of the American Historical Association on my own research on the YWCA. I have been approached by Oregon State University Press as a possible publisher for the results of our research (probably a short monograph jointly written by Rebecca Shoemaker and PSU faculty). I anticipate writing a series of historical articles on the YWCA, women's organizing, and Portland women in the twentieth century. Melissa Gilbert and I have also discussed writing together on feminist pedagogy and advocacy research in the context of our work on this project. Much of the scholarship we produce on the YWCA in Portland will be published and evaluated along traditional academic lines.

Final Reflection

Collaborations offers students and faculty an exciting opportunity to do socially engaged research. The need for such work--for women to recover and interpret their own history--was a major impetus to academic women's studies over twenty years. Two reasons make it a fitting inquiry today. First, Portland's women's community is "young" compared to that of other urban communities in the U.S., especially in the east. Like many Western states, Oregon lacks a deep tradition of higher education for women or of secular female institution building (like social settlements).[3] Thus the YWCA occupies a unique historical position in Oregon and offers a

---

[3] Marylhurst College was for women between c.1893 and c.1974. On women's church-based organizing in Portland see: Jan E. Kurtz, "'Giving No Orders, but Always Paying

particularly accessible and rich overview of women lives in the Portland community. Second, the YWCA itself is undergoing huge institutional transformation, contemplating, for example, the sale of its current downtown center. To foster education and communication around these issues, the YWCA history project can connect Portland women across generations, neighborhoods, and institutional boundaries at a time of rapid growth and change in the city's, University's, and YWCA's own history. An exhibit at Oregon Historical Society will make available to the general public what we hope will be an extremely informative and bracing story of women in Oregon history. It seems likely, too, that the YWCA/USA will circulate our work as a model for other local histories or perhaps even send the exhibit on a tour of branches across the country.

Finally, Collaborations provides value by focusing on a still largely undocumented area of Oregon history: women in their many roles and communities. Through course work, public forums and lectures, publications, and exhibits, Collaborations strives to foster local reflection on teaching and learning history and contribute to current national discussions about service, feminism, educational reform, and volunteerism and religion in American life. As we in the late-twentieth-century United States search for meaningful community and try to recover (supposedly) lost traditions of volunteerism and service, this project inquires into what we think we have lost and what have yet to learn from the social movements of women in American history.

APPENDIX

Syllabus, Spring 1997

Deficits:' The Evangelical Woman in Oregon's Protestant Churches, 1870-1900," unpublished paper, 1997 and Michael Springer, "The Ladies' Relief Society of Portland, OR: The Influence of the Changing Sphere for Women, 1870-1920," unpublished paper, 1997. Of interest also is Andrew N. Bryans, "Mary Frances Isom and Sarah A. Evans: Progressive Reformers Who Redefined Woman's Sphere in the Pacific Northwest," unpublished paper, 1997; and Ron Solomon, "Beatrice Cannady: Fighting Racism with the Sword of Love," unpublished paper, 1997; and Gloria E. Myers, A Municipal Mother: Lola Greene Baldwin, America's First Policewoman (Oregon State University Press, 1995).

HST 410/UNST 410
The Portland YWCA   in the World War Two Era

Professor Patricia A. Schechter
Tu, Thu 2-3:50
359 CH

Office: 492F Cramer   email: patricia@ch2.ch.pdx.edu

Introduction:

This course is one in an on-going series of capstones designed to research and write the Portland YWCA's history in anticipation of its centennial celebration in 2001. Our focus will be on the 1940s. Themes include: war work and patriotism; working women's politics and organizing; black migration and civil rights; feminism and women's social activism; Japanese internment and relocation; youth and teen culture. After background reading and discussion, students will shape a research agenda and carry out research in the YWCA archives and in other repositories in Portland. The course will culminate in a public presentation on our findings to the community.

Texts:

Hewitt and Lebsock, eds. <u>Visible Women: New Essays in American Women's Activism</u>
Weiss and Friedman, eds., <u>Feminism and Community</u>
Packet -- available at Clean Copy

Texts will be available for purchase in class during the first week of meetings and thereafter available at In Other Words bookstore, 3734 S.E. Hawthorne St.

All assigned readings and most titles from the supplemental bibliography will be available on reserve at Millar Library.

Requirements: (10% each toward final grade)

1. Portfolio/Student assessment
2. Précis on Annual Minutes (2-3 pp.)
3. Reflection on all summaries (2-3 pp.)
4. Draft research prospectus (5-7 pp.)
5. Final research prospectus (5-7 pp.)
6. Outline for theme paper
7. Draft theme paper
8. Final theme paper (10-15 pp.)
9. Public Presentation
10. Attendance and participation

Assignments:

Week I.   Introduction

April 1:   What is Community-Based Learning?
April 3:   What is the Portland Y.W.C.A.?

Reading for discussion:
        <u>Packet</u>: Lynn
        <u>Visible Women</u>: Roydhouse

Week II.   Historical Foundations

April 8:   U.S. Women's Institutions and Organizing

Reading for discussion:
        <u>Feminism and Community</u>: Freedman, hooks, Lugones
        Packet: Sklar
        <u>Visible Women</u>: White, Frederickson, Janiewski

DUE: STUDENT ASSESSMENT/PORTFOLIO

April 10:   The Women, the West, and the War

Reading for discussion:
        Packet: Matsumoto, Skold, Solinger, Coontz
        <u>Visible Women</u>: Hewitt, Hine

DUE: MINUTES PRéCIS ON MINUTES--COPIES TO BE CIRCULATED

Week III.   Theory

April 15:   What does it look like, what does it mean?

Reading for discussion:
        <u>Visible Women</u>: Chafe, Evans
        <u>Feminism and Community</u>: Freedman, hooks, Lugones, (review)
          plus: introduction and choose two (2) additional essays

DUE: WRITTEN REFLECTION ON MINUTES--COPIES TO BE CIRCULATED

April 17:   The making of women's institutions and communities...

DUE: DRAFT RESEARCH PROSPECTUS -- COPIES TO BE CIRCULATED

Week IV. Research Outlines

April 22:   What do we know? What do we need to know?
April 25:   Themes devised and assigned

DUE: FINAL RESEARCH PROSPECTUS

Week V.   On Site Archival Work

April 29:
May 1:

Meet with YWCA archive interns to view photographs and brainstorm with former capstone student Kelley Burke

Week VI.   On Site Archival Work

May 6:
May 8:

Week VII.   Reflection and Writing

May 13:
May 15:   DUE: OUTLINE FOR THEME PAPER

Week VIII.   Reflection and Writing

May 20:
May 22:

Week IX.   Reflection and Writing

May 27:
May 29:   DUE: FINAL PAPERS

Week X: Presentations

June 3:   Trouble-shooting, wrap-up, and reflection
June 5:   Public Forum/Presentations

Bringing Scholarship to the Public:
The Academic Practitioner

Warren J. Rauhe
Associate Professor and Director,
Landscape Architecture Program
Michigan State University
March 1998

A Portfolio of Outreach Scholarship
Developed as part of the W.K. Kellogg Foundation Funded
Project on the Peer Review of Professional Service

The Project

The case study project illustrated herein is the development of a master land use plan for Beaver Island, Michigan, a 5 mile wide by 11 mile long island located in the northeast portion of Lake Michigan. While under continuously increasing pressure for development, the island is at the same time a significant natural ecosystem that is reflective of the natural history of the area. Accommodating and guiding these conflicting demands on the same natural resource base clearly required a master land use plan that was sensitive to the multitude of factors and reflected the consensus of what the future quality of life would be for the residents of Beaver Island.

Background

Warren J. Rauhe is currently the director of the Landscape Architecture Program at Michigan State University and is a tenured associate professor. Prior to joining the faculty in 1987, he had more than 15 years of professional experience in a landscape architecture practice. Since 1987, he has pursued an academic career path that focused on teaching and outreach activities in the area of community planning and development.

At Michigan State University, outreach as…"a form of scholarship that…involves generating, transmitting, applying, and preserving knowledge for the direct benefit of external audiences in ways that are consistent with university and unit missions (University Outreach at Michigan State University: Extending knowledge to serve society, October, 1993, p. 1; emphases added)."

Warren's outreach objectives are the overriding purpose of bringing scholarship to the public, specifically in the area of community development as it pertains to future direction and economic/quality of life improvements. He has further focused on consensus building during the planning and design of the environment within any given community. His specific objectives are as follows:

1. Import theory and practice from other professions to apply to community development. (Organizational theory from the business world, for example.)
2. Combine professional expertise with academic practice. (Teaching/student learning experience in a community-based project.)
3. Leave the community an operational design that will, in a very practical manner, meet community needs.
4. Communicate the successes and failures, to one's peers in both academia and practice.

Over the past 10 years, Warren has pursued a series of outreach activities that have tested various approaches of planning for community development at a multitude of scales and complexity. The common thread throughout those activities was to apply knowledge in a manner that could be observed, recorded, analyzed, and then adjusted for application in another community. The consistency was not the project focus or type, but the *consensus building* process that was employed, and its continual refinement. The case study project illustrated here

1

represents an example project that is typical of outreach activities that span Warren's 10 years at Michigan State University.

Description

The Beaver Island case study project was selected from a larger set of Warren's outreach activities and illustrates creation and application of new knowledge in a specific community setting, while at the same time testing out, evaluating, adjusting, and re-testing the methods of carrying out those activities.

The Beaver Island project grew out of a strong community driven need to guide future growth and development. The Island's two township plan commissions requested Michigan State University's participation and expected, as a final product, a master plan that they could officially adopt. Funding came from the local townships, a private foundation, and MSU. This project combined the research, professional, and teaching experience of Warren J. Rauhe and was the focus of a capstone design course in the Landscape Architecture Program, taught by Warren. The research basis was two-fold Geographic Information System (GIS) based landscape analysis and consensus building strategy. Warren's 20-year plus professional experience in land use planning augmented the work on this project.

The issue of building community consensus during the planning and design process is critical to the success of any local planning effort. The significance of the consensus building element in the Beaver Island project was that it became a continuous thread throughout the entire planning process. Warren's outreach activities were a central part of the planning process from start to finish.

Diagnosis

The Beaver Island project addressed the topics of preparation, context/principal/characteristics, theoretical/methodological principles, and situation specific elements. The project characteristics included a sequence of public input and consensus building sessions, semester long student projects as input to the planning process, a balance of economic development and environmental preservation, and a very lengthy planning time frame (4 years from start to final plan adoption). Warren's expertise and experience on this project ranged from instructor in an active learning environment and applied research in GIS and consensus building, to professional expertise in actually producing the final plan document.

The community and its stakeholders gave the case study project high priority. Methodology and evaluation existed in this case study project, but it was not as formal or structured as one would see in a traditional research mode. Goals and available resources have been, for the most part, in concert with each other. An over-riding concern, however, is that resources have been limited to "project performance" and not available at a sufficient level to conduct appropriate follow-up work. The most significant contextual impact of the case study project was the increased level of participation and local involvement. Methodology was also refined and adjusted throughout the project as the consensus building process was evolved.

Design

Conflicting goals of economic development and environmental preservation quickly emerged. The design of the project and thus the planning process evolved into lengthy philosophical debates, rather than specific planning solutions. This philosophical basis then transitioned into a specific land use plan for the Island. Extensive client ownership developed to the point of local citizens telling the MSU planners/designers to "get out of the way, it's our plan." This transition to local ownership of the process and resulting plan had been designed into the project from the beginning and it was especially gratifying to see this occur, although community involvement had been taken to a high level of risk to create this transition. The Beaver Island project included proper process pre-planning, a willingness to expose the entire process to public input, allowing sufficient time for consensus to form, and utilizing non-traditional consensus building techniques.

Delivery

Delivery mechanisms included multiple meetings, continuous feedback loops at all phases of the project development, graphic and written documents, and major on-site reviews and participation. Delivery techniques included routine teaching, research, and professional practice methods. In addition, delivery methods were adapted from outside of the traditional physical planning and design professions. (e.g., techniques used in business, corporate planning were modified and used.) Over the project's 4-year period, delivery was modified and "improved upon" as feedback from successes, and failures, was analyzed. The most effective delivery occurred when the widest spectrum of participants was included in both the planning process and the consensus building, even though it resulted in longer time frames. Unexpected developments were minimal with the exception of maintaining a consistent and high level of local involvement during the extended planning period.

An objective evaluation of the Beaver Island project would illustrate a lack of traditional academic rigor as to methodology, documentation, modeling, and hypothesis. Because much of the work of this outreach/professional service activity tested out approaches and gathered feedback from local stakeholders, issues of "lack of rigor" emerged. Those issues prompted a study of methodology from the field of behavioral science and its applicability to a similar project.

Outcomes and Impacts

Outcomes of the Beaver Island project were varied and occurred on multiple levels; process and product, academic and professional.

Process, academic - The academic process was an active learning mode for teaching, as students worked on a community project as part of an MSU class. Traditional steps of description, diagnosis, design, and delivery were followed. The community brought a problem to MSU, which also resulted in a traditional service process.

Process, professional - The relationship of community to the university was parallel to the client/consultant relationship. A "scope of services" was agreed upon by both parties and this scope was then executed, step by step.

Product, academic - The teaching piece produced student work as part of a regular MSU course. (Appendix A-1.) The research piece produced peer reviewed published proceedings. (Appendix A-2.) The service piece recommended solutions for the community.

Product, professional - Professional design work, professional planning work, a report, drawings, and supporting text were produced. (Appendix A-3.)

Impacts - In this study project, the goals of the community were met. The final results were formally adopted as the community's official land use plan. The local stakeholders were satisfied and the results directly affected public policy decisions. It is clear that the intended issues and individuals were impacted in a positive manner. The project left the community in a position to direct their own actions with improved and expanded capacity. Resource people at MSU have been contacted by the community for additional assistance and the University has had direct access to additional projects within the community. Active learning in the classroom, a published article, and a service project have all provided new and expanded opportunities. Impact has also been felt on the broader research agenda of consensus building approaches in communities, although this has lagged behind the other impacts.

In summary, the outreach evaluation dimensions of significance, context, scholarly characteristics and contributions that are contained in Michigan State University's outreach matrix have been addressed by the Beaver Island project. The consensus building element of the planning process was the continuous thread throughout the duration of the project and laid the foundation for future teaching, scholarly, and service activities of Professor Rauhe.

Annotated List of Case Study Items

Appendix A-1: Course prospectus for LA 445 - Advanced Project Design and various student projects. (Michigan State University course materials and student project reports.)

Appendix A-2: Rauhe, Warren; Conners, Dean; and Burley, Jon Bryan. (1994.) <u>Beaver Island: Bridging Geomorphology, Ecological Processes, and Environmental Planning and Design</u>. 1994 URISA Proceedings. (A peer reviewed publication.)

Appendix A-3: Rauhe, Warren; Richardson, Dana; Martin, John; and Paquet, Stacey. (1994.) <u>Master Plan: Beaver Island, Michigan</u>. (The official land use plan document for Beaver Island.)

"Bringing Scholarship to the Public, the Academic Practitioner" - A Reflection

Starting in 1987 and for the next several years, outreach projects that I completed were not based in scholarship. Communities needed help to solve economic or quality of life concerns and my experience in planning and design was exactly what was needed; i.e., a consultant. As I settled into academia and the purpose and expectations of what an assistant professor had to do to be successful slowly came into focus, scholarship became the key consideration in outreach activities. The generation and transformation of knowledge for multiple audiences became the central thread of my activities. Given my background, education, and experience, this was accomplished in a highly applied manner.

An overriding premise that developed, perhaps particularly due to my business background, was generating multiple outcomes with one approach. In academic terms, an outreach activity must have teaching, creative/scholarly work, and service benefits. There are also multiple audiences: academic, professional, and the public. Each had its own expectations and "final product needs." In some cases, the process itself was the product. (In consensus building activities, this is especially true.)

With all of this in place, outreach scholarship became quite complex and terribly time consuming. A product for one audience was not necessarily an acceptable product for another audience and thus one could easily feel that outreach activities just added more work to a traditional scholarship approach such as traditional research. In the same view as if a "tree falls in a forest and no one hears it, was there a sound?;" if a "community based outreach activity solved a problem, but no peer reviewed article was published, was there scholarship in that activity?"

My personal outreach activities are not meant to be a substitute for traditional research scholarship. They represent a new paradigm. It is no longer enough to be good at traditional scholarship; i.e., research, measured by all the traditional devices such as _____…you fill in the blank. A successful academic in the 21st century must be *relevant* in all 3 areas of teaching, creative/scholarly work, and service. Must one excel in all 3? No, but at a minimum, you cannot simply focus on one at the expense of the other 2. Outreach activities become the ideal mechanism for becoming a relevant academic. "Bringing scholarship to the public, the practicing academic" is a very real way to survive and thrive.

Allow me to make a few closing observations.
1. My work as an academic must be relevant to my students, academic peers, profession, and the public at large.
2. The academic reward system is changing, must change more, and be more reflective of what "counts" in today's society and marketplace. Our strength lies in how our scholarship can improve lives.
3. Outreach scholarship is extremely time consuming and unpredictable. Outreach takes place "out in the streets," not in a controlled laboratory.
4. Pre-planning and getting multiple results from the same resources is critical. Doing more for less actually works to our advantage.
   In summary, a more focused and systematic evaluation of results, direct feedback from communities, and communicating more with my academic colleagues would add increased depth to my outreach scholarship. The work is terribly relevant as it connects academia with societies' needs, and this must continue to be the case. My experience to date is a "work in process."

The Broadway Shalom Wellness Center: Reaching Traditionally Difficult-To-Access Inner City Population

Sandy C. Burgener, Ph.D., R.N.C.
Indiana University
School of Nursing

I. PURPOSE:

The service activities inherent in my faculty role as Associate Professor of Nursing at Indiana University involve the development and implementation of a small network of church-based, nurse-managed clinics. The Broadway Shalom Wellness Center was established in March, 1994, as a cost-effective approach to meeting the health care needs of defined, under-served populations in inner-city Indianapolis using a culturally sensitive, church-based model of care. The overall project goal was to test the effectiveness of utilizing an established community organization, specifically Broadway United Methodist Church, to reach a traditionally difficult-to- access, inner-city population. As many people relate in some way to a church, temple, or other place of worship, collaboration with such an organization can provide access to under-served populations through both its geographic location and outreach interests, facilitating access to minority populations not readily open to formal health care providers (King et al., 1993). Additionally, offering health services through churches increases the cost effectiveness of care because the church can support the clinic's physical needs. With a second site located in the Roberts Park United Methodist Church, the Center's staff provides primary care, health promotion, and disease management services across the life span to the local indigent populations through an advanced-practice nurse-managed clinic, within collaborative practice agreements with appropriate area physicians.

Currently no conceptual models exist in the literature or practice which clearly describe the collaboration between community-based organizations and academic units, and the effect of this type of collaboration on health-related outcomes. One evolving outcome from this project is the development of understandings of the necessary components for this type of collaborative model, including the necessary health-related resources to affect meaningful outcomes. This type of "action research" or field-based knowledge development represents the type of knowledge generation essential to a practice-based discipline, such as nursing. Without clear support for interventions to improve the health status of the nation's most vulnerable people -- such as inner-city, poor minorities -- nursing as a discipline would fall short of fulfilling its role

1

as a major discipline in the health care arena.

Inherent in any service-related activity should be an examination of why one activity is appropriate for an individual faculty member. The determinants of this project's appropriateness included: 1) The obvious need in the local and larger community was made evident through statistics documenting unmet health-related needs for indigent populations in inner-city Indianapolis. This particular need matched with my previous background in design of care programs for community-based populations, evidenced by my funded studies in the design of home-based interventions for elderly persons with irreversible dementia. 2) A large body of previous research provided convincing evidence that advanced practice nurses are uniquely qualified to meet health-related needs of individuals presented with complex concerns, in a cost-effective and competent manner. This research and the personal experiences of administrators within the Indiana State Department of Health (ISDH) provided the impetus for designated funding to develop and implement nurse-managed clinics designed to serve populations with identified unmet health care needs. My own background and certification as a Gerontological Nurse Practitioner provided the necessary understanding of the unique knowledge and skills of advanced practice nurses, specifically the combining of biomedical and behavioral knowledge, and the potential contribution of advanced practice nurses to improving the health of the target population. 3) My previous research as a Robert Wood Johnson Post-Doctoral Fellow allowed me to investigate the appropriateness of utilizing existing community organizations, such as churches, to assist in meeting the larger community's needs.

The societal need for this service project is evident when examining the health statistics for the target population:

- Many persons are on Medicaid, Medicare, or lack adequate health insurance. Approximately 18% of the 7,500 residents are uninsured.

- The median household income of $13,555 is less than half the City/County $29,152 median.

- 45-55% of residents are below the 1989 Federal poverty level (City/County, 16%).

2

- 26-35% of area residents receive some type of public assistance.

- The five-census tract area has a medically-underserved area (MUA) score of 59.3.

- The 1994 black infant mortality rate is 19.8% (City/County rate is 8.9).

- 46% of black mothers and 32% of white mothers 18-19 years old receive inadequate prenatal care.

- Drug-related deaths for both genders of African Americans have increased from 3.7/100,000 in 1979 to 7.4/100,000 in 1989.

- Heart disease, malignant neoplasms, and cerebrovascular disease are listed as the three leading causes of death.

II. PROCESS:

The Center has been functioning for 4½ years, with sustained success in meeting previously unmet health care needs and with successive funding from state, federal, and foundation sources. My role in this development process has been multi-faceted and relates to my role as faculty and my own clinical expertise. As the Center's co-director, a major responsibility has been the design and implementation of data collection systems to assure the Center is meeting the goals inherent in this project. A second major responsibility has been the communication with a variety of local and state organizations involved with health care to assure that all the Center's clients receive the necessary available services and to assist the local and larger community in recognizing the strength inherent in this relatively novel care model. Also, acquisition of continuous revenue streams remains an essential concern, requiring continuous communications and negotiations with public payers (Medicare and Medicaid) and the local business community. My role has also included direct "hands-on" management of the clinic's staff and activities, including supervision of graduate students and development of some clinic programs, such as the in-home care; depression and dementia evaluation services; data base development and oversight; and development of assessment instruments and protocols for specific clinic programs, such as the smoking cessation/prevention program for adolescents. I have also assumed a major responsibility for grant writing, with primary responsible for grant

3

development related to specific clinic activities and outcomes. These varied activities have utilized my expertise as an educator, researcher with an aging focus, and Gerontological Nurse Practitioner in the design and implementation of systematic, practice-based studies, while expanding my knowledge concerning negotiations with public and private entities, requirements of Federal reimbursement programs, and resource coordination for delivery of multifaceted health care programs. As a project co-director, 15% of my time, representing 6 hours/weekly, is supported by my faculty position. In reality, my responsibilities require approximately 20 hours/week, so this role represents a significant service commitment.

Several other aspects of this project helped assure that "if we build it, they will come", including the strategic location within a church that has an outreach mission and a recognition in the local community as open and accepting. Careful assessment of the community's needs was carried out, with ongoing input from the community being assured through inclusion of community members on the clinic's advisory board. Clinic personnel (outreach worker and secretary) were hired from the local community to assure that "word" about the clinic would get to those needing services and that persons coming to the clinic would be greeted by familiar persons. All students and clinic personnel receive training in cultural sensitivity issues, helping assure appropriate approaches with clients. Also, all clinic sites are staffed by consistent personnel to assure consistency in care and increased client comfort. Working with area physicians and health care organizations assures that continuity of care will be maintained, while accessing a wide variety of services for clients.

III. THE PROJECT'S IMPACT:

The knowledge gained from this project supports the effectiveness of utilizing this care approach to meet the complex health care needs of a defined population. The variety of measurable outcomes, including cost-effectiveness of care, allow this model to be well-supported. Additionally, as churches exist in virtually every area of the country, including rural areas not well-served by traditional health care providers, this care model is readily transferable to other situations and location. The Center's impact on a variety of constituencies, most important on clients, will be briefly described.

Impact on the service recipient: Evidence for the Center's effectiveness includes:

- Clients with hypertension receive significant reductions in blood pressure (mean systolic pressure lowered from 172 to 147; mean diastolic pressure lowered from 99 to 84).

- Obese clients show continued weight loss (mean loss of one pound/month)

- Decreases in blood cholesterol levels are evident in hypercholesteremic clients.

During the current year:

- Approximately 90 clients weekly received care.

- Approximately 3,500 to 4,000 client contacts are projected for the total year.

- Over 120 children received immunizations.

- Approximately 200 children received care for episodic illnesses.

- Well-child examinations were conducted for over 125 children and adolescents.

- Pregnancy Prevention, Parenting, and Violence Prevention Programs were conducted for area adolescents, with positive health-related outcomes.

- 27 women were tested for HIV with extensive counseling initiated.

- Approximately 80 clients received mental health counseling.

- Approximately 303 women and 45 men received a complete cancer screening.

- Cancer detection rates approach national averages for breast, cervical, and prostate cancers.

The impact of the Center's services on client outcomes is evident in the year-end report (see Appendix A-1), the findings from a client satisfaction survey (Appendix A-2), unsolicited letters from clients emphasizing the quality of care and outcomes (Appendix A-3), and the recognition by the larger scholarly community of the importance of these client outcomes (Appendix A-4).

Impact on the institution: As a "learning lab" the Center provides students and fellow faculty members with a rich source of clinical experiences. Because most clients have very complex health care needs, the students gain comprehensive information about a variety of health problems in clinical practicums in the graduate nursing program, nutrition, medicine, and community health majors. Students' evaluations are consistently positive, as noted in Appendix B-1. Because this population is of particular interest to public policy makers, a limitless variety of research studies are possible within the clients and services provided. Faculty and students have routinely participated in national and regional presentations of outcomes from this project (Appendix B 2-6). The School of Nursing and University have also received local recognition through published writings describing the Center's activities and accomplishments (Appendix B-7). This type of recognition validates the School's and University's commitment to serving the local and larger community and demonstrates a successful activity to meet this commitment.

Impact on discipline: In addition to the project's development as an effective practice model for advanced practice nurses, several other project outcomes have implications for the larger discipline. Professional knowledge has been generated and disseminated around several areas: 1) the effectiveness of advanced practice nurses serving in traditionally medically-underserved areas; 2) the structure and function of a true collaboration between a public entity, such as the University, and local community organizations, such as the church, to meet the needs of the larger and local community; 3) measurement of relevant client care outcomes within existing and developing complex, multi- disciplinary data bases (see Appendix C1-2); 4) the development of continuous "revenue streams" to support this type of clinical practice model (see Appendix C-3); and 5) creation of new insights and understandings regarding the scholarship of practice (see Appendix C-4). Scholarship regarding all of these areas fits well within the School's and discipline's commitment to serving populations in need of effective health care.

Individual Development: This project has been fundamental in meeting a variety of professional and growth goals, including maintaining clinical competency in my area of specialization, fulfilling research goals relevant to care of underserved or indigent populations, testing a church-based model of care as a mechanism to reach clients not generally accepted by traditional health care providers, and providing students and other faculty with an opportunity to learn in a richly-diverse and complex setting. My cumulative experiences have allowed me to

6

more clearly understand the political and policy complexities of caring for a population not able to pay for care. My own understandings about the necessary components of a scholarly practice have increased, along with an increased valuing of clinical research endeavors. These activities have also broadened my professional recognition as a scholar in another field (see Appendix D 1-3), as I was previously known primarily for my work with elderly persons suffering from Alzheimer's dementia. Having presented at several peer-reviewed national and regional scholarly meetings and received requests for invited presentations both regionally and nationally, the importance and recognition of this work as scholarship for nursing practice has broadened my own recognized scholarly activity. New challenges and opportunities for learning are also being developed as larger networked data-bases are being developed for the Center.

IV. REFLECTIVE CRITIQUE:

While obvious outcomes are monitored, other outcomes speak to this project's success. The interest of area providers and organizations in collaborating with the Center is one indicator of the recognition by the local community of the Center's success (see Appendix E-1). The willingness of a variety of local funders to support this project was based largely on our "reputation" as a qualified, accessible, and successful provider meeting previously unmet health care needs in a particularly problematic area of the city. Also, continuous support by a large national foundation, the Robert Wood Johnson Foundation, gave further credence to the convincing evidence for the Center's ability to reach clients with services that may greatly impact on their health, quality of life, and total costs of care. Requests from other regional community-based health providers for consultation on development of their own clinic provides additional support for the project's effectiveness. Students' evaluations of their clinical experiences also attest to the value of this setting for assisting in meeting the professional development goals for a variety of health-related disciplines.

Important, as well, this type of scholarship carries with it a different focus on my own development as opposed to my research scholarship. In my research scholarship, my primary concern has been the development of knowledge for the discipline or to meet the needs of a

7

particular population, while "fitting in" or fostering the development of my own research career and program. While this service project was developed to meet the specific needs of a defined population, the fit of the scholarship to my own research program was less important, evidenced by the fact that it did not really fit. I question whether the "fit" is the most important issue here, or if meeting community needs with the expertise and background one brings to the project should not be the most important concern.

Another important aspect of this service activity concerns the issue of "accountability". Within this service model I am not just accountable to the University, School, or a funding body, but I am now accountable to a larger community and constituency. If I make a mistake or do not reach an outcome in research scholarship it is often considered as acceptable, or part of a pilot project, or just not supportive of a research hypothesis. But, if I make a mistake or do not meet the expectations of a variety of constituents as part of this service activity I am immediately affecting people's lives and possibly their health, while negatively impacting on the School's and University's image. In this sense, this type of service project carries with it a sense of accountability different from other types of scholarly activity -- or fewer "degrees of freedom" than traditional research models.

ANNOTATED LIST OF ITEMS TO INCLUDE IN APPENDICES

Appendix A: Examples of Impact on Service Recipient

Appendix A-1: Moore, S., & Burgener, S. C. (1997). Shalom Wellness Center: Year End Report: Project Year 01, Robert Wood Johnson Local Funding Partners Initiative.
> This report contains a detailed description of the Center's outcomes from the first year of funding (the Center's fourth year of functioning) from the Robert Wood Johnson Foundation.

Appendix A-2: Client Satisfaction Data: Shalom Wellness Center. (1997). Indiana State Department of Health: Evaluation of Nurse-Managed Clinics Projects, 1996-1997.
> This report describes the results of a client satisfaction survey conducted with a random sample from the Center's client base. Client scores indicated a "high" level of satisfaction with provider quality of care, accessibility of the Center's clinic sites, ease in getting appointment times, and the overall atmosphere of the Center.

Appendix A-3: Letter from mother of child receiving a complete physical exam through a summer camp screening program, September, 1997.
> This letter describes the positive results from a screening exam conducted on an 8-year old child. The child was referred for corrective lenses for visual difficulties (undetected in previous exams by other providers). The consulting ophthalmologist informed the mother the child had the visual defect since birth and might have eventually suffered blindness if this had not been detected and treated at this time.

Appendix A-4: Moore, S., & Burgener, S. C. (1995). "A Church-Based Model of Care: Impact on Cardiovascular Disease". American Public Health Association Annual Meeting, San Diego, CA.
> This peer-reviewed, competitive presentation described the changes in clients' cardiovascular status as a result of care received within this advanced practice nursing care model.

Appendix B: Examples of Impact on the Institution (including students):

Appendix B-1: Graduate nursing students' evaluations indicating the quality of clinical experiences obtained through the Center.

Appendix B-2: Burgener, S.C., Moore, S., & Murray, C. (1995). "A Church-Based Model of Care: Impact on Cardiovascular Disease". Midwest Nursing Research Society Annual Meeting, Kansas City, MO.
> This presentation focused on describing the approaches to care inherent in this model and changes in clients' cardiovascular status as a result of care received. A graduate student involved in clinical experiences at the Center assisted with giving this presentation.

Appendix B-3: Burgener, S.C., & Moore, S. (1997). "Effectiveness of Nurse-Managed Clinics", Diversity in the New Public University Conference, Gary, IN.

> This presentation specifically described the impact of collaborations among educational institutions, community organizations (such as churches), and local health care agencies in impacting on quality health outcomes with persons needing care while fulfilling the local mission of a public university.

Appendix B-4: Moore, S., & Burgener, S. (1997). "The Effectiveness of an Advanced-Practice Nursing Clinic using a Church-Based Model of Care", American Public Health Association Annual Meeting, Indianapolis, IN.

> This peer-reviewed, competitive presentation included an emphasis on the sustainability of nurse-managed clinics, including the acquisition of continuous funding sources.

Appendix B-5: Burgener, S.C., Moore, S., & Riley, J. (1996). "A Church-Based Model of Care: A Cost-Effective Community Partnership for an Advanced Practice Nursing Clinic", Midwest Alliance in Nursing, Indianapolis, IN.

> One of the Center's practitioners participated in delivering this peer-reviewed presentation focusing on the Center's cost-effectiveness in providing client care, also describing the evolution of the Center-church partnership.

Appendix B-6: Moore, S., & Burgener, S.C. (1996). "An Advanced Practice Nursing Clinic within a Community Partnership Model", Women in Philanthropy Conference, Indianapolis, IN.

> This invited presentation described the effectiveness of this model in reaching a traditionally difficult to access population in the provision of health care services.

Appendix B-7: Sample of local newspaper articles describing the Center's work and outcomes, including the Indianapolis Star.

Appendix C: Examples of Impact on the Discipline

Appendix C-1: Burgener, S.C., & Moore, S. (1997). "Relevant Client Outcomes in Nurse-Managed Clinics", Tennessee Nurses' Association, Measuring Outcomes for Nurse-Managed Clinics Conference, Vanderbilt University, Nashville, TN.

> This invited presentation represented a keynote address at a state-wide conference in Tennessee to inform advanced practice nurses regarding the current state of knowledge in measurement and tracking client outcomes from an advanced practice nursing practice.

Appendix C-2: Moore, S., & Burgener, S. C. (1997). "Measuring Client Outcomes: How to Measure Success in Nurse-Managed Clinics", Health Care for the Homeless and Poor Conference, Indianapolis, IN.

> This invited presentation focused on the practical aspects of measuring clients outcomes, describing both quantitative and qualitative approaches to outcome measurement.

Appendix C-3: Examples of contracts written with local organizations to begin to assure continuous revenue streams for the Center: 1) Indiana State Department of Health, Early Breast and Cervical Cancer Detection Program; 2) Head Start of Indianapolis.

Appendix C-4: Burgener, S.C. (under review). Scholarship of practice in a practice profession: Insights from the field. Image: Journal of Nursing Scholarship.
> This article describes the qualities inherent in scholarship of practice and differentiates this type of scholarship from traditional academic research models. Insights gained from this project and my participation in the Kellogg Project are reflected in the manuscript.

Appendix D: Individual Development

Appendix D-1: Leadership Award for Excellence in Geriatric Care, Midwest Alliance in Nursing, September, 1996.
> This competitive, regional award is given to a nurse exemplifying excellence in care to older adults.

Appendix D-2: Fellow, Institute for Action Research for Community Health (IARCH) and WHO Collaborating Center, Indiana University, 1993-present.
> The appointment as a Fellow in the IARCH Center reflects my contribution to solving and knowledge of community health issues.

Appendix D-3: Consultant, Indiana State Department of Health, East Chicago Advanced Practice Nursing Clinic, Doris Blaney, P.I., January, 1996-June, 1997.
> This consulting role was initiated by the Indiana State Department of Health due to the success of the Center is achieving quality outcomes and reaching a large number of under-served clients.

Appendix E: Recognition by Local Community
Listing of over 40 agencies with which the Center interacts routinely to provide comprehensive, high quality care.

Free The Children: Testing the Capacity and Methods for
Locally Based Efforts to Address Poverty

David N. Cox
Department of Political Science
The University of Memphis

Objective and Context of the Project:

The initiative for addressing the needs and problems of
the poor in the United States has shifted among national,
state and local levels from time to time. Recently there
has been a devolution of that initiative to state and local
levels. Whether actions by any given locality can
significantly reduce poverty among its citizens, and, if
possible, how to go about it remains unclear.

Experience across all levels has produced several
lessons regarding efforts to treat poverty. One, the more
comprehensive the effort, the greater the chance of success.
Two, the earlier the interventions in the lives of persons
experiencing poverty, the greater the chance and magnitude
of success. Three, people experiencing poverty must be
active participants in the selection, design, and
implementation of efforts to treat poverty. And four,
effective antipoverty efforts must be sustained through
time. That sustainability requires the involvement of
institutions with principal control over community

resources. In sum, comprehensive efforts that involve the
poor in their design and execution, engage the collaborative
efforts of local community institutions through time, and
are aimed at youths have been found to be more effective in
treating poverty. Accomplishing those conditions within
localities, though, has been problematic.

Reflecting these lessons, a not-for-profit agency
called Free The Children (FTC) was created in Memphis,
Tennessee, in 1988 under the leadership of the mayor of the
urban county in which Memphis is located, Shelby County. By
the language of its creation, it was to be a collaborative
involving the poor and local institutions to engage in a
coordinated comprehensive effort to treat poverty in a
targeted area of North Memphis. By its title, it was to
focus on efforts aimed at youths. It was one of a set of
like initiatives created in the United States in the 1980's
to try to treat poverty at the local level. What FTC set
out to achieve and how it sought to do it placed it in the
midst of national policy experiments to treat poverty.

My outreach activities were mainly concerned with two
principal tasks for the organization. One was to serve as
Project director for the creation and implementation of an
effort called Project ACHIEVE within FTC that would provide

a model for developing and delivering comprehensive
collaborative programming with the potential for
sustainability. The other was to serve as a consultant to
identify and conceptualize the roles for FTC to accomplish
the conditions related to the successful treatment of
poverty. My work with Project ACHIEVE took place between
1989 and 1992. The task for FTC took place in 1990. I was
involved with the program on a full-time basis for 9 months
during the 1989-90 academic year. Following the first
9 months, the rest of my time was supported by a 15-percent
buyout of my 9-month academic contract and 25 percent during
the summer.

My goals were to learn about the capacity of localities
to affect poverty, management strategies to accomplish
collaborative coordinated activities, how to involve
community residents and institutional elites in
collaborative planning and program implementation,
strategies to increase the retention rate and academic
achievement of minorities, and structural arrangements that
can sustain comprehensive collaborative programming.

What I Brought to the Activity:

Comprehensive collaborative programming has often foundered on a range of factors. Potential stakeholders are commonly unable to identify and sustain shared interests sufficient to create the needed cooperation. Institutions don't respect and trust community residents, community residents don't trust community institutions, residents and agencies disagree on the causes and appropriate solutions to poverty, agencies battle over program turf and control, and provider and coordinating agencies experience continuing mission drift as they compete for scare resources. Communication identifying shared interests with supporting administrative/management structures and strategies to sustain those interests are required to accomplish the collaboration. Participation in scholarship addressing these factors was consistent with the mission of the University, the mission of the units in which I was located, and my academic specialty and experience.

Included in the mission of The University of Memphis are the statements that the university: (1) is an urban university; (2) responding to the challenging responsibility of being located in a culturally diverse region, its

4

teaching, scholarships, and research contribute to the growth of the area; (3) develops, integrates, disseminates and applies knowledge; and (4) fulfills its outreach mission through its contributions to the needs of the community.

I am a member of the faculty of the Department of Political Science in the university, have served as chairperson of the department, and have served as director of two graduate programs in the department, the Master of Public Administration (MPA) and the Master of Health Administration (MHA) programs. The missions of both programs include research and instruction related to the development and delivery of programs that: (1) increase the efficiency, effectiveness and equity in the public and not-for-profit sectors (MPA Program Mission Statement); and (2) seek to provide an environment for the development of policies, programs, and delivery systems contributing to healthy persons and communities (MHA Program Mission Statement). Outreach related to the development of roles, structures, and strategies for a not-for-profit agency aimed at accomplishing comprehensive coordinated programming to treat poverty are consistent with the mission of the university and the unit and programs within the unit where I am located within the university.

Reflecting my role in the unit, my Ph.D. training was in urban politics and administration. My subsequent research and teaching have addressed a range of issues exploring the conditions for the physical, social, economic, political, and cultural development of urban and metropolitan areas. As examples, I have studied the impact of election rules in the representation of minorities, the effect of urban administrative structures on efficiency and equity in the delivery of urban services, and management strategies for accomplishing change and improved public, health, and not-for-profit service agency effectiveness. In addition, I have conducted evaluations on the administrative performance and effectiveness of organizations. That education and those experiences provided me with the preparation to begin the analysis of the communication, structural, and strategy needs of FTC.

Intellectual Framework Informing My Approach

Various sets of literature formed the intellectual approach to my tasks with FTC. Regarding my work with FTC as a policy reform organization, one was the literature that

debates the potential for locally based leadership
initiatives, leadership strategies, community agency
structures, and community agency strategies to affect
poverty in any particular place. FTC provided an
opportunity to test whether locally based activity could
have those effects and the strategies and structures that
can best accomplish those effects. An intellectual
framework informing my work with collaborative components of
FTC and the project within FTC in which I sought to build a
collaborative model was research on the processes for
identifying shared interests among stakeholders and the
negotiation of rules, agreements, and administrative
incentives to transform those shared interests into
coordinated collaborative action. Specifically, research on
the use of language to develop shared understandings and
commitments, incentives to reward collaborative behaviors,
and communication media and styles to sustain those
understandings, commitments and behaviors provided guidance
for accomplishing collaboration and as a means for building
on those insights. A third literature that informed my work
was research on developing organization and program missions
and linking or turning those missions into action. Finally,
a fourth intellectual framework was specific to the subject
matter of the project that I directed. That project was
aimed at increasing the number of minorities entering

health-related professions by increasing the number in the pool eligible to enter college. That required knowledge of the factors affecting minority academic retention and achievement, cultural approaches to understanding those behaviors, and structures and incentives of educational institutions that affect those behaviors. Some of those factors were concerned with learning styles associated with ethnicity and gender, the development of a positive identity of self and enhanced self esteem, teachers' incentives for change and effective instruction, and curriculum revisions leading to appropriately rigorous content and effective pedagogy.

My hypotheses were: (1) a properly directed and structured locally based initiative could have a significant effect on reducing poverty in a given community; (2) an organization and program mission could be effective toward achieving positive and collaborative action, but to do so required action involvement by stakeholders in the development and implementation; (3) systematic communication aimed at openly identifying the interests and incentives among potential stakeholders could form the basis for effective ongoing collaboration; and (4) a combination of enhanced counseling/cultural experiences, mathematics and science curricula with substantial hands-on applications, and rewards and recognition for students and teachers for improved performance could improve the retention rates and academic performance of minority students. The choice of my hypotheses was based on my professional experiences and research to that point and the literature specific to each of the tasks.

The Process:

I first focused my attention on treating the needs of Project ACHIEVE. Though I knew that FTC as an organization lacked focus and organization, since the project didn't receive funding approval until June 1989 and the school year started in late August, it was imperative that a project management plan be developed and agreed to immediately. Reflecting the literature and an intuitive reading of the setting, my priorities in working with the project were to develop trust among the partners and to create a project decision making and management structure as part of creating the management plan. To that end, I met separately with each of the partners and reviewed their separate plans. Based on those reviews, I then created a master project summary identifying areas where the separate plans had shared assumptions, areas where there were differences, proposed activities that were separate, proposed activities where there was overlap, and activities based upon what I had learned from my literature review on mathematics and science performance for minorities that would be appropriate but were missing from any partner's plans. I first reviewed the summary separately with each partner to make sure that I had correctly interpreted its proposals and to answer questions in a non-hostile and non-threatening setting about the plans of the others. That step provided the opportunity to defuse misunderstandings and identify real issues. It also helped to give credibility to my role as a communicator and facilitator among the partners rather than another competitor. Subsequent to this step, I then convened a 2-day planning retreat among the partners to create the project's management plan.

An important step that I took while building the agenda for creating the management plan was to begin to design the eventual decision making and management structure for the project. Given the intellectual framework that I was using, it was clear, given the scale of the project and the initial conflicts among the partners, someone with authority in each organization to make decisions and commitments for that agency was needed on the governing board. Since the success of the delivery of the project's programming depended on the understanding, capabilities, and commitment of persons responsible for day-to-day administration of those programs, it was also important that key project administrators also participate. Based on my recommendation, a project coordinating committee comprised of the Associate Superintendent from the school system, the Vice President for Academic Affairs of the college, and the Vice Chancellor of the medical school was created. In addition, each participating institution had a project director for the project on the committee. The Principal of the high school, a teachers' representative, and the President of the high school's community advisory committee represented the schools and parents. This group met at least monthly over the life of the project. As a measure of its success, though several of the initial participants were replaced over time, the members eventually came to help one another across organizations to accomplish project goals and formed the core for several other collaborative projects and successful grant applications.

The planning retreat turned out to be a critical management step and learning experience. As a management step, and with an agenda built from the work prior to the meeting, the committee was able to forge an agreement on a management plan that focused the mission of the project on trying to improve the performance of underachieving minorities, divide responsibility for activities among the partners with a coordinated calendar of events, make budget distributions to support those activities, and foster a sense of trust and shared commitment among the members. With a few adjustments, that plan formed the basis for a successful competitive renewal grant and the outline for the project through the following years. The project provided year-around services for more than 2,000 students within 3 years. In addition, 45 community organizations were eventually recruited and coordinated in providing services for the project.

As a learning experience, the formation of the committee and outcome of the retreat provided an outline and insights for me to address the organizational tasks facing FTC. With Project ACHIEVE launched in September 1989, I turned a part of my attention to developing a mission statement and statement of goals and roles for the organization. In September, I drafted a model for an economic development plan that was eventually adopted as the FTC economic development plan. A copy of that plan is attached. Drawing from my research on FTC, interviews of board and staff members, review of the literature, and experience in getting Project ACHIEVE underway, I completed a draft outline for the mission, roles, and organization of

FTC.   That draft formed the basis of the agenda for a March

1990 FTC Board retreat.   At that meeting, the board adopted

the mission statement and the six goals or roles that I had

posited for the organization.   The mission statement was

revised in 1993 to include the term "personal empowerment."

The mission statement and goals are described on page 1 of

the document titled "A Documentation of Free The Children,

Inc." attached.   The description of FTC roles or goals came

to guide the discussion of activities that were and were not

appropriate for the organization.

In regards to the organization of FTC, the planning and

management model developed for Project ACHIEVE came to be

used for the other interorganizational projects undertaken

by FTC.   A governing committee with highly placed

institutional representatives and programmatic heads was

created to guide a major successful economic development

project called the Hurt Village/Self Initiative Project.

The communications processes used for the creation and

subsequent management of Project ACHIEVE were regularly used

for other projects.   The management and communications

models used for the project were eventually presented by

invitation of the U.S. Justice Department at a national

forum on interagency collaboration for crime prevention.

THE OUTCOMES: The Impact of the Activity

The Impact of the External Partner

The mission statement, description of roles and goals, and project management structures that I developed have continued to be used by FTC and have been disseminated to other organizations. FTC is still in operation in 1997, 9 years after its creation. Regarding Project ACHIEVE, the project had several significant successes in keeping minority students in the educational stream and increasing the number eligible to enter college. Evaluations of the project's effects may be found in the documents titled "Northside High School and Project ACHIEVE: A Record of Achievement," a report by the project, and "Project ACHIEVE: A Summative Evaluation," a report by Mathematica Project Research, Inc. As described in the Mathematica evaluation, ". . .during the years that Project ACHIEVE operated, personal and institutional relationships were forged that have already facilitated other cooperative activities." Included are joint degree programs and joint grant proposals producing more than $3,070,000 in collaborative funding for fostering minority academic achievement. Project activities were disseminated to 24 other schools during 1994-95, supported by a highly competitive $300,000 National Science

14

Foundation grant. Project activities formed the basis for a

successful $15,000,000 application by Memphis City Schools

for a National Science Foundation Urban Systemic Initiative

grant. Regarding project effects, Mathematica concluded,

"Project ACHIEVE seniors in each graduating class

experienced more favorable outcomes than their classmates."

The Impact on Me

The experience affected every aspect of my scholarship.

The literature reviews and research that I did in

preparation for my participation in the project introduced

me to new information about the conditions of

interorganizational arrangements and management, strategies

and approaches to improving the academic performance of

underachieving minorities, approaches to economic and

community development for impoverished urban areas, and the

politics and processes of institutional reform. I have used

that new information in a variety of ways.

I used the committee and management frameworks

developed with FTC in guiding interorganizational efforts in

a variety of subsequent tasks. I was the author of a

successful $300,000 National Science Foundation grant to

expand Project ACHIEVE to other schools. The grant served

as a prototype and lead-in for the Memphis City Schools
$15,000,000 Urban Systemic Initiative. I, along with
another colleague, Dr. Stanley Hyland, used that model and
process in setting up several interdisciplinary research and
outreach efforts within The University of Memphis, including
a $500,000 Community Outreach Partnership Center grant from
the U.S. Department of Housing and Urban Development and a
$300,000 planning grant from the Memphis Housing Authority.

The literature reviews that I completed became the
basis of syllabi and courses that I have subsequently taught
in public administration, health administration, urban
administration, and urban problems (syllabi attached). The
materials that I reviewed, structures and processes that I
created, and experiences that I gained in working across
organizations have become important components of each of
those courses. The research and work that I did as a policy
advisor for FTC in economic development for poor
neighborhoods has informed a major portion of the course
that I teach on urban problems. In regard to research, the
experiences with FTC and Project ACHIEVE have largely guided
my research agenda over the past 6 years. I have also
written and presented papers addressing and describing how
localities can have the capacity to affect poverty and
conditions required for them to do so, about strategies for

developing sustaining interorganization service networks,
about strategies for increasing the number of minorities
qualified to enter college and health-related professions,
and on the use of not-for-profit agencies for policy reform.
A list of those presentations is attached.

Impact on the Institution and Department or Other Unit

My work with FTC and Project ACHIEVE contributed to the
institution and my unit in a number of ways. I am currently
involved in revisions in the MPA program curriculum guided
by what I learned about public, not-for-profit, and private
sector collaboration and coordination. The experiences that
I gained and networks I developed were instrumental, in
partnership with another faculty member, Dr. Stanley Hyland,
in developing a major proposal leading to more that $600,000
in external funding in national competition to foster
university-community urban outreach. The grant also served
as a catalyst for the creation of a university level center,
the Center for Urban Research and Extension, to foster urban
outreach and research. The work of the center focuses on
engaging interdisciplinary university outreach for community
building. Examples include building integrated urban
information systems, design and finance of affordable
housing, and the design and implementation of effective

health and recreation systems. The work also contributed to the development of a range of other externally funded research opportunities for persons within the university and community that, in combination with my work, total more than $3,000,000 within the last 6 years in funded research and outreach support. A list of those opportunities is provided.

References:

1. Interorganizational Management Bibliography

2. A Documentation of Free the Children, Inc., 1995

3. Project ACHIEVE: A Summative Evaluation, Mathematica
   Policy Research, Inc.

4. Memphis Minority Mathematics and Science Achievement
   Partnership Project Evaluation

5. Publications and Presentations related to FTC and
   Project ACHIEVE

Outreach Project:

Evaluation Of School Restructuring

Steven M. Ross

Counseling, Educational Psychology, and Research
The University of Memphis

Purpose

<u>Context for Project</u>

In 1995-1996, the Memphis City Schools (MCS) district was selected as one of 10 national jurisdictions for implementing New American Schools (NAS) restructuring models system-wide. Launched by President Bush's Goals 2000 program, and supported by private foundation funding, the mission of NAS was to improve American education by redesigning school organizations and delivery methods to promote active learning, higher student motivation, and improved performance.

During the 1994-1995 school year, the dean of the College of Education at the University of Memphis worked with Memphis City Schools to establish a NAS jurisdiction. A fundamental component was the facilitation of the restructuring initiative through partnerships with local corporations, teacher unions, local and state educational agencies, local and state government, and higher education. In fulfilling the latter role the University agreed in a formal "Memorandum of Understanding" to: (a) coordinate the formative evaluation of the restructuring initiative; and (b) revamp the College of Education's preservice teacher education program to support successful restructuring designs.

My outreach project was oriented around two main areas of scholarship. The first was traditional in nature, involving the planned formative evaluation research on the school restructuring. The culminating products of this research were to be several research papers co-authored by different faculty researchers including myself. The second focus was the "scholarship of practice" that was applied in addressing the challenges of working with a school district in a pressured context with multiple stakeholders. My role was to supervise the participation of 17 University faculty researchers and 4 colleagues from Johns Hopkins University, within a system (a large urban school district) that historically did not welcome outsiders' involvement, and that was apprehensive about our activities and potential role.

Societal Framework

The need for this outreach project emanated from Memphis City Schools' involvement in a large-scale restructuring project and accountability interests for itself and the community in determining its success. The expertise that our research team offered, and our location in the same city as MCS made us uniquely qualified to address the evaluation issues in a cost-effective manner. Specifically, the major evaluation questions were: (a) How did schools choose the various designs? (b) Was teacher training adequate? (c) Did principals and teachers understand and support the design? (d) How effectively did individual schools implement their respective designs? (e) How was student learning affected by the restructuring? Added to these questions were ones relating to the scholarship of practice: (f) What processes were involved in collaborating with the school system to implement the evaluation project? (g) How successful was the evaluation in terms of providing useful data, involving University faculty as researchers, and maintaining good relations with school district leaders and staff?

Participants

The primary stakeholder in the project was the MCS superintendent. Through her advocacy of MCS becoming a NAS jurisdiction, she was making a substantial commitment for the district with regard to policies, educational philosophy, and funding. A second stakeholder was a district administrator charged with overseeing the University's evaluation work. A third stakeholder was New American Schools (NAS) and their evaluation agent, the PICA Laboratory (a pseudonym). Although NAS had been highly supportive of the University's involvement in creating the jurisdiction, we suspected that it was less favorable toward our evaluation interests, given the possibility that our conclusions would not represent their views. A fourth stakeholder was the College of Education, as represented by the dean and the various department chairs.

Preparation

The resources for the project were fairly limited. It was assumed that sufficient faculty would be willing to donate time to participate in the research due to limited funding for operating expenses. Key events in the planning process were as follows:

- Memorandum of Understanding, spring, 1995
- Orientation meeting for participating school principals, spring, 1995
- Orientation meeting for University researchers and MCS staff, spring, 1995
- Orientation between the research coordinator and faculty researchers, fall, 1995
- Orientation between PICA researchers and faculty research team, fall, 1995
- Monthly meetings with research team, starting summer, 1995

Methodology

<u>Attainable Goals and Design</u>

The critical product of the planning (task definition phase) was the clarification of project goals. One goal was the production of intermittent brief reports and a culminating report at the end of summer, 1996. The final team of faculty researchers and graduate assistants were recruited and trained, and a management team with myself as leader was created. The basic design was to use multiple measures (interviews, surveys, observations, etc.) to obtain as complete and reliable information as possible for addressing each research question (see research reports in the appendix for more details).

<u>Monitoring of Project</u>

Regular meetings were held with the faculty researchers to discuss project activities and assignments. Because the data collection needs were clearly defined, and the instrumentation prescribed, our degree of success in implementing the project was expected to be more objectively determinable than in typical outreach projects.

<u>Reflection</u>. Overall, the above methodology proved to be effective, although more frequent meetings with school district representatives in attendance would have improved communications among project staff.

Process

In this section, I will provide reflections, descriptions, and evidences of developments that impacted on the success of the project and the fidelity of its implementation with the planned strategy.

<u>Phase I: A Promising Start (June-December, 1995)</u>

We initiated the project smoothly and successfully and continued it without incident for the fall, 1995 semester. During this period, I coordinated the entire evaluation process and served as the contact for approving data collection activities, by either local or outside groups, related to the MCS restructuring initiative. Given this defined power and its explicit approval by the superintendent, we were able to implement the evaluation project with few impediments. The district research coordinator, who might normally have assumed many of the "gatekeeping" and decision-making activities, remained occupied with other major responsibilities.

<u>Reflection</u>. The research coordinator's attitude did not seem unusual to me for several reasons: (a) I felt that, based on prior experiences with her, our personal relationship was positive; (b) she was over-committed with other projects in the district; and (c) the superintendent had overtly supported my role as evaluation coordinator at

several prior meetings. In retrospect, given that I was an "outsider" to MCS, I should have recognized the liabilities of my assuming these responsibilities.

By the semester break in December we had completed all planned data collection activities and were looking toward continuing the project in January. The faculty researchers appeared to be profiting from their experiences while learning that working with a school system, in contrast to what some of them had experienced previously, could be both productive and congenial. Only one incident occurred that was troubling and foreshadowed eventual problems. When we requested a supporting letter for a research proposal the research coordinator's response was negative, indicating concerns that the research would be unacceptably "intrusive" and, more troubling, questioning the compatibility between the school system's interests in the research and the University's. Through negotiation with the superintendent I obtained a modified letter that forwarded a less-than-enthusiastic endorsement of the project.

Reflection. Later, I realized that I had failed to sufficiently develop the research coordinator's investment in the project. Two possible consequences were (a) alienating her; and, as a result, (b) weakening my standing with the superintendent.

Phase II: Problems Surface (January-February, 1996)

The new year started well with our scheduling of school visits. The research team was enthusiastic and feeling confident about their roles in collecting data from schools. In early February, one of the research leaders from PICA (NAS' contracted evaluators) called, asking me to schedule times two weeks later when his team could visit schools and interview principals and teachers. When the PICA researchers arrived the next week they were dissatisfied with various details, and interacted uncomfortably with the University researchers.

Reflection. I sensed, but was not fully cognizant of, the severity of the problem that was developing. To bolster our position with MCS I asked my research team to analyze the data from the teacher survey that we conducted in the fall. We compiled this information and presented it in a "preliminary" report (see appendix) that we submitted to the superintendent prior to her planning meeting with NAS officials.

Phase III: Stormy Times (February-March, 1996)

In late February, the NAS president met with school district administrators and questioned why PICA was having "such difficulty" implementing its research plan. As it was described to me by someone present at the meeting, the superintendent expressed surprise and immediately questioned the research coordinator about what she knew. The research coordinator, in turn, was caught off guard and put in the position of defending her lack of involvement with the evaluation and her knowledge of the discord between the two research groups.

I knew now that we would be encountering major difficulties. I contacted the PICA and NAS leaders about the conflicts, but they professed innocence in initiating trouble. One overt sign of a deteriorating relationship with the school district was the discontinuation of communications between MCS and the University on the NAS initiative. Through the end of February and middle of March, several events took place related to NAS (e.g., visitors, ceremonies, planning meetings) to which we would normally have been invited but of which we were not notified by MCS.

Reflection. I was convinced that the situation would get worse and decided to take direct actions both to "test the waters" of the University and MCS relationship to improve our position. One component of my strategy was to develop a more central role for the dean, who not only held a high administrative position, but was well-respected by the superintendent and other MCS leaders. Another part was to arrange a meeting between the superintendent, the research coordinator, the dean, and myself to determine the status of our collaborative work on the district restructuring.

Phase IV: Conflicts Surface (March-April, 1996)

Based on my personal experiences with the superintendent, I knew within minutes of the start of the March meeting that it would not go well. The research coordinator asserted her assumption of complete control over the NAS research. More foreboding in its implications, she began questioning the role of, and need for, the University's research with regard to MCS interests. She expressed the view that, while the University could probably serve the district by providing technical assistance, our direct involvement with NAS gave us a stake in the outcomes that might compromise our objectivity as researchers. She further indicated that she now saw PICA as potentially well-equipped to provide evaluation information that would serve the district's needs at no cost.

Reflections. It was now clear that our involvement with the restructuring program was being restricted. In discussions with the dean, who also perceived the climate and our situation as having deteriorated, we decided that it was time to establish him rather than me as the primary University stakeholder. The logic was that he personally brought to the table a large and complex set of collaborations, and mutual dependencies, between the college and school district.

We initiated the above plan and took actions to shore up other fronts. We wrote, in the dean's name, a conciliatory letter to PICA to document our willingness to cooperate with them to achieve our mutual goals. I wrote to the dean a letter analyzing the differences between our research and PICA's research (see appendix). The dean then attached my letter to one that he wrote to the research coordinator and the superintendent, asserting the University's interests in the NAS research and its expectancies.

Phase V: The Moratorium (April 3, 1996)

Without advance notification to us, the research coordinator sent to all school principals, on April 3, 1996, a letter calling for a moratorium on all research by external "organizations," explicitly including the University of Memphis and PICA. This action terminated, until further notice, not only our NAS research, but all studies in MCS being conducted by our research center, University faculty, and graduate students. Needless to say, it caused immediate panic and ongoing frustration among all concerned. In addition, the tone of the letter and the action itself raised questions among the school principals regarding what the University had done to precipitate the decision and, more critically, our status with the district. This event was a significant setback.

Reflection. I felt frustrated by these events, but concluded that positive action rather than passivity would serve us best. My main idea was that we could best serve the interests of the University and the school district by being as productive as we could, as if no problems had occurred.

The strategy adopted was to: (a) increase communications with the research coordinator and other administrators regarding the nature of our research, in general and compared to PICA's; and (b) try to work as cooperatively as possible with the research coordinator regarding the reinstatement of other research projects. Also, at that time (but then unknown to me), PICA was handling the moratorium less amicably and creating some negative reactions from the district toward PICA.

Phase VII: A Break-Through in Boston (May 1, 1996)

Fortuitously for me, the research coordinator and I were both asked by NAS to serve on a special committee on performance assessment, with the first meeting to be held in Boston. Our previous positive association (before all of this year's events) and our mutual concern for the district among this national group seemed to bond us as we interacted with each other and others at the meeting. On several occasions, she alluded to the "unfortunate circumstances" of this year and the need to plan things better for next year (a hopeful sign about our future prospects in MCS). She also acknowledged (and this was an important point for me) the potential of the University to support district evaluation needs more effectively than outside groups (such as PICA). I left Boston aware that the situation with our project was still tenuous, but feeling that clear gains had been made. On May 21, 1996, the moratorium was removed. We were therefore freed to continue data collection as best we could in the remaining time.

Aftermath: Summer, 1996

During the summer, my research team and I worked on analyzing the data and writing final papers for scholarly publication (see *Impacts* section below). In the middle of the summer, the University was invited by the superintendent to be the primary evaluators of the MCS restructuring in 1996-1997. In addition, she awarded the University a contract close to $100,000 to evaluate each of 34 restructuring schools. Although this project would be considerable work and potentially sensitive given the high stakes involved for the school principals, I felt it would provide us with clear entry into the schools to pursue our research interests. As the summer continued, communications increased between MCS and the University. We began the fall feeling optimistic and enthusiastic but also cautious given last year's experiences. The contract was signed in October, and, at the time of this writing this (January, 1997), we are collecting data at the schools. The second year of the outreach project is proceeding well thus far.

Scholarship Impacts

The outcomes of my outreach project will be discussed below in relation to the impact categories on the external partner, myself, the institution, and the discipline/professional field (knowledge base). Each of these categories includes the conventional scholarship products of research reports and journal publications, but also the products of scholarship of practice acquired from the project experiences.

Impacts on the External Partner

Traditional scholarship. During the academic year MCS received 2 preliminary research reports, 1 AERA monograph, and 6 journal articles (see appendix) describing various aspects (historical, procedural, and evaluative) of their restructuring initiative. As conveyed by school district representatives, the preliminary reports were useful to their understanding of restructuring outcomes and influenced their planning during the year. The 6 papers, given to MCS leaders in early summer, were positively viewed as a valuable contribution from the University. One of the MCS administrators who read the papers has since requested my participation at various MCS functions.

Scholarship of practice. I believe that the present leadership in the school district gained, as we did, a better understanding of how to work collaboratively with an outside organization. It also seems certain that the MCS leaders acquired greater appreciation of our (the University's) commitment and value to them.

Impacts on Me

Traditional scholarship. The outreach project proved a fertile context for generating scholarly documents and publications of high interest in the field. I also gained recognition as a researcher and expert in school restructuring.

Scholarship of Practice. Through the project, I became more knowledgeable about how to work with school administrators on sensitive projects. I also gained understandings about school organizations and restructuring designs that were helpful to my teaching. Finally, I gained skills and increased confidence in conducting applied school research.

Impact on the Institution

Traditional scholarship. Through our publications and presentations, the University, college, and our research center are gaining local and national recognition for scholarship in the area of school restructuring. One tangible result that probably would not have occurred in the absence of the evaluation project was the selection of the research center to co-host the International Congress on School Effectiveness and School Improvement, held in Memphis in January, 1997. Through the outreach project, 17 of our faculty participated as researchers, co-authored papers, became directly involved with schools, and increased their knowledge about school research and school practices in general.

Scholarship of Practice. All participants from the University, including the dean, the faculty researchers, and the graduate students, seemed to acquire valuable experience and knowledge in the effort to collaborate with the school system. As a result of their involvement, the faculty appear much more knowledgeable, realistic in their expectancies, and better prepared to handle the everyday challenges that occur in conducting applied school research.

Impact on the Professional Field/Knowledge Base

Traditional scholarship. As described above, the project produced substantial scholarly products, including 6 publications in a leading international journal. I was also invited to make presentations at various conferences (e.g., Council of Chief State School Offices, International Congress of School Effectiveness and School Improvement, AERA), specifically because of my involvement in the Memphis restructuring. In addition, Sam Stringfield (Johns Hopkins University), Lana Smith (The University of Memphis), and I edited a book on the restructuring that was published by Lawrence Erlbaum Associates in December, 1996. Finally, we received a contract from MCS to continue our research in 1996-97 and a contract from Dade County Schools (Miami) to conduct related research on their restructuring schools. These research projects are producing findings that are of considerable practical and scholarly interest in the field.

Scholarship of Practice. The incidental "lessons learned" from my outreach experiences are less comfortably disseminated to external audiences than they are internally. Nevertheless, parts of our conference presentations and of one journal publication have dealt with the issues of university-school partnerships, based on our experiences. However, potentially, *this* outreach report will become the primary vehicle through which the "incidental" knowledge gained from my project will be best communicated to fellow academicians.

Reflective Critique

My experiences in trying to manage a high-stakes project in the complex and highly political environment of the school district were illuminating in many ways. I learned about the importance of communicating with, and developing buy-in from, all present and potential key stakeholders, not just the ones who appeared in power at a given time. I learned about the importance of being adaptable to changes in climate or policies that could occur unexpectedly at any time. I also learned about the power of persistence, guided by reflective analysis about the problem situation and the application of well-planned strategies to resolve difficulties. I believe that, as a result of the outreach project, I am much better prepared to work effectively in similar contexts in the future.

Appendix

In an the full Outreach support, the appendix would contain the documents described below.

1. Preliminary Teacher Survey (Fall, 1995)
2. Snap-Shot Reports (Winter, 1996)
3. AERA Monograph (Spring, 1996)
4. Abstracts of the 6 manuscripts accepted for publication in a special issue of the international research journal, <u>School Effectiveness and School Improvement</u>.
5. A copy of my analysis of the PICA and the University research needs.

Reforming the Process of Change

Pennie G. Foster-Fishman, Ph.D.
Assistant Professor, Psychology
Michigan State University
March 1998

A Portfolio of Outreach Scholarship
Developed as part of the W.K. Kellogg Foundation Funded
Project on the Peer Review of Professional Service

Prologue

*The greatest thing in the world is
not so much where we are,
but in what direction we are moving.*

Oliver Wendell Holmes.

When I was first asked to participate in this project, I was excited to be part of an endeavor that was attempting to expand our understanding of scholarship, both in its form and documentation. Little did I realize that the greatest personal reward from this project would be the insights I gathered about myself and my work through the writing and reflection required by this endeavor.

As a community psychologist, I spend a considerable amount of time working in the field -- an occupational hazard that can leave little time for critical reflection about the process of my work. This project forced me to *think* not only about how I do my field work but also where these actions have led me, my students, and my community partners. At first I found this task quite foreboding and in conflict with the academic style of writing. In fact, my first few drafts of this chapter contained very little reflection. It was only as I read drafts written by some of my more courageous colleagues that I recognized its absence in my own writing.

As I began to reflect more on my work in general, and this one project in particular, I realized the important role such reflection can play in my own professional development as well as in improving the quality of my work. While I have always valued and emphasized the important role process plays in university/community partnerships, I had done little to document this process in the past. While I have always been committed to creating value-added change in the sponsoring communities, I have never before considered documenting this impact beyond what was required for my research or evaluation project. With an expanded perspective on what I should be documenting, I have found myself attending more to the processes and multiple outcomes in all of my projects. Still, I have found the process of reflecting easier than the documentation of this reflection. I believe the following chapter illustrates this struggle.

The Purpose

The Context.

Significant reform is currently under way in the human service delivery system and with it a growing recognition that the current system is often fragmented, territorial, and ineffective at meeting the multiple needs of many consumers. Coupled with this recognition is the emerging realization that the resources available for service provision will continue to decline. Current local, state, and federal governments have adopted policies and practices aimed at increasing service efficiency and improving client outcomes. While the specific character of these reforms varies somewhat from state to state, within Michigan a shift to a collaborative, strengths-based approach to service delivery forms the corner stone of social service system reform. The importance of these reform elements is evident in legislation, policies, and practices at the state and local level. Adoption of these reforms is tied to access to resources and is promoted through the formation of service goals and program agendas.

Recent assessments of similar reform efforts in other states suggest that substantial obstacles exist and are impeding the adoption of these changes. If reform efforts are to have a significant, sustained impact on the service delivery sector, it is critical to understand those forces that facilitate and impede adoption of innovation within the human service system. This outreach effort provided an excellent opportunity for examining the factors associated with the adoption of service innovation in Michigan.

The Setting.

A key player in many of the Michigan reform efforts are the county-wide interagency coordinating councils. Across the state, these councils, consisting of the leaders of the key service providing organizations in a county, have sponsored service delivery reform pilot programs, encouraged interagency collaboration, and developed a county-wide vision for service provision. The interagency council in Creek County (ICC) is recognized as one of the more successful coordinating bodies in Michigan. It has experienced tremendous growth in membership since its inception in 1989, including leaders and representatives from over 35 public and private human service delivery organizations in the County. This Council has also implemented several innovative service delivery programs.

Despite the ICC's efforts and an increase in service delivery dollars, county-wide indicators have worsened over the last few years. Immunization rates are some of the lowest in the state, out-of-home placements have increased, teen age pregnancy is on the rise. These indicators caused great consternation among Council members, and led some to argue for a systematic evaluation of their reform efforts.

The Evaluation.

In January, 1995, the ICC invited the Applied Developmental Sciences Program at Michigan State University (ADS) to conduct an evaluation of the reform efforts in Creek County. Given my affiliate faculty status with ADS and my interests in human service delivery reform, I was invited to lead this collaborative effort. In March, 1995, I presented my evaluation philosophy to the ICC. In April, 1995 the ICC formally developed a partnership with ADS.

1

I invited my colleague Deborah Salem to help me design and implement this evaluation. In May, 1995, Debby and I began to meet with one of the ICC workgroups to determine which questions should be prioritized and which methodologies should be implemented. In the end, we designed, in close collaboration with a subcommittee of local service providers and leaders, an evaluation strategy that would primarily target two service level outcomes closely linked to the reform efforts occurring across the state: the adoption of a strengths based approach to service delivery, and interagency coordination. This four year evaluation project plans to collect, in years 1 and 3, survey data from providers and leaders representing all relevant organizations on the Council as well as a small group of non-participating, but critical service organizations in the county. In years 2 and 4, data will be collected from a small, representative sample of consumers. We are currently in year 2 of this project.

Link to My Program of Research.

I have a primary interest in understanding and improving human services delivery. I have investigated the processes of multiple stakeholder collaboration in the laboratory and in the field. I have applied organizational culture theory to understand the successes and failures of organizational and ideological transformation, specifically human service delivery reform. Therefore, the system level outcomes matched well my current program of research and the context provided an excellent opportunity for me to explore several research questions.

Research Question 1: *How do internal and external belief systems influence the adoption and implementation of new service delivery paradigms?* Attitudes and behavior are often constrained by the demands, character, and norms of the contexts within which individuals live and work, and the values and beliefs within the external environment. If not aligned with the goals and ideologies of the intended reform, the belief systems within the organizational, community, and institutional environments can diminish the success of the change program. Attention to the multiple ecologies that may shape the success of human service delivery reform is particularly important, given the open, loosely coupled system character of the human service delivery system. In this project, the impact of the belief systems within different ecologies on staff attitudes towards, and implementation of, system reform is examined. Such an examination will help us to identify possible intervention points for system reform efforts.

Research Question 2: *What factors impact the processes and outcomes of multiple stakeholder collaborations and service coordination efforts?* Despite their popularity, little is known about the effectiveness of multiple stakeholder coalitions and the impact they have on service outcomes. This setting provided an excellent opportunity for examining the process and outcomes of one coalition, in general, and the impact coalition membership has on service coordination, in particular.

Available Resources.

As part of its community/university partnership model, ADS commits to jointly fund or seek funding for all of initiatives. For years one and two, we received $28,000 from several internal sources and $26,000 from the County and three local foundations. Substantial in kind contributions from the Department of Psychology were also provided, including space, computer equipment, and supplies as well as one research assistant for one academic year.

Institutional Mission and Priorities.

     This project serves well the land grant mission of the university -- to identify practical uses for theoretical knowledge and to share this information with a community audience. It also serves the purpose of my interest group, the Ecological/Community Psychology Program, to facilitate the healthy development of individuals and the settings they live and work in.

The Process

Developing a Strong Community/University Partnership.

     As a community psychologist, I believe in developing a strong collaborative relationship with evaluation setting members. In all of my evaluation efforts, community members are active partners in determining which questions to ask, designing the methods to be employed, collecting data, and interpreting results. To help identify which outcomes should be prioritized in this evaluation, my co-principle investigator and I facilitated three mini-retreats in the summer of 1995 for the members of the ICC workgroup charged with implementing this project. This group agreed that the two most important changes occurring in the County were 1) the adoption of a strengths-based approach to service delivery, and 2) the emphasis on service delivery coordination. Noting that these two outcomes were broader than any one reform initiative, the group agreed that this evaluation should not solely focus on the impact of one initiative, but instead should investigate the overall change across the County on these two indices. In practice, this meant that the evaluation would have to target the range of service providing organizations in the county. These decisions were presented to and approved by the ICC in September, 1995. An evaluation subcommittee, consisting of workgroup members and a few key ICC leaders was developed to work collaboratively with us in this effort.

     To build and sustain a positive relationship with the key players in the County and subcommittee members, I began to pursue several venues for developing a presence within the County. Subcommittee meetings were held every 3 to 4 weeks. I began to attend the monthly ICC meetings. I held weekly conversations with the ICC Coordinator, our primary liaison to the County. These visits not only strengthened my relationships with County residents, but also greatly enhanced my understanding of the issues and dilemmas facing this County. I would often use my conversations with council members or my liaison to test some of my "hypotheses" about life in Creek County and the norms and expectations of the service delivery system.

Linking Theory with Practice.

     To create a project that would answer a community need and address my research questions, I engaged in two parallel processes. At the evaluation subcommittee meetings, I would ask the members to identify factors they felt influenced service providers' ability to adopt a strengths-based, coordinated approach to service delivery. I would document their ideas and then, back at the university, review the literature on the outcomes, the process factors they identified, and other factors suggested by previous research. Following this literature review, I would

3

present a summary of the factors at the next subcommittee meeting, highlighting ones that converged with their own ideas and inquiring about factors that were not identified in both arenas. Using these multiple sources, a conceptual model for the project began to emerge (See Attachment 1). Both the subcommittee and the ICC accepted this model and reported that it provided them with a more complete understanding of, and rational for, the difficulties their County has experienced. While this process resulted in an evaluation design that would answer our research questions, make a contribution to the literature, and meet some of the needs of the County, it also inhibited our ability to fully explore some new areas of research in this study. The time frame imposed by the ICC often did not correspond with the time needed to conduct a thorough literature review. In addition, the need to include variables deemed important by the subcommittee necessitated the elimination of some other theoretically interesting factors.

Once we were in agreement about the factors to target, the evaluation team developed drafts of the measurement instrument and sent these drafts to the committee to critique and review. We used committee meetings to discuss sample selection, survey distribution methods, and brainstorm survey items. This process took approximately 6 months.

Evaluation Methodology.

Survey data was collected from human service providers and managers across 32 organizations. The organizations in this sample represent a broad range of human service agencies (e.g. domestic violence shelters, Head Start, substance abuse programs, Community Mental Health, Public Health) and service domains (e.g. mental health, physical health, education, judicial) providing a very representative picture of the services offered in the County. Given the diversity of organizations targeted, data collection strategies were modified to meet the unique needs of each organization. Throughout the course of our data collection process, we met monthly with the evaluation subcommittee to critique our data collection strategies, revise them as needed, and generate assistance in distributing and collecting surveys.

Staff and Leader Survey Instruments. These surveys measured provider involvement in the human service initiatives in the County, perceptions of the organizational and institutional environments, attitudes toward a strengths-based model and service coordination, current client practices, and breadth and depth of interagency coordination. Open-ended questions were asked about the barriers to and the potential impacts of the reforms.

The Outcomes

Impacting Local Policy and Practices.

I presented the evaluation findings to the ICC in October, 1996 and in January, 1997. Three reports (one describing staff attitudes, one describing staff behaviors, one describing leader attitudes and behaviors) were distributed to organizational leaders. Each organizational leader was also given a separate report which compared and contrasted their employees to other human service providers in the County (See Attachments 2-5 for copies of these reports). This feedback was so well received that we were invited to conduct three additional presentations in the County. First, a community forum was held in March, 1997 where staff, managers, and consumers were invited to attend. The ICC also invited us to review and discuss the evaluation implications at their February and March, 1997 meetings.

4

At this point in the process, our project began to evolve from a pure evaluation to an organization and system development endeavor. The ICC began to examine the implications of our evaluation findings and made the review of current county policies and practices a priority (See Attachment 6 for copies of the ICC minutes). For example, at the March ICC meeting, leaders were assigned the task of evaluating, in their home agency, two of the organizational policies our studies identified as critical to the success of these reforms: 1) client confidentiality practices; and 2) flex time policies and supports for staff involvement in reform initiatives. At the May, 1997 meeting, some leaders reported on their current policies and plans for revisions, if needed.

While, in general, the reactions to our evaluation findings have been positive, our evaluation also seems to have exacerbated several tensions within the ICC. Historically, the ICC has maintained a somewhat traditional hierarchy in its relationship with its workgroups, which are staffed by managers and line workers. Despite a desire by the workgroups to be treated as partners in the change process, they are still perceived and treated as the "worker bees" of the ICC. Our findings highlighted this and other systemic barriers to change. Specifically we found that organizational and institutional barriers, not provider characteristics, were the critical factors impeding system reform efforts in the County. Workgroup members embraced these findings as a legitimate voice to their experiences and frustrations. On the contrary, some leaders either ignored or questioned the importance of our findings and recommendations. This reaction was most apparent by the refusal of several leaders to engage in the self-audit of their organizational policies described above. This reaction spawned several workgroups to question the ICC's commitment to foster real system change within the County. This resistance also illustrated the difficulties in fostering a shared work agenda among multiple, powerful, stakeholders.

Impacting Statewide Policy and Practices.

Immediately following our first presentation, the ICC discussed our findings with and distributed our feedback reports to policy makers around the state. This dissemination has led to invitations to present our findings to four additional audiences. In January, I presented our findings to over 100 providers and leaders at the United Way of Michigan State Conference. In February, my co-investigator and I presented our findings to the system reform evaluation committee, a group appointed by Governor Engler to oversee and evaluate his reform initiatives. This committee, consisting of top public administrators, was so interested in our findings that they encouraged MSU and the ICC to co-sponsor a public policy forum, inviting elected and appointed public officials from across the state to hear our results. We are currently planning this public forum. I was also invited to present our findings at a technological assistance workshop held for all of the interagency council coordinators in the state and at a welfare reform conference held for Michigan human service leaders. In all of these presentations, the response to our findings has been quite positive; many audience members have indicated that the findings speak to their own experiences and requested additional copies of our reports to distribute to their colleagues. The feedback reports have been so widely distributed that human service leaders from other states and counties have begun to contact us for more information.

We were also invited to write a brief article on our study for Perspectives, an MSU publication that is distributed to over 5,500 policy makers, leaders, providers, and faculty across the state. This article was published in summer, 1997 (See Attachment 7).

Contributing to a Knowledge Base.

This research potentially advances both the science and practice of service delivery reform. It provides a theoretical framework for assessing the internal and external factors that influence human service delivery reform; it is one of a few studies that will investigate the changes in interagency network structures longitudinally and the role of ICCs and interagency teams in fostering system reform. A paper based on this work has been presented at the third Head Start National Research Conference. We also presented our experiences in developing a collaborative university/community partnership at a departmental colloquium in November, 1996. We have submitted our first paper on this study to the American Journal of Community Psychology. This paper describes and tests our conceptual framework. Four additional papers are in process and will be submitted in 1998. Three presentations on this study were made at the 6th Biennial Conference for Community Research and Action.

Unexpected Developments.

At a pivotal ICC meeting held about 9 months into the evaluation planning process, I was invited to present an overview of our plans and progress to date. During this meeting, several powerful ICC members noted their concern about the nature and content of this evaluation, stating that evaluation dollars should only be spent on targeting change within people, not system reform. These individuals began to make the distinction between "means versus ends" and how this evaluation was an example of "means" not "ends".

This meeting demoralized many of the subcommittee members. They felt that the Council had undermined their process. In response to these concerns, we began to discuss, as a group, why this dynamic might exist at the Council and how similar processes have played out in its history. As a result of these discussions, the evaluation team from MSU, in conjunction with the subcommittee members, displayed a poster at the Society for the Psychological Study of Social Issues Annual Conference describing the development of the Council in terms of this and other dynamics. We are in the process of writing a paper that describes these issues.

Enhancing Local Capacity.

Our findings indicated that involvement in one of the County's interdisciplinary teams designed to implement a family-centered service model significantly facilitated providers' adoption and implementation of these service delivery reforms. Providers involved on these teams were more likely to coordinate with a broader agency network and to offer services in a strengths-based, consumer driven manner. The coordinators of these teams used this finding to support the continuance of these teams in the County and to procure additional funds (See Attachment 8 for a letter of support from one team leader). This finding also encouraged other counties in Michigan to expand their interdisciplinary team efforts. In addition, this evaluation further enhanced the ICC's standing in the state.

Strengthening My Capacity.

Participation in this project has expanded my skills as an evaluator, grantee, scholar, and teacher. The skills I have developed and the reputation I am developing as an evaluator has created additional evaluation and external grant opportunities for me. The lessons I have learned on how to construct a valid, reliable survey instrument and design feasible data collection strategies have improved the design of my other evaluation projects. I have integrated many of these lessons into my graduate seminars. I have also learned two new statistical procedures as a result of this project: Hierarchical Linear Models and Network Analysis. Through my participation in this project, I have also developed a more clearly articulated and focused program of research and have been able to augment other studies by examining complementary research questions. To continue this area of study, I am planning to submit a grant to either a federal funding agency or a foundation in 1998.

For three of the five graduate students involved in this project, this was their first exposure to a large scale evaluation. Several have stated how this experience prepared them for their own thesis work. One student, who used data from this project for her master's thesis, has decided to specialize in human service system reform. Two students were also able to complete a practicum course requirement through their involvement.

A Discussion of Lessons Learned

The Need for Additional Resources. During year-one data collection, I realized that this project was and continues to be significantly underfunded. As the first large scale project I have directed, I underestimated the resources needed to conduct a study of this size. While this lack of resources has, to date, produced no perceptible impact on my ability to fulfill our promises to the County, it has created some undue burdens on my time. Perhaps the most tangible impact this lack of resources has on the project is the constant need to balance limited time among preparing scholarly publications, producing timely feedback reports, and responding to requests to present results to other service providers and leaders across the state.

The Challenge of Targeting Multiple Sites. Perhaps one of the greatest difficulties we experienced in this project was collecting data from 32 different organizations. Although all of the ICC leaders verbally agreed to participate in this evaluation, we quickly learned that verbal consent may be a necessary but is certainly not a sufficient condition for guaranteeing easy access to employees. Some leaders would often speak to the value and importance of our project at the monthly ICC meetings, yet would provide significant resistance to our data collection efforts. In many ways, this inconsistency well illustrated one tension present within most collaborative bodies: the need for participating leaders to maintain autonomy yet support the group process. Not surprisingly, the leaders with whom I had developed a more personal relationship were less resistant to our efforts. Unfortunately, with 32 organizations targeted in our study, and limited resources, it was impossible to develop such a relationship with each individual leader. I now know to rely more on insiders to help negotiate entry into organizations.

Recognizing Your Integration into the Local Ecology. One indicator of a successful outreach project is the extent to which the project becomes integrated into and adopted by the sponsoring community. Such integration signifies the community's acceptance of the project and the likelihood that the project will be sustained over time. Thus, throughout the course of the project, as ICC support for and involvement in our project expanded, we viewed this integration as an indication of our success in developing a positive collaborative relationship with the County. However, we began to realize that such success can also result in another form of integration, one where the evaluation project and its staff become players in the tensions and dynamics inherent to that setting. Many of the issues we identified between the ICC and its workgroups seemed to also characterize our own relationship with the ICC; many of the tensions and disagreements within the ICC seemed to be reflected within the multitude of responses our evaluation elicited. If anything, I have learned that I should begin to use my ability to assess the culture and climate of a setting in order to predict the issues that may emerge in reaction to my project. Such insight would better prepare me for the complex interpersonal dynamics that are so embedded within an outreach endeavor.

Annotated List of Attachments

Attachment 1: Conceptual Model for the Project

Attachment 2: Feedback Report 1: Factors influencing staff attitudes towards service delivery reform efforts

Attachment 3: Feedback Report 2: Factors influencing provider adoption and implementation of a collaborative, strengths based approach to service delivery

Attachment 4: Feedback Report 3: Factors influencing leader adoption and implementation of a collaborative, strengths based approach to service delivery

Attachment 5: Feedback Report 4: Individualized reports to each organizational leader: Comparing and contrasting your providers' attitudes and behaviors with those of other service delivery staff in the county

Attachment 6: Minutes from meetings of the Interagency Council in Creek County (ICC)

Attachment 7: Allen, N. E., Foster-Fishman, P.G., & Salem, D.A. (Summer, 1997). Human service delivery reform: One Michigan county's experience. Perspectives, 3(3), 6-7.

Attachment 8: Letter of support from one county team leader

DELINQUENT YOUTHS AND THEIR FUTURES: CAN OUTREACH ON THE PART
OF THE UNIVERSITY MAKE A DIFFERENCE?

by

G. Roger Jarjoura
School of Public and Environmental Affairs
Indiana University-Purdue University Indianapolis

DELINQUENT YOUTHS AND THEIR FUTURES: CAN OUTREACH ON THE PART OF THE UNIVERSITY MAKE A DIFFERENCE?

There is a perception that juvenile delinquency is all too common. In fact, evidence indicates that a substantial amount of juvenile offending can be attributed to a rather small group of chronic offenders. Indeed, while most juvenile offenders desist after one arrest, those who have been arrested three, four, or five times are highly likely to continue re-offending. Rather than focusing get-tough policies at the general teenage population, our efforts are better served in trying to reduce the likelihood of recidivism among the juvenile offender population. A key aspect of such efforts must focus on aftercare (treatment provided to assist in the transition back to the community).

Aftercare is traditionally a neglected component in juvenile justice programs. This project is designed to provide aftercare support to juvenile offenders and training experiences to college students as part of an ongoing partnership between a university and a state department of correction. My work focuses specifically on planning for and developing linkages with community resources to assist in the transition of the youths from the institution back to their communities. As the external partner, the Department of Correction (DOC) has much to gain. With organizational priorities that pay relatively little attention to the provision of aftercare programming, there is a great need for additional resources. This project supplements the services being provided at no cost to the DOC. In addition, my own role brings an integration of the existing knowledge base and provides an example of how best to base policy on existing research.

Background

While teaching and conducting research on the juvenile justice system, I was continuously faced with evidence that juvenile aftercare was the weakest component of the juvenile justice system. My own volunteer work with juvenile offenders at the state correctional facility exposed me to youths with lots of potential who invariably failed upon release because of a lack of effective supports in their communities. My research agenda laid the theoretical foundation for the current project. A review of the literature pointed to several conclusions: 1) Getting tough with juvenile offenders is more likely to exacerbate the problem than provide any real reductions in juvenile delinquency; 2) The most effective treatments are cognitive in nature, targeting the thought processes of youths, but do not have long-lasting effects if the youths return to the same environment from which they came; and, 3) Enhancing protective factors as part of a comprehensive aftercare intervention can better sustain the positive effects of correctional treatments, reducing the likelihood of re-offending.

Criminological theories also provide a foundation from which to structure this project. Based on the explanations derived from social learning theory and symbolic interactionism, I believe that delinquent behavior is shaped through interactions with others. While parents and teachers can often be effective prosocial role models, delinquent youths are more likely influenced by their peers and the antisocial examples of family members. The goal of this project, therefore, is to provide learning opportunities targeted at improving the decision-making and problem-solving skills of the youths and to provide opportunities for these youths to develop positive relationships with prosocial others.

This project will also add to the existing knowledge base on juvenile aftercare. Based on the research that shows that these youths are among the most troubled adolescents, to meet their needs related to emotional problems, skill development, and deficiencies in their environments, collaborative efforts between existing agencies are likely to be the most effective. Thus, the best scholarship in this area suggests that aftercare workers must be more service broker than case manager. This project considers ways to structure the involvement of mentors to provide support and act as service brokers. Outcomes from this project will inform the field on successful approaches to building integrated efforts.

This project is also important in that it fulfills the different missions of the contexts from within which it operates. It serves to fulfill specific aspects of the mission of the School of Public and Environmental Affairs (SPEA)—my unit within Indiana University-Purdue University Indianapolis (IUPUI)—by reinforcing continuing relationships with public agencies and nonprofit organizations, and by combining academic course work with practical experiences that may ultimately help students find jobs and enhance their careers. This project also fulfills several aspects of the mission of IUPUI by serving as a model for collaboration and interdisciplinary work through partnerships between the university and the community, by enhancing the public and private lives of students through effective academic programs, and by developing

2

and applying knowledge to issues of social well-being through teaching, research, and service. Finally, the DOC benefits by being able to fulfill part of their mission to enhance their aftercare programming with a mentoring component. Providing community-based aftercare programming can ultimately enhance the reputation of DOC with the general public.

Development of the Project

In the summer of 1994, I began working as a volunteer at the Indiana Boys' School, a state-run juvenile correctional facility. The following spring I was asked by the institution to develop a service learning course which would involve students from IUPUI working at the institution as part of the course. It became clear as I taught that course (which has now been offered six times) that planning for and providing aftercare was virtually neglected by the institution. This led to a year-long effort at developing and pilot testing an aftercare program provided by students and faculty on a volunteer basis from IUPUI. I began working with two groups of youths. This allowed me to get a sense of the needs of these boys once they are released and the resources in the community available to them. I have been fortunate that at all levels of the DOC, there has been great support for this program. We included a randomized evaluation design for the first 18 months of the program and DOC has developed some training programs for my students. In addition to the mentoring program, the staff at the facility and at DOC have become more willing to seek out other forms of support from my students and I, which, in turn has led to more varied forms of involvement on the part of the University at the facility.

My strategy has been to access services from as many different community partners as possible. We continue to build partnerships with local service providers and hosted a state-wide conference (September 1997) on juvenile aftercare to facilitate the building of coalitions for aftercare programs. Finally, based on a successful model program based initially in the Department of Psychology at Michigan State University, I built in the mentoring component which involves the college students working one-on-one with the youths. The evaluation of this program has become a major part of my personal research agenda. The design of the evaluation involves a randomized experiment.

3

The basic design of our program was shaped by discussions with all of the involved parties: groups of IUPUI students, DOC personnel, and groups of youths at the facility. Further redesign of the program has occurred as the program has been in operation. Once per semester, I meet with DOC administrators to further clarify how we can best operate our program within their structure. By maintaining contact with the youths after their release, we are constantly aware of key issues we are still not addressing very well. By conducting exit interviews with the mentors, and assessing the mentor/mentee relationships, we learn how better to equip and motivate our mentors. Finally, through developing partnerships with other agencies, we are learning how best to access needed services.

As the program has evolved, we have learned as much from our failures as we have from our successes. We originally conceived that by developing a plan and identifying resources in the communities, the youths would follow through upon their release. We learned, however, that for most of the youths we need to be there to walk them through the initial steps. We also found that we needed to focus on the whole of each youth — it was not enough to focus on employment and school issues. These youths also need to know where to go for low cost health care, low cost mental health counseling, how to arrange transportation, ways to facilitate safe sex and birth control, and perhaps most important, how to structure their leisure time. I am encouraged to discover the actual breadth of services available. In fact, more often than not, service providers are interested in developing linkages to our program since they are in need of ways to identify potential clients. We have created a partnership with Goodwill Industries in which they provide employment assistance to our youths. We are working with a network of local churches and community centers to provide support within the local neighborhoods these boys return to. We are also currently working with the YMCA to develop opportunities for structured leisure activities.

The role of the mentor in the transition back to the community is another area in which experiences have helped shape the structure of this program. From working with over 50 youths through the prerelease and post-release periods, I learned several important lessons. First, it is crucial that the relationship between the mentor and the youth be established prior to the release of the youth. Second, the first week after release is vital to the successful compliance of the youth with his reentry plan. Third, the ways in which the youths

4

deal with obstacles that arise will really determine the ultimate success of those youths. The involvement of mentors at these times has often made the difference between the youths experiencing success or going back to a correctional facility. Finally, mentoring is particularly effective if it can be maintained over the long term.

Impact of Program

This project has major implications for my teaching. First, students are gaining a real sense of the nature of the juvenile justice system. In addition, students gain a true understanding and empathy for juvenile offenders and the etiology of delinquent behavior. Finally, students develop an awareness of how much help is required from the private sector for juvenile offenders to be successful. These outcomes are evident in the written assignments submitted by students and in their comments when surveyed at the end of their experience.

I believe this project is significant in another regard. Most scholars lament from time to time the lack of impact their research has on the applied field. For one specific agency, this project allows me to model the way in which we learn from the research literature in designing an intervention. The evaluation results, should they point to positive effects, are likely to serve as justification for building up the community-based aftercare programming at DOC.

This program will also benefit the community to the extent that criminality is reduced. If we can facilitate the transition into the labor market for these youths, we will also reduce the likelihood that these youths will be supported by the social welfare system. This project, in furthering the mission of both SPEA and IUPUI, has the potential for enhancing the public image of both the School and the University.

Outcomes

The evaluation of this project is ongoing. There are, however, some preliminary and formative outcome measures I can point to. Of 42 youths who have been assigned a mentor, 11 have returned to a correctional facility. This low figure is encouraging, but at this point we have no comparison data. In

September 1997, we hosted a statewide conference with the goal of building a coalition of aftercare providers to inform policies at the state and local levels, as well as within the DOC. This conference was well-attended by service providers and was the first of what will be annual conferences on juvenile aftercare. We are currently expanding the provision of our prerelease curriculum and have made arrangements to play a more active role in the treatment team at the facility.

Other measures will result from the evaluation. Each youth develops a reentry plan as part of the prerelease program. The action steps on the plan form the basis for what I call markers of progress. In follow-up interviews we will track the compliance of the youths with the components of their plans. Mentors record the amount and nature of contact each week with each youth in the program. At one year after the date of release, we will check official records for evidence of subsequent criminal activity and technical parole violations. The evaluation will also document the benefits this project presents to the DOC, the correctional institution itself, the community, the University students, SPEA, and IUPUI. Surveys with program participants (including the youths, the mentors, and the staff at the facility) will be used to assess the progress of the program, focusing specifically on ways in which the project has enhanced the lives and work environment of these groups, how the program fell short of expectations, and how the program might be restructured to better meet their needs. DOC administrators will be asked to address the ways in which the project is related to the mission of the agency, results in value added to their programs, provides services which are otherwise unavailable, and may be modified to better contribute to the organization.

Future Plans

At this point, there are several areas for change which have been identified. Based on the coalitions we are building, we are moving more into the role of brokers for community-based providers. This program can be expanded to other campuses in other areas of the state. We need to do a better job of screening mentors, and make changes in our recruitment strategies, so as to increase the pool of eligible mentors. Supervision of mentors is also an area we need to enhance. We plan to increase our expectations of mentors, particularly in terms of the length of their commitment. We will also provide more structured programming to encourage more regular involvement on the part of the youths.

Several new questions have arisen as a result of the ongoing evaluation of this project. First of all, I cannot help but wonder whether we are doing harm by introducing mentors with a relatively short-term commitment to the youth. I also question whether we are indirectly subjecting these youths to a higher probability of re-involvement with the criminal justice system by increasing the level of supervision by an adult. If so, this is the kind of outcome which will ultimately reduce the appeal of our program to these youths. In addition, because some of the youths get back into trouble once they are no longer working with their mentor, I wonder if we are able to bring about sustainable change or are we simply delaying the inevitable failure of these youths? Finally, because it is so critical to the long-term success of these youths, I question whether it is possible to get the community to recognize the importance of aftercare.

APPENDIX

As illustrative materials, the following items would be appended to this document to further support the case being made for the quality of scholarship of this project:

1. Surveys would be conducted with each of the following:

    - mentors
    - youths
    - DOC administrators

    The focus of these surveys will be to assess the following:

    - in what ways has this project enhanced their lives or their work environment?
    - in what ways has the program failed to meet their needs or those of the youths/DOC?
    - if it were up them, how would the program be restructured?

2. Copies of papers written for practitioner and outreach journals.

3. Letters solicited from DOC administrators which answer the following questions:

    - in what ways are the activities of the project related to the mission of their agency?
    - in what ways has the project resulted in value added to DOC?
    - in what ways does this project provide services which would be otherwise lacking?
    - what are some additional ways to structure the program to contribute to the mission of the agency?

4. Documentation of partnerships which enhance scope and quality of program:

    - details of community service programming for youths through Youth as Resources
    - letters of support for program from local juvenile court judges demonstrating the need and benefits of program
    - letter of cooperation from partner agencies:
        - local community centers
        - employment preparation service, Goodwill Industries
        - local churches
    - details of positions funded through federal work study and Americorps programs which attract students who can make commitments as mentors for up to two years

REFLECTIONS ON THE PROCESS

Writing this document has been a valuable experience for me. I had not previously thought seriously about what "scholarship" means. It has helped to think about the nature of scholarship for two reasons. First, it validated for me that my own work can be so classified. I am in a field--criminology/criminal justice--in which much of the research, by design, is applied. Yet, applied research is often considered more as service than research, particularly as to evaluation of my work. They socialized me in graduate school to value research more highly than service, yet I have a strong commitment to serving the criminal justice field through applied research. Writing this document and participating in the discussions with other participants of this project has helped me see how to justify the scholarship in what others would often discount as merely service.

Second, by working to document the scholarship in the project described here I believe I have enhanced the quality of the project. Since this project is ongoing, I can reflect on how best to justify the scholarly nature of the work. This led to much reflection about the work itself, which led to revisions in the approach taken and a more rational approach to measuring outcomes. I am convinced of the value of ongoing reflection and believe my project is better than it would have otherwise been.

I have learned a great deal at each stage of this project and have developed some new habits in my work that will serve me well in the future. As an assistant professor, the timing of this project for me was fortunate. I have recently had to make my case for tenure and promotion and was better prepared because of my involvement on this project. As a faculty member who believes strongly that we have an obligation to serve the community outside the university, this project and the other scholars I have had the opportunity to work with inspire me to continue to do more.

Professional Development for Michigan Veterinarians

James W. Lloyd, D.V.M., Ph.D.
Associate Professor, Large Animal Clinical Science
& Agricultural Economics
Michigan State University
March 1998

A Portfolio of Outreach Scholarship
Developed as part of the W.K. Kellogg Foundation Funded
Project on the Peer Review of Professional Service

Goal

   The goal of this outreach program is to enhance the production of livestock in Michigan through professional development of practicing veterinarians.

Description

   Program Overview--Since 1990, this outreach program has sought to enhance the professional development of Michigan veterinarians. Following an initial needs assessment, which revealed both topics of interest and administrative preferences for this diverse group of learners, a cadre of educational methods has been employed toward the objective of achieving higher levels of cognitive learning. Methods have included: technical publications, seminars, workshops (both stand-alone and as part of a larger curriculum), demonstration projects, collaborative problem solving, a practice-based teaching program (involving professional veterinary students), and orchestrated peer teaching (according to Rogers theory of innovation).

   Without exception, the principles of andragogy have been followed during development and delivery. Ongoing program monitoring has led to numerous mid-stream modifications and enhancements. In veterinary medicine, this outreach program is unique because it: 1) describes the diversity in learner needs for professional development, and 2) develops an equally diverse blend of educational methods to meet those defined learner needs.

   Nature of the problem--Recent social and economic trends have combined with a cascade of technological advances to compound both the importance and difficulty of livestock production management. Progressive management skills are desperately needed to maintain and enhance the economic viability of Michigan's animal agriculture. In this setting, the veterinarian's role in livestock production has been transformed. Traditional service demands emphasized medical and surgical expertise for curative purposes. These skills now need to be blended with concern for factors such as management, nutrition, reproduction, facilities, epidemiology, and economics to manage livestock health toward production-related goals and objectives including both profitability and product quality. Veterinary practitioners must be able to identify and solve complex management problems, and professional development programs in non-traditional disciplines that incorporate higher level cognitive learning are needed. Because of the need for expertise in multiple disciplines and the extreme learner diversity, it is reasonable for these programs to be developed by a university.

   Program Origin--My first recognition of the need for enhanced professional development occurred when I was working as a private veterinary practitioner. Ultimately, this realization led me to pursue my own graduate training. Although occasional seminars and workshops had been offered by faculty from the College of Veterinary Medicine at MSU in the past, there did not appear to be an overall plan to guide program development and implementation. This struck me as a serious programmatic deficiency, in light of the situation in the industry and the accessibility aspects of the Land Grant Philosophy. Because my initial faculty appointment included a 20% time commitment to outreach, I decided to work toward addressing the problem. Development of this outreach program was also consistent with my teaching and research agendas, which were focused on the economics of livestock production and health management.

1

Program rationale--Leaders in both veterinary medicine and animal agriculture have widely recognized the management challenges being faced by livestock producers and their veterinarians, as indicated by increasingly widespread publication on the economics and epidemiology of animal health management in both scientific and lay journals. Further evidence of this issue's importance is provided by the financial support obtained for various aspects of this outreach program, which was obtained either directly from the livestock industry, from individual livestock producers, or through the substantial registration fees of participating veterinarians. Finally, this outreach program is entirely consistent with national trends in agriculture, which have seen successful management programs become increasingly more progressive as livestock operations have decreased in number and increased in size and as consumer interests in food safety have risen.

Stake holders--The key stake holders in this program are livestock producers and practicing veterinarians in Michigan, consumers of livestock products, and Michigan State University. By virtue of the project's publications and presentations, there has almost certainly been an additional impact beyond Michigan's borders in livestock production, veterinary medicine, and academia.

Diagnosis

Industry and professional interactions--Beyond my own bias as a former practitioner, I identified the need for this outreach program through interactions with the veterinary profession, the livestock industries, and professional colleagues across the MSU campus. These ventures have included active involvement in organized veterinary medicine, working relationships with the livestock industries, and numerous multidisciplinary projects at MSU. The list of committees contained in Appendix A, is indicative of those on which I have served to achieve such interactions.

Needs assessment--Following the initial problem identification, I conducted a formal needs assessment with the assistance of Professor Howard Hickey (Department of Educational Administration, MSU) to further characterize the needed outreach program. This process consisted of both a survey and a focus group meeting, which convened representatives from the veterinary profession, the livestock industries, government, and academia to discuss survey results. From this meeting came a better rapport with allied livestock industry groups and an improved understanding of how to establish effective delivery processes for the reported lifelong education needs. From the needs assessment I discovered wide demographic differences in both topics of interest and administrative preferences. Findings from the needs assessment are published, in part in the works listed in Appendix B.

Design

The Land Grant Philosophy holds that the knowledge contained in the university should be accessible to the citizenry for application and problem solving in the real world. Such is the approach of this outreach program: new approaches to livestock health management should be developed on Michigan farms by veterinarians and producers, based on the knowledge that is available at the university. To be truly accessible, a variety of educational methods needed to be employed based on the inherent diversity of the veterinary profession. Individually, perhaps none of the principles or methods employed in this program is unique in its application. However, the blend of these factors in a single, orchestrated outreach program is singular in veterinary education, if not beyond.

2

Based on the complexity of the livestock health management problems involved, the expertise employed by this outreach program was necessarily multidisciplinary and collaboration was crucial. Clinical skills needed to be blended with technical expertise from disciplines such as animal science, agricultural economics, agricultural engineering, food science and epidemiology. In addition, the challenge of delivering effective learning required the involvement of specialists in education.

Challenges encountered--Practicing veterinarians constitute a very diverse learner group. Because each veterinary practice is unique in the service it provides, and each practitioner is unique in the skills and knowledge s/he commands, I found a wide variation in individual learning needs, interests, and styles that went beyond the demographic differences defined by the needs assessment. In addition, another challenge occurred when it became apparent that many practitioners were convinced of the need for new skills in the long run, but were somewhat uncertain about the willingness of their clients to pay for these new services in the short run.

Critical principles--To address the diverse target audience, several principles were employed to form a foundation for educational program planning and development. First, I developed a portfolio of programs that was applicable across a spectrum of learner needs. As it turns out, this portfolio spans Bloom's domain of cognitive learning, from basic knowledge and comprehension (where I have developed publications, classroom activities, and seminars) to evaluation and formation of value judgements (where I have engaged in collaborative problem solving). In many cases, different program levels were developed sequentially for the same learners.

Professor Joseph Levine (Department of Agricultural and Extension Education at MSU) assisted me in integrating Knowles' theory of andragogy and pedagogy into the program design. Knowles' theory holds that mature learners are more likely to achieve success if instruction takes an andragogical approach, recognizing and building upon the learners' life experience while adopting an attitude of teacher-learner equality. This is in contrast to the pedagogical approach, which positions the teacher in an authoritative posture. Because the learners in this project are practicing professionals, I have adopted a strictly andragogical approach. Even in classroom and seminar settings, it has been useful to present material on a colleague-to-colleague basis, as opposed to a teacher-to-student approach.

Program design was further influenced (this time with the assistance of Professor Hickey) by Rogers' theory of innovation, which holds that new techniques are much more likely to be adopted from peers who are perceived as leaders in the field (early adopters) than from outside sources. For this reason, I have specifically targeted opinion leaders in the veterinary profession for the initial wave of education, and have developed opportunities for them to speak about and demonstrate their new skills to audiences of their peers. Finally, to help provide the practitioners with an opportunity to market their new skills, I have also targeted livestock producer groups in an effort to stimulate a derived demand for these new veterinary services.

Resources--The resource base for this outreach program was both sufficient and creative. Evidence of the resource sufficiency is contained in the fact that the program has continued to develop successfully, while evidence of the creativity is found in the variety of funding sources. These sources included several university grants obtained to support certain aspects of the program (Appendix C).

Delivery

Educational approaches employed--Because of the wide variety of educational needs, an equally broad array of educational approaches has been employed. At the foundation of these are the technical publications which target three distinct groups: fellow educators, veterinary practitioners, and livestock producers (Appendix D contains examples).

Along with the technical publications have been numerous educational meetings for veterinary practitioners. These have included seminar-type scientific presentations, primarily using an andragogical approach to develop lower levels of cognitive learning (basic knowledge and comprehension). Workshops have also been designed that seek to develop intermediate levels of cognitive learning (application and analysis) over a 1 to 2 day time period. Many of these workshops were presented as part of an organized curriculum designed as a certificate program (examples are listed in Appendix E).

To develop the practitioners' capabilities beyond the classroom, in effect to pursue higher levels of cognitive learning (synthesis, evaluation, and value judgements), demonstration projects and collaborative problem solving were undertaken. These activities involved visiting client farms with workshop participants to apply methods that were taught in the classroom. In addition to helping these particular veterinarians develop a better grasp of their new skills, these farm visits provided material for teaching cases to be used in future workshops (and in the veterinary curriculum), and they helped identify particular areas where the seminars and workshops needed to be enhanced. Between 1988 and 1996, at least 15 such visits were made across Michigan.

Another educational method that has helped many practitioners achieve higher level cognition is a practice-based teaching program where veterinary students are placed in private practices and the practicing veterinarian serves as clinical instructor. Teaching the latest techniques requires that the practitioners be able to synthesize, evaluate, and provide value judgements, and students serve as a knowledge conduit from the university to the profession through their questions and input. I personally led the program's development and implementation, and have served as program coordinator since its inception.

Following Rogers' theory of innovation, the final educational method that has been employed involves the development of situations where practitioners (Rogers' early adopters) serve as teachers and role models for their peers. To achieve this activity, I helped initiate a special session at the annual Michigan Veterinary Conference where practitioners are selected to give presentations (Practice Tips) based on their known active participation in many of the aforementioned educational activities. In addition, I successfully nominated one of our leading practitioners for a prestigious, statewide award for outstanding veterinary practitioners (1996 Birth of a Purebred Award, Dr. Garold Koester).

A summary of educational methods employed and their target audiences is presented in Table 1.

Monitoring methods--To monitor this outreach program, we relied on the learners' professional expertise for evaluation of the program's quality and relevance, and watched for changing behaviors. To obtain feedback, each seminar and workshop had a structured evaluation for participants to respond through both standardized and open-ended questions. In addition, perpetual informal interaction has

4

occurred with veterinarians across the state on almost a daily basis in the course of administering the practice-based teaching program. Such interaction provides an invaluable means to obtain feedback on virtually all aspects of the outreach program, and has led to numerous programmatic modifications.

Documenting the impact of this program on Michigan veterinarians and livestock producers would have been easier if I had been able to successfully design an overall evaluative strategy at the outset. Such an approach, which would have monitored the relative success in livestock production for clients of veterinarians who had participated in this program (as compared to their peers), was not feasible within our resource constraints.

Unexpected developments--Originally, it was expected that individual programs would not need to be developed beyond the workshop stage. However, it became apparent that, in the case of some learners, full adoption of the new skills did not always occur following the seminars or workshops. Therefore, demonstration projects and collaborative problem solving were introduced where needed.

Two other changes in program design resulted from unexpected circumstances. The first was identification of the need for stimulating a derived demand for new veterinary services among livestock producers, which led to programs (such as those listed in Appendix F) targeting early adopters in the livestock production arena using seminars and demonstration projects in an andragogical approach. Second, circumstances in the veterinary curriculum made it necessary to develop the practice-based teaching program after the main portion of this outreach program was well under way. These circumstances provided an ideal and unique opportunity to meet curricular objectives while achieving higher levels of cognitive learning with the veterinary practitioners.

Even though the findings of the needs assessment were followed closely, two specific workshops were developed that did not attract sufficient registrants to be conducted (one in beef cattle health management and one in equine nutrition). Although this was disappointing, it helped me realize that additional factors not included in the needs assessment, such as the total amount of time an individual can allocate to continuing education and the related need to prioritize among available programs, are important to the choices veterinarians make in professional development.

Outcomes

This outreach program has been highly visible in the veterinary profession and in the Michigan livestock industry. Evidence of this is contained in the high number of leading veterinary practices that have been involved. Of the 200 (approx.) large animal veterinary practices in Michigan, the 65 that participate in the practice-based teaching program are among the largest and most progressive, and are widely considered as leaders of our veterinary community. In addition, these practices serve a correspondingly high proportion of Michigan's livestock industry. By far, the most common reason that practitioners provide for their participation in the program is that it provides a method of pursuing continuing education.

Evidence that knowledge has been generated and applied in a scholarly fashion in this outreach program is contained in my accompanying list of publications and speaking engagements. Many of the publications are in peer-reviewed, scientific journals, and many of the presentations were invited at national and international meetings. These have included presentations to fellow educators on the process of professional development for veterinarians. I have also been invited to give many professional development presentations to veterinarians across North America emphasizing my particular technical expertise (content), and I have been invited frequently to make technical presentations to livestock producer groups across the country. Examples of these presentations are listed (by target audience) in Appendix G. These presentations to educators, veterinarians, and livestock producer groups indicate that the scope of this outreach program has actually grown beyond Michigan. One portion of this outreach program also received an award for innovation in teaching, and two others received awards for outstanding extension activity. These awards are listed in Appendix H.

Benefits to non-university groups and evidence of changing behaviors--The primary groups to benefit from this outreach program have been Michigan livestock producers, their veterinarians, and consumers of their products. Livestock producers benefit from improved economic efficiency and profitability, and a more stable market for their products. Veterinarians benefit through enhancement of their service and, consequently, improved sustainability of their businesses. In effect, through the successful education of Michigan's veterinarians, their professional capacity is increased by leveraging the body of knowledge contained within the university. Consumer benefits are realized through improved product quality available at a lower price. In addition, groups allied to the livestock industries (such as the feed and pharmaceutical industries) also benefit from enhanced economic stability in the livestock sector. The most convincing evidence to support the existence of these benefits is the consistently positive evaluations obtained from workshop participants and seminar attendees and their continued willingness to pay for such programs.

The evidence of changing behaviors in the veterinary practitioners is encouraging. Specifically, an expansion of services that the practitioners are providing beyond traditional medicine and surgery has occurred into consultative arenas. Though it is not possible to determine the exact degree to which this outreach program is directly responsible, it is difficult to imagine that some of the specific services would be currently available to Michigan livestock producers had this program not been developed. Most notable among these is the economic analysis, either formal or informal, that increasingly accompanies the development and implementation of dairy health management programs. Evidence that this is the case includes several practitioner-originated Practice Tips sessions during the past two years at the Michigan Veterinary Conference that emphasized economics.

Other indicators that expanded consultation is occurring include widespread adoption of an hourly-basis for fees (as opposed to strictly piece-work), and a practitioner-initiated informal discussion group on developing consultative services. Evidence of the impact on livestock producers is contained in their willingness to pay for the new skills of their veterinarians.

Benefits to the university--In general, this outreach program has resulted in an increase in cross-disciplinary collaborations within the university, and has greatly improved communication between the university and the professional veterinary community. As stated by both university administrators and members of the veterinary profession, this outreach program has resulted in an enhanced overall rapport between academia and the practicing professional community, thereby improving the university's capacity to meet the needs of its constituents. Access to the university is much broader, and university access to the veterinary community has greatly expanded. One direct result has been improved employment opportunities for students.

6

Impact on outreach--An increased number of faculty has been engaged in service with this program, especially when the certificate program and the practice-based teaching program are considered. My interest in practitioner education led me to participate on lifelong education planning committees for both the College of Veterinary Medicine and the Michigan Veterinary Conference, where issues are broader than the scope of this specific program.

Another impact is being realized through a kind of outreach multiplier effect. This outreach program directly impacts practitioners and then places them into the leadership positions of teachers and role models. In this capacity, the practitioners have a much broader scope of influence than that relating solely to the application of new skills they acquire as a result of a particular workshop or seminar. The scope includes virtually all aspects of the professional career, from basic medicine and surgery, to practice management and ethics. In this manner, this outreach program has a strong, indirect influence on veterinary students (future colleagues), professional peers (current colleagues), and livestock producers (clients).

Finally, from the focus group phase of the needs assessment that I conducted came the suggestion that a certificate program be developed for professional development of food animal practitioners. Such a program has now been successfully conducted twice at MSU. Although I did not serve as coordinator of that program, I consulted on both the administrative details and desired content based on the needs assessment findings. In addition, I have taught quite extensively throughout the program.

Impact on teaching--This outreach program has also had a number of noteworthy impacts on my teaching, leading to new opportunities for student learning. The practice-based teaching program has led to a markedly improved caseload and faculty-to-student ratio in the professional veterinary curriculum, whereby veterinary students obtain an abundance of first-hand experience in the real world for both clinical and practice management issues. Student evaluations of the courses involved (listed in Appendix I) have been overwhelmingly positive.

The demonstration projects and collaborative problem solving have led to a wealth of teaching cases. These cases provide both a high quality and quantity of teaching material for me to use in undergraduate courses, in the veterinary curriculum, and in post-DVM education. The courses most directly influenced are listed in Appendix J.

Finally, graduate students in both agricultural economics and animal science have participated actively in demonstration projects, collaborative problem solving, and practitioner workshops. As a result, they have gained invaluable experience in both real-world problem solving and teaching.

Impact on research--The most obvious impact on my research has been the development and pursuit of a completely unanticipated line of inquiry to investigate methods of professional development for practicing veterinarians. From this has come the realization that both topics of interest and administrative preferences differ substantially between various demographic groups of learners. To expect success, it is now evident that professional development programs for practicing veterinarians need to be targeted to a specific, well-defined market.

Beyond these findings, my research program has been enhanced because the educational programs have provided both an immediate outlet and test of relevance for research results at both the veterinary practitioner and livestock producer levels. The application of research results in the context of this program has been a valuable source of new research questions. The specific areas of my research that have benefited the most from this program are the development of methods for economic analysis of livestock health management programs, the economics of reproduction in dairy cattle, and the occurrence of drug residues in meat and milk.

Future directions

In the future, progressive outreach programs will need to take full advantage of computer technology where appropriate. This program is no exception. Expanded use of the Internet will allow practitioners improved access to the resources available in academia.

To date, this outreach program has focused almost exclusively on livestock, and consultative services have been heavily emphasized. In the future, the potential exists to use a similar educational approach to include additional animal species and additional subject matters. I expect veterinary practice management to be foremost among these.

Critical Reflection

This outreach program has been an extremely rewarding experience. In general, I have found practitioners to be more demanding learners than are college students. Information must be immediately relevant and presentation must be clear and concise to meet the educational needs of this market. At the same time, the immediate feedback and long-term support obtained as a result of successful endeavors is extremely gratifying. This interaction with the real world has helped me maintain a critical relevance in the balance of my academic activities.

A multidisciplinary approach to both design and delivery has been a key to the success of this program. Although these collaborations have been crucial, it would have been useful to spend more time with Professors Hickey and Levine early in the program to help me more fully understand the educational principles involved from the outset.

Overall, my experience with this program has taught me that scholarship in outreach is similar to scholarship in research or teaching: planning, documentation, and dissemination of results are all vital steps. Similarly, the capacity to adjust to unexpected developments and the ability to define the next logical step based on results obtained to date are critical features. In the face of increasingly scarce resources for higher education, scholarship is an increasingly important component of outreach programs.

APPENDIX A--Committee Membership
    Dairy Type of Farming Team, Michigan Agricultural Experiment Station, 1988 to 1991
    Food Animal Practice Committee, Michigan Veterinary Medical Association, 1990 to present
    Research and Extension Committee, Michigan Cattlemen's Association, 1990 to present
    Lifelong Education Committee, College of Veterinary Medicine, 1991-94, 1995 to 1997
    Preharvest Food Safety Committee, Michigan Department of Agriculture, 1995
    Program Committee, Michigan Veterinary Conference, 1995 to 1997

APPENDIX B--Needs Assessment Publications
    Lloyd, J.W., L.D. Lloyd, and H. Hickey. Continuing education for veterinarians in Michigan, *Options: Michigan Association of Adult and Continuing Education (MAACE) Scholarly Journal*, 7(2):7-8, 1992.
    Lloyd, J.W., L.D. Lloyd, H. Hickey, J.B. Kaneene, and D.C. Sawyer. Veterinary lifelong education interests in Michigan, *Journ. of Vet. Med. Ed.* 19(4):118-122, 1992.

APPENDIX C--Funding Sources
    Lloyd, J.W., H. Hickey, J.B. Kaneene, S.J. Levine, and D.C. Sawyer. Improving skills of Michigan veterinarians and livestock producers. Source: Assistant Provost for Lifelong Education, Michigan State University. Period: 1990-1992. Total grant: $13,124.
    Rust, S., and **J. Lloyd**. Beef Safety and Quality Assurance Program. Sources and amounts: National Cattlemen's Association, $2000; Michigan Beef Industry Commission, $2500; CES Food Safety Task Force, $4800. Winter 1991. Total grant: $9300.
    Kaneene, J.B., **J.W. Lloyd**, and S.B. Smalley (co-principal investigators). Utilization of chemical residue information in Extension food safety education programs. Source: USDA/ES. Period: 1992-1996. Total grant: $40,000.

APPENDIX D--Technical Publications
Refereed journal articles (peer-reviewed)
    Hady, P.J., and **J.W. Lloyd**. Using a bio-financial approach to appraise performance of the dairy business, *Compend. Contin. Educ. Prac. Vet.*, 16(8):1075-1083 & 1104, 1994.
    Gibbons, S.N., J.B. Kaneene, and **J.W. Lloyd**. Patterns of chemical residues detected in U.S. beef carcasses between 1991 and 1993, *J.A.V.M.A.*, 209(3):589-593, 1996.
Proceedings
    Lloyd, J.W. Financial aspects of dairy farm expansion and improvement: The veterinarian's role. In: *Proceedings of the 79th Annual Convention, Wisconsin Veterinary Medical Association*, Madison, October 14-16, 1994.
    Lloyd, J.W. Why is everyone milking more cows, and where does the veterinarian fit in? In: *Proceedings of the 1997 Michigan Veterinary Conference*, Lansing, January 23-26, 1997.
Extension and technical reports
    Gibbons, S., **J. Lloyd**, S. Rust, and S. Smalley. Drug residues: Risking the dairy beef investment, Michigan/Indiana Holstein News, March, 1993.
    Lloyd, J.W., G.D. Schwab, and M.S. VanderKlok. The economic impact of pseudorabies on the Michigan swine industry in 1993, Michigan Agricultural Experiment Station, Research Report 541, October 1995.

APPENDIX E--Scientific Presentations to Veterinary Practitioners
Seminars
    Lloyd, J.W. Epidemiology and economics of lameness in dairy cattle. 1995 Michigan Veterinary Conference, Lansing, January 26-29, 1995.
    Lloyd, J.W. Give me the bottom line. Do production and profitability intersect? 1996 Michigan Veterinary Conference, Lansing, January 25-28, 1996.
Stand-alone workshops
    Dairy production medicine: Reproduction and performance, Michigan State University Lifelong Education Program, Kellogg Biological Station, Hickory Corners, Michigan, December 12-14, 1990--developed and coordinated by **J. W. Lloyd**.
    Residue-free dairy products: Issues for Michigan veterinarians, Michigan State University Lifelong Education Program, E. Lansing, December 7, 1991--developed and coordinated by **J. W. Lloyd**.

<u>Curricular workshops</u>

Radke, B.R., and **J.W. Lloyd.** The economic aspects of culling decisions, Heifer Management, Planned Parenthood, and Culling Module, Dairy Health Management Certificate Program, Michigan State University, Kettunen Center, Tustin, Michigan, September 11, 1994.

Lloyd, J.W., B.R. Radke, P.J. Hady, and M. Wustenberg. Dairy production and health management economics, Module #2, Dairy Health Management Certificate Program, Michigan State University, Kellogg Biological Station, Hickory Corners, Michigan, January 11-13, 1996.

APPENDIX F--Scientific Presentations to Livestock Producers

Lloyd, J.W., and G.D. Schwab. Should I consider contracting services? 1994 Dairy Management Conference, Michigan State University Extension, Lansing, March 1-2, 1994.

Lloyd, J.W. The relationship of culling to efficiency and profitability. Michigan Professional Dairy Farmers Association, Ithaca, Michigan, February 12, 1997.

APPENDIX G--National and International Scientific Presentations
<u>Fellow educators</u>

Lloyd, J.W., J.B. Kaneene, and L.D. Lloyd. Michigan lifelong education interests in veterinary epidemiology and animal health economics, Conf. of Res. Workers in Animal Diseases, Chicago, November 1991.

O'Brien, D.J., **J.W. Lloyd**, and J.B. Kaneene. A principal components analysis of factors critical to participation in veterinary lifelong education programs, Conf. of Res. Workers in Animal Diseases, Chicago, November 1992.

<u>Veterinarians</u>

Lloyd, J.W. Dairy cattle lameness: epidemiology and economics, 131st Annual Meeting, American Veterinary Medical Association, San Francisco, July 1994.

Lloyd, J.W., B.R. Radke, P.J. Hady, and M. Wustenberg. Dairy production and health management economics, Université de Montréal, Saint-Hyacinthe, Québec, December 1-3, 1995.

<u>Livestock producers</u>

Lloyd, J.W. The importance of dairy health management to economic efficiency and profitability, American Dairy Science Association Annual Meeting, Corvallis, Oregon, July 15, 1996.

Lloyd, J.W. The importance of dairy health management to economic efficiency and profitability, Colorado Farm Show Dairy Days, Greeley, January 29, 1997.

APPENDIX H--Honors and Awards

Commendation (for Extension activity), Michigan Cattlemen's Association, 1992
State Team Award, Milk Quality Assurance Program, Michigan State University Extension, 1993
Creativity in Teaching Award, Merck Agvet, 1995

APPENDIX I--Courses Involved in the Practice-based Teaching Program

LCS 621	Equine Practice Clerkship
LCS 631	Food Animal Practice Clerkship
LCS 677	Veterinary Preceptorship

APPENDIX J--Courses Benefiting from Teaching Cases

LCS 633	Dairy Production Medicine Clerkship
LCS 637	Advanced Dairy Production Medicine Clerkship
LCS 643	Food Animal Fundamentals Clerkship

Table 1. Summary of educational methods and their target audiences.

Educational Methods	Target Audiences		
	Veterinarians	Livestock Producers	Educators
Technical publications	*	*	*
Seminars	*	*	*
Workshop (stand-alone)	*		*
Workshop (curricular)	*		
Demonstration project	*	*	
Collaborative problem solving	*		
Practice-based teaching	*		
Orchestrated peer teaching (Ala Rogers' theory of innovation)	*	*	

Reflections and Future Challenges

As we completed this *Guide,* we were aware there remained significant insights that could not be described well in the guidelines or recommendations offered elsewhere in the volume. Some of the thinking that follows emerged from our own reflections and conversations and some from the writings of the faculty participating in the Kellogg project. So in this chapter, we offer both guidance and challenge for those campuses undertaking to follow the path of our collaborative team of faculty in pursuit of "making visible" the scholarship of professional service/outreach.

The Struggles of Documentation: Resisting Tradition

Reflecting back over the three years that preceded this *Guide,* we can only describe the work of the Kellogg project's sixteen faculty members to document their professional service/outreach as a series of struggles. Early in the project, those struggles were unnamed, felt at an emotional level, and difficult to articulate. Our first "Aha!" experience came amidst that early tension when, as a group, we and the faculty realized its source.

In our naivete, we had proposed a framework for the faculty members to use in their initial documentation efforts, but they were struggling to fit their service scholarship to its structure, seeing it as one that reflected the protocols of traditional scholarship. "We're doing something unique, and we don't want to document it in a traditional way," they said. Warren Rauhe (Landscape Architecture) spoke for many in the group, "My outreach activities are not meant to be a substitute for traditional research scholarship. They represent a new paradigm."

Once the faculty acknowledged their intense resistance to a traditional research framework and their determination to frame the scholarship of professional outreach/service with categories vastly different from it, the search for an appropriate framework proceeded with less tension —but no less difficulty.

Ultimately, the group came around to many elements of a traditional research framework. All scholarly work is defined by the universal categories of goals, questions, and methods. The scholarship of professional service requires a theoretical foundation in much the same way as traditional scholarship. The struggle to be completely unique had been abandoned by the end of the first year, and the resulting framework (diagrammed in **Chapter Three**) is a blend of traditional components and components relevant to service/outreach.

As the documentation struggle continued, the faculty wrestled with style issues again, in an effort to find an alternative to traditional research reports. Steve Ross (Psychology/Research) talked about his decision:

> I decided to write this report in a style that emphasizes the outreach scholarship of my project as distinguished as much as possible from the research scholarship component. I decided that a report focusing on actual findings of the evaluation study might create a weak version of

our actual already completed reports and journal publications, and thus communicate research achievements in an outreach medium, the opposite of my intentions. In contrast, I adopted a narrative style using a story-telling orientation and personal reflections on the process of the project — what was done, what occurred, and what decisions were made in the context of implementing the project.

As intended, the projects differed from one another, and their disciplinary contexts added more variation to both structure and style. Even in the cases of Dannelle Stevens (Education) and Cheryl Rosaen (Education), both of whom worked with professional development schools, the professional service was unique for each of them, the institutional context varied significantly, and consequently their scholarship required different forms of description and evidence. They found many insights in reviewing and critiquing each other's documentations, as did all of the faculty members. Those reflections provide strong support for the collaborative process.

THE STRENGTH OF COLLABORATION

In spite of their disciplinary differences, the Kellogg faculty were able to guide one another and draw insights from work that little resembled their own. That collaborative aspect of the project was a strength and a balm to the struggle. Cheryl Rosaen describes it well, "The documentation process is not one that should be tackled alone." We ourselves are quite clear that the documentation project would not have yielded the richness of insights without the intense collaborative nature of the process. We gained such wisdom from the discussions, from the cooperative thinking, from the struggles. Patricia Schechter speaks for all in the project group:

> I profited both personally and professionally from the shared intelligence, creativity, and integrity of the faculty participants. The opportunity to delve deeply into the political and philosophical implications of our work, to revise and refine our documentations in a genuine community of scholars will serve as a model of inquiry and reflection in my career.

The collaborative reflection experienced by these faculty members is something we encourage for any campus engaged in an effort to recognize and reward the scholarship of professional service. The benefits of ongoing reflection for the documentation of professional service/outreach are extensive, even for the individual scholar.

SCHOLARLY DOCUMENTATION: IMAPCT ON PROFESSIONAL SERVICE/OUTREACH

Earlier in this *Guide,* we advocated for documentation as an ongoing process, not as a summative report at the end of a community project. Those faculty participants actually engaged in professional service during the three years of our project had the opportunity to experience that ongoing quality of documentation. (Some faculty members had already completed community outreach/service when our project work began.) The faculty members who documented as they engaged in outreach came to realize the impact of documentation on the community project. For example, Roger Jarjoura (Public Affairs) commented,

> By working to document the scholarship of the community project described within, I believe I have enhanced the quality of the project. Since this community partnership is ongoing, I can reflect and revise the work continuously. Already my documentation efforts have led to revisions of my approach and a more rational approach to measuring outcomes. I am convinced of the value of ongoing reflection and documentation and believe that my project is better than it would have otherwise been.

Clearly, the process of describing their service work prompts faculty to reflect and assess that work, often leading to refinements or revisions. While some faculty members began adjusting the evidence they collected as a result of ongoing documentation, others modified their approaches or their communications or their evaluation methods.

The potential for rethinking community work as a result of documentation offers a challenge to those engaged in partnership activities, one that requires collaborative reflection and revision. The faculty participants in the Kellogg project acknowledged a number of challenges at the close of their collaborations.

CHALLENGES TO DOCUMENTATION OF PROFESSIONAL SERVICE/OUTREACH

As more faculty members embrace professional service/outreach, and as more institutions support their work with revised roles and rewards systems, we expect more challenges to the documentation process to emerge. The myriad of community partners, community service activities, and evidence alternatives offers an initial challenge, while making the engagement of faculty in service/outreach compelling and stimulating. The unpredictability that comes with that diversity and the unknown quality of community service expand the challenge, but they also lend support to the idea of documentation as ongoing.

Other challenges are described eloquently by Cheryl Rosaen:

> The interconnection of my community outreach work with other aspects of my faculty role helped maintain a richness in my work but made writing about it difficult. How would I explain the interconnectedness? Would this complicated picture interfere with understanding the important issues embedded in the work or its contributions to the field?

Making the Case for Professional Service described the multiple objectives that typically characterize professional service. Capturing that complexity can only be achieved by an "interrelated combination of pertinent work samples and products, together with a narrative explication of them" (Lynton 1995: 28). Even with such combinations of evidence and narrative, faculty in the Kellogg project struggled to communicate the sophisticated quality of their service projects and to portray the richness of the work. Says Cheryl Rosaen:

> A second challenge was one of capturing the developmental nature of my work and not making it appear more linear or rational than it was. The outcomes evolved out of the work, instead of being clearly defined at the onset.

In the documentations, the faculty members worked to make examples of immediate impact distinguishable from examples of broader impact, "a very demanding writing task," she reported.

A third challenge was one predicted in 1995 in *Making the Case*. The title of that volume was selected with the specific intent to "connote that the individual [faculty member] must be an active participant, not a passive object, in the documentation of the intellectual process" (Lynton: 28). Yet such documentation is atypical for faculty. As noted earlier in **Chapter Four,** faculty typically reveal little of self in research scholarship, and certainly very seldom describe problems, concerns, and failures. In our early efforts in the Kellogg project we found ourselves frequently urging a faculty participant to "talk about yourself, not just the project." Most of the group confessed the difficulty of doing so — "It's not the usual way to write about our scholarly work."

FINALLY

Knowing beforehand what challenges we will likely encounter can ease the task before us in higher education. As we said at the outset of this *Guide,* we think that the conversations and reflections of our project participants can be a source of encouragement and inspiration for faculty who commit to professional service and then set about to document the scholarship of that work. And we intend its insights to serve as a source of information, examples, and guidance for institutions, as their faculty and administrators explore new roles for faculty and appropriate rewards for their efforts.

Finally, we urge your thoughtful study and deliberations as you and your campus "make the case" for professional service/outreach, then undertake to "make visible" the resulting scholarly work.

REFERENCES

Boyer, Ernest L. (1990). *Scholarship Reconsidered: Priorities of the Professoriate.* Princeton, NJ: Carnegie Foundation for the Advancement of Teaching.

Elman, Sandra E., and Sue Marx Smock. (1985). *Professional Service and Faculty Rewards: Toward an Integrated Structure.* Washington, DC: National Association of State Universities and Land-Grant Colleges.

Farmer, James A., and Steven F. Schomberg. (1993). *A Faculty Guide for Relating Public Service to the Promotion and Tenure Review Process.* Urbana-Champaign, IL: University of Illinois.

Glassick, Charles E., Mary Taylor Huber, and Gene I. Maeroff. (1997). *Scholarship Assessed: Evaluation of the Professoriate.* San Francisco, CA: Jossey-Bass Publishers.

Lynton, Ernest A. (1995). *Making the Case for Professional Service.* Washington, DC: American Association for Higher Education.

———— . (September/October 1983). "A Crisis of Purpose: Reexamining the Role of the University." *Change* 15: 18-23, 53.

Zlotkowski, Edward. (January 1998). Presentation at the Service-Learning Colloquium, AAHE Conference on Faculty Roles & Rewards, Orlando, Florida.

A COLLECTION OF DOCUMENTS FOR REWARDING FACULTY PROFESSIONAL SERVICE

MICHIGAN STATE UNIVERSITY

"Points of Distinction: Planning and Evaluating Quality Outreach"
Developed by the MSU Evaluating Quality Outreach faculty working committee, this guide provides information, criteria, and tools to help academic units and individual faculty members identify outreach opportunities and measure results.

"Matrix: Four Dimensions of Quality Outreach"
A twelve-page booklet that serves as a matrix for evaluating quality outreach at Michigan State University. The matrix describes four dimensions of quality outreach: significance, context, scholarship, and impact. It outlines components to consider, offers sample questions to assess each component, and suggests qualitative and quantitative indicators. [See **Table 2** on page 19.]

"Guidebook: Planning and Evaluating Quality Outreach"
Sections in this fifty-two-page guidebook cover unit planning and evaluation, individual faculty planning and evaluation, and project evaluation. A matrix describes four dimensions of quality outreach: significance, context, scholarship, and impact. An appendix contains tools for defining outreach, unit planning, priority setting, rewarding quality outreach, evaluating unit outreach, developing a faculty outreach portfolio, and evaluating individual outreach.

Contact: Lorilee R. Sandmann, Director, University Outreach, Office of the Vice Provost for University Outreach, Michigan State University, 6 Kellogg Center, East Lansing, MI 48824-1022; ph 517/355-4589

PORTLAND STATE UNIVERSITY

"Policies and Procedures for the Evaluation of Faculty for Tenure, Promotion, and Merit Increases (Adopted June 12, 1996)"
These promotion and tenure guidelines define scholarship to include discovery, integration, interpretation, and application, plus offer an overview of faculty responsibilities. They also provide a description of the scholarly agenda expected of the faculty, criteria, and documentation for evaluating scholarship. One section describes community outreach in detail, and recommends indicators of quality and significance.

"Redefining Scholarship for the College of Liberal Arts and Sciences (December 30, 1994)"
This report was written by a faculty committee given the task of clarifying the model of scholarship that forms the basis for evaluating and rewarding faculty

activities. It defines scholarship and its application to teaching and outreach; lays out the criteria by which an activity can be judged as scholarly, and describes the kinds of faculty profiles that might both promote individual scholarly agendas and combine to serve departmental missions. Suggestions are included for how scholarship can be documented and used for faculty development.

Contact: Rod Diman, Vice Provost, President's Office, PO Box 751, Portland, OR 97207-0751; ph 503/725-3422

INDIANA UNIVERSITY PURDUE UNIVERSITY INDIANAPOLIS (IUPUI)

"IUPUI Task Force on Service (September 17, 1996)"
A committee report that summarizes current practice in professional service; locates service within IUPUI's mission; defines professional service; and provides criteria for evaluating professional service, application of the criteria, documentation of professional service, conclusions, and a timeline for actions of the task force on service at IUPUI.

"Indiana University Faculty Service Fellows Program: Strategic Directions Project on Defining, Documenting, and Evaluating Professional Service: Report From First Year of a Three Year Project (April 25, 1997)"
Report of a three-year project funded by Indiana University's Strategic Directions Initiative to engage faculty from system campuses in preparing portfolios of their professional service and sharing those portfolios with other faculty members, academic department chairs, and campuses. The report defines professional service and discusses the background of the project, quality indicators for professional service, application of quality indicators, and documentation issues.

Contact: Robert Bringle, Director, Center for Public Service and Leadership, IUPUI, 815 W. Michigan Street, University College, LY 3118, Indianapolis, IN 46202-5164; ph 317/274-6753

UNIVERSITY OF ILLINOIS AT URBANA-CHAMPAIGN OFFICE OF CONTINUING EDUCATION AND PUBLIC SERVICE

"A Faculty Guide for Relating Public Service to the Promotion and Tenure Review Process"
This guide was written by James A. Farmer, Jr., and Steven F. Schomberg and the Senate Committee for Continuing Education and Public Service (1990-1993). It provides guidance in defining the scope of public service, lists distinguishing characteristics of activities considered as public service, and provides examples of pub-

lic service activities. It describes potential sources of confusion in defining service, and provides suggestions for planning, documentation, and evaluation.

For copies, send email to strader@ux1.cso.uiuc.edu. Or contact Gloria Buhrmester, 302 East John Street, #202, Champaign, IL 61820; ph 217/333-4258

THE UNIVERSITY OF GEORGIA

"Public Service and Outreach Academic Rank Guidelines for Appointment and Promotion (May, 1997)"

This document discusses the university's alternative appointment for faculty who wish to devote most of their time to public service. It describes the purpose and philosophy of this "Public Service and Outreach" career ladder, the definitions and requirements of the public service rank, professional functions, appointment procedures, promotion process, suggested documentation to be used to prepare the service dossier, and form letters for outside recommendations.

"The Walter Barnard Hill Awards for Distinguished Achievement in Public Service and Outreach"

Describes the university's Hill Awards, inaugurated in 1992 to recognize distinguished achievement in public service and outreach by faculty members and service professionals. The material covers purpose, eligibility, process, documentation, and award criteria, and includes a description of award winners. The Hill Awards recognize achievements in program and project development, management, extension and public service instruction, technical assistance or consultation, applied research and studies, and instructional or media materials development. Each awardee receives a permanent salary increase of $2,000.

Also discussed is the Hill Distinguished Public Service and Outreach Fellow award, which is comparable to a distinguished professorship and is the highest award offered in public service and outreach at the university. This second program recognizes faculty who have made extraordinary contributions to service programs. It comes with a further salary increase of $1,000, as well as a supplemental fund for the awardee to use to advance his or her program of work.

Contact: Tom Rodgers, Associate Vice President for Public Service and Outreach, The University of Georgia, 300 Old College, Athens, GA 30602; ph 706/542-6125

CALIFORNIA STATE UNIVERSITY, MONTEREY BAY

"Interim Criteria for Review, Promotion, and Tenure"
> This twenty-page document describes the interim criteria for promotion and tenure at a new campus. It links the university's mission and a definition of scholarship that includes the scholarship of professional application. Examples are provided and documentation and criteria for evaluating professional service are described.

Contact: Jeanne Picard, Assistant to the Vice President for Academic Personnel, California State University, Monterey Bay, 100 Campus Drive, Monterey, CA 93940; ph 408/582-3361

UNIVERSITY OF CALIFORNIA-DAVIS

"Why Public Service: A Guide for Faculty at the University of California-Davis (1985, June): Report of the Committee on Public Service of the Davis Academic Senate and the Public Service Research and Dissemination Program. University of California-Davis: Academic Senate"
> Several documents written by this committee reflect on the mission of UC-Davis as a land-grant university and its responsibility to provide service to the state. It provides survey research done with the faculty at UC-Davis, reporting their involvement and interest in public service, as well as descriptions of different public service activities appropriate for UC-Davis to engage in.

Contact: Kathy vonRummelhuff, Assistant to the Academic Senate, Public Service Committee, University of California-Davis, Davis, CA 95616; ph 530/752-3920

MONTCLAIR STATE UNIVERSITY

"Faculty Scholarship Incentive Program"
> Describes a program in which faculty develop two-year scholarship plans that allow them to weight each form of scholarship (discovery, teaching, pedagogy, and application) at a different level or percentage for evaluation. For instance, a faculty member might agree to spend 30% of his/her time on teaching, 20 percent on discovery, and 50% on service. The document provides examples of how this program works and how faculty are then evaluated on their scholarship according to their percentages.

Contact: Richard Lynde, Provost and Vice President for Academic Affairs, Montclair State University, Upper Montclair, NJ 07043; ph 973/655-4383

UNIVERSITY OF WISCONSIN

"The Wisconsin Idea and Outreach"

"The Commitment to the Wisconsin Idea: Guide to Documenting and Evaluating Excellence in Outreach Scholarship (1997)"

These documents describe the philosophical background for the outreach mission of a land-grant college and, specifically, for the outreach mission of the University of Wisconsin. Department and individual faculty outreach are then described as extensions of this mission. Separate sections cover outreach research, outreach teaching, outreach service, and the combinations of these three, with examples of each. The second document provides examples of how to document professional outreach and criteria for evaluating excellence in outreach scholarship.

Contact: Carol Crary, Outreach Development Office, University of Wisconsin Madison, 750 University Avenue, Madison, WI 53706-1490; ph 608/262-4353

UNIVERSITY OF ALABAMA AT BIRMINGHAM, SCHOOL OF EDUCATION

[Untitled]

Description of a merit pay system that weights service equally with teaching and research in merit pay decisions within a school of education. The document includes examples of kinds of professional service, the documentation required, and forms for providing documentation.

Contact: Clint Bruess, Dean, School of Education, UAB Station, Birmingham, AL 35294; ph 205/934-5363

FACULTY PROFESSIONAL SERVICE: SELECTED RESOURCES

Boyer, Ernest L. (1990). *Scholarship Reconsidered: Priorities of the Professoriate.* Princeton, NJ: Carnegie Foundation for the Advancement of Teaching.

Summary: Can America's colleges and universities, with all of the richness of their resources, better serve the nation and the world? Can we define scholarship in ways that respond more adequately to the urgent new realities both within the academy and beyond? These questions frame this critical work. Boyer begins by exploring the history and development of our views of scholarship in American universities. He then proposes a new way of looking at scholarship, as having four components: teaching, discovery, integration, and application. He makes recommendations for how colleges can use the mosaic of talent that faculty bring to their jobs in the service of the diversity of college missions, especially missions that meet critical community needs. Boyer looks ahead to a new generation of scholars, and he proposes ways to structure faculty careers so that over time faculty can excel and be rewarded for multiple forms of scholarly excellence.

Braskamp, Larry A., and John C. Ory. (1994). *Assessing Faculty Work: Enhancing Individual and Institutional Performance.* Jossey-Bass Higher and Adult Education Series. San Francisco, CA: Jossey-Bass Publishers.

Summary: This book emphasizes the role of assessment in fostering development of individual faculty members and their institutions. Part one describes the role of faculty assessment, outlining inadequacies in current approaches and emphasizing the role of collegial activity to individual and institutional assessment. Part two defines the work of faculty and explores faculty expectations through the concepts of classifying work and the importance of expectations. Part three outlines collecting and organizing assessment evidence, including strategies for collection, source credibility, and the portrayal of faculty work. Part four examines appropriate uses of evidence and provides practical guidelines for enhancing individual and administration use of assessment. Part five presents methods of collecting assessment evidence: written appraisals, rating scales and checklists, interviews, observations and videotaping, indicators of eminence, quality, impact, achievement and outcome measures, and records and portfolios. Appended are extensive practical resources and samples including forms, measurement instruments, guidelines, and surveys.

Crosson, Patricia H. (1985). *Public Service in Higher Education: Practices and Priorities.* ASHE-ERIC Higher Education Report, no. 2. Washington, DC: ERIC Clearinghouse on Higher Education.

Summary: This monograph provides an overview of the history and rationale for the service mission in higher education. It presents metaphors and rival perspectives on forms of service and the evolution of the ideal of service, and describes examples of different forms of service, such as service to community colleges, urban communities, state and local governments, and businesses. The authors examine the context and nature of these partnerships. The final section presents organizational structures, policies, and reward systems that can encourage public service. Concluding recommendations suggest a new research agenda for the study of public service in higher education.

Diamond, Robert M., and Bronwyn E. Adam. (1995). *The Disciplines Speak: Rewarding the Scholarly, Professional, and Creative Work of Faculty.* Washington, DC: American Association for Higher Education.

Summary: This one-stop source offers statements on rewarding faculty work from nine disciplinary/professional societies: religion, history, geography, math, chemistry, the arts, business, journalism, and family/consumer science, plus the National Education Association. In their introduction the authors call for a reward system responsive to the needs of faculty, departments, and institutions.

Glassick, Charles E., Mary Taylor Huber, and Gene I. Maeroff. (1997). *Scholarship Assessed: Evaluation of the Professoriate.* A Special Report of the Carnegie Foundation for the Advancement of Teaching. San Francisco, CA: Jossey-Bass Publishers.

Summary: *Scholarship Assessed* begins where *Scholarship Reconsidered* left off. Begun by Ernest L. Boyer and completed by Glassick, Huber, and Maeroff, this book examines the changing nature of scholarship in today's colleges and universities. It proposes new standards for assessing scholarship and evaluating faculty work by placing special emphasis on methods for documenting effective scholarship. Based on the findings of Carnegie's National Survey on the Reexamination of Faculty Roles and Rewards, this is a practical guide for campuses looking for specific criteria to evaluate scholarly work and ideas for methods to document and evaluate faculty. It ends with a discussion of the qualities of a scholar.

Holland, Barbara. (Fall 1997). "Analyzing Institutional Commitment to Service: A Model of Key Organizational Factors." *Michigan Journal of Community Service Learning*, pp. 30-41.

Summary: Although exploration has begun related to expanding, sustaining, and institutionalizing service-learning, there is little understanding of the dynamic relationship between organizational factors related to service-learning and actual levels of institutional commitment. Each institution must develop its own understanding of its academic priorities, including the role of service as an aspect of mission, and set clear goals for a level of commitment that matches those priorities. Holland proposes a matrix that links organizational factors to levels of commitment to service as one possible approach to setting institutional goals, realistically assessing current conditions, and monitoring progress toward desired levels of implementation of service-learning.

Lidstone, James E., Patricia E. Hacker, and Fred M. Oien. (1996). "Where the Rubber Meets the Road: Revising Promotion and Tenure Standards According to Boyer." *Quest* 48(2):100.

Summary: This article in the journal of the National Association for Physical Education in Higher Education builds on Boyer's argument that the next step to acknowledging multiple forms of scholarship on campuses is to identify ways to fairly and equitably evaluate faculty scholarship within the context of the professoriate in general, and in higher education institutions in particular. The authors argue the case for differential application of standards within and among universities, based on the diversity of missions and goals. Following that, they give examples for how Boyer's classifications have been applied to promotion and tenure standards at one Midwest comprehensive land-grant university. Administrator and faculty (new and old) commentaries support the new standards.

Lynton, Ernest A. (1995). *Making the Case for Professional Service.* Washington, DC: American Association for Higher Education.

Summary: Professional service/outreach by faculty based on their professional expertise can be an intellectually challenging activity, as well as a critical element in fulfilling campus missions — if properly conceptualized, performed, evaluated, and rewarded. This monograph covers why professional service is needed, and how it can be documented and evaluated, with case study examples of five actual projects.

———— . (1991). "The Mission of Metropolitan Universities in the Utilization of Knowledge; A Policy Analysis." NERCHE Working Paper #8. Boston: University of Massachusetts at Boston.

Summary: In the ecology of knowledge in modern society, efforts to enhance the use of knowledge are every bit as essential and as challenging as activities toward the creation of knowledge. An emphasis on use of knowledge defines the mission of comprehensive or metropolitan universities; it demands a broadened conception of scholarship and a high degree of interaction. To fulfill their missions, such institutions must develop appropriate internal and external bridging mechanisms and make appropriate adaptations in the preparation, evaluation, and rewards of their faculties. The paper describes recommendations for rewarding faculty for application and use of knowledge.

———— , and Sandra E. Elman. (1987). *The New Priorities for the University.* San Francisco, CA: Jossey-Bass Publishers.

Summary: This book explains how the university must shift its priorities in order to adapt, survive, and effectively serve the needs of society in the new information age. The authors demonstrate that the current emphasis in most universities on the quest for new ideas is too narrow — revealing that the technological, economic, and social changes over the last forty years have created a need, not so much for new knowledge but for new ways to accumulate, interpret, and apply existing knowledge in the real world. They show that the traditional focus on basic research does not fulfill the information needs of modern society, and explain that the definitions of scholarship and professional activity must be expanded to include applied knowledge and the dissemination of knowledge. They describe specific ways universities can meet these new priorities, for example, through procedures for bringing together faculty from different departments to do applied research, communicating findings to those in the community who can apply them, making use of the resources that outside organizations have to offer, and more. The authors also argue that universities need to focus on preparing individuals to apply knowledge both on the job and as private citizens. And they explore how curricula in all areas can be adapted to more effectively suggest real-world applications.

O'Meara, KerryAnn. (1997). "Rewarding Faculty Professional Service." NERCHE Working Paper #19. Boston: University of Massachusetts at Boston.

Summary: Scholars of higher education have long recognized that existing reward systems and structures in academic communities do not weight faculty professional service as they do teaching and research. In the past five years, however, many colleges and universities have found innovative ways to define, document, and evaluate faculty professional service in traditional promotion and tenure systems. Other institutions have created or expanded alternative faculty reward systems, including faculty profiles in service, merit pay, and post-tenure reviews emphasizing service. Based on data from a nationwide sample, this paper discusses innovations in rewarding faculty professional service, and offers conclusions and recommendations.

Rice, R. Eugene. (1996). "Making a Place for the New American Scholar." New Pathways Working Paper, no. #1. Washington, DC: American Association for Higher Education.

Summary: What does it mean to be a distinctly American scholar? What is the role of the scholar in a dynamic, changing democracy? These questions, raised by Ralph Waldo Emerson's famous address of 1937, "The American Scholar," begin Rice's examination of higher education, the larger purposes of American society, and the history and development of current visions of scholarship. Rice describes how faculty have been more and more pulled toward research while society and undergraduate education are even more in need of teaching and service. Building on inquiries into how knowledge is acquired and utilized — different ways of knowing — he sets aside the polarities in the contemporary setting and proposes an alternative perspective. Rather than fostering academic careers in which faculty are disconnected from society, American higher education can form new models for faculty careers that, over the season of an academic life, encourage faculty to engage in multiple forms of scholarship. Rice suggests a reward system that cultivates knowledge anchored in practice, a reworking of the tenure system, and a continuous review of senior faculty.

This paper is a call for a broader view of scholarship: one that is congruent with the rich diversity of American higher education; one that is more appropriate, more authentic, and more adaptive for both our institutions and day-to-day working lives of faculty.

Schomberg, Steven F., and James A. Farmer, Jr. (Fall 1994). "The Evolving Concept of Public Service and Implications for Rewarding Faculty." *Continuing Higher Education Review* 58(3).

Summary: As described in this paper, the main theoretical representations of public service were used as the basis for asking faculty members at a Midwestern, land-grant university their views of public service. The faculty view public service as a set of activities that use faculty expertise to address societal needs directly or to help others to do so, for the benefit of the public, and as a contribution to the welfare of society. The authors discuss the implications of this definition for compensation and tenure and promotion decisions. They argue that systems models such as Peter Senge's provide a more powerful means of interpreting the relationship among teaching, research, and public service than do the analytical attempts to differentiate among these missions.

Singleton, Sharon E., Catherine A. Burack, and Deborah J. Hirsch. (April 1997). "Faculty Service Enclaves." *AAHE Bulletin,* 3-7.

Summary: Offering protected conditions necessary for ideas to develop, yet isolated in indifferent, even hostile campus environments, faculty service enclaves can be powerful forces for grassroots change toward the "service culture" ideal. This article describes a seven-campus study of New England institutions with commitments to service. Interviews with chief academic officers, deans, department chairs, and directors of service-learning programs revealed six empowering traits of these service enclaves: leadership, flexibility, institutional support, consistency with institutional mission and culture, integration with research and teaching, and visibility. At institutions where the level of commitment to service was high, these groups thrived in productive collaborations with the external community. However, at the other institutions, where those conditions did not prevail, the groups found themselves struggling for resources and support as they carried out their service projects. Service enclaves that do not enjoy the same credibility as other academic programs often are scrutinized more harshly by campus members. This makes deliberate efforts at internal visibility all the more important.

EXAMPLES OF SUPPORTING EVIDENCE

- Results from surveys of clients, community partners, other stakeholders
- Diagrams of collaborative processes
- Charts of accomplishments of teachers, clients, community partners
- Monographs
- Portfolios of student work
- Newspaper reports
- Letters and memos that document process and communication
- Student evaluations
- Testimonials from community partners
- Minutes from meetings that document process
- Policy changes or developments
- Recommendations from community partners
- Syllabi from community programs
- Archives
- Graphics, collage, visual display of collaborative achievements
- Chronological chart or table illustrating process
- Funding of related projects
- Needs assessments
- Legislation, with demonstrated influence of service work
- Case studies of community agency, neighborhood, or project

About AAHE and Its Forum on Faculty Roles & Rewards

History

In 1990-91, the faculty rewards system surfaced as a national issue. Colleges and universities across the country launched task forces to reexamine faculty expectations, evaluation, and rewards. To seize the moment — frame and articulate the agenda — and give status, direction, and practical guidance to this emerging, nationwide reexamination, AAHE created the Forum on Faculty Roles & Rewards, with FIPSE support.

Current Issues

The Forum is now in its seventh year and has succeeded far beyond its planners' original expectations. Its focus on reexamining faculty priorities and the reward structure has resonated broadly across higher education. The Forum's annual, national conference not only has become a nexus where connections are made between campus leaders and institutions but also has come to function as an incubator for new ideas and prototypes for innovative practice. Under the Forum's auspices, a separately funded New Pathways project has entered a second phase — "Academic Careers for a New Century: From Inquiry to Practice" — and that project will continue to build over the next three years as one of the Forum's central themes. The work of the Forum has evolved into a significant catalyst for change at a time when change is most needed.

Resources and Services

The Forum sponsors the AAHE Conference on Faculty Roles & Rewards, regional meetings, workshops, special projects, and publications. It works with key faculty, provosts, deans, and department chairs in reexamining faculty priorities, the structure of the academic career, and the reward system. Trustees of universities and colleges and legislators who work on issues of higher education policy are also involved. Since beginning the New Pathways project, the Forum also has served as a resource for institutions, administrators, faculty, and governing bodies reexamining faculty careers and employment arrangements, including tenure processes and policies.

Publications

AAHE publications addressing the Forum's concerns include a fourteen-paper series of Working Papers on issues of faculty employment and the monographs *The Collaborative Department: How Five Campuses Are Inching Toward Cultures of Collective Responsibility* (Jon Wergin, 1994); *Making the Case for Professional Service* (Ernest Lynton, 1995); and *The Disciplines Speak: Rewarding the Scholarly, Professional, and Creative Work of Faculty* (Robert Diamond and Bronwyn Adam, editors, 1995). To receive a catalog, call AAHE's Publications Order Desk (x11) or visit AAHE's website (www.aahe.org).

Future Focus

As the Forum proceeds, its focus will be on moving "From Fresh Ideas to New Practice." To do this, the Forum will broaden and deepen its work by reaching out in several new directions: toward the departments, the disciplinary associations, additional types of institutions, and other groups working on innovation in higher education. Several mechanisms will be expanded or established as the Forum continues to grow:

National conference. The annual AAHE Conference on Faculty Roles & Rewards will continue, with the aim of making it financially self-sustaining.

Clearinghouse. The Forum's clearinghouse function will expand, augmented by new sector-specific networks on faculty roles and rewards via the Internet.

Regional meetings. The planners of regional meetings on faculty roles and rewards will continue to be supported and assisted, with investments of additional Forum staff time in cultivating this efficient and highly effective means of getting faculty across the nation actively engaged in the work of the Forum.

Lines of work. The Forum will continue to seed "lines of work," moving on to a set of second-generation issues and continuing to bring together the key actors doing ground-breaking work on an issue to create practical, usable "products" that can have an impact on faculty.

Over the next three years, primary attention will be given to the New Pathways project. In collaboration with a newly formed Project on Faculty Appointments, at Harvard University, the Forum will move from inquiry and discussion of the changing academic career to working with colleges and universities on the concrete implementation of new approaches and effective practice. Issues will be targeted that have the potential to make individual faculty careers more vital, and that provide institutions with the flexibility needed to anticipate and respond to a rapidly changing educational environment. The work will be focused on three areas: faculty appointment policies, the tenure process, and post-tenure review.

More Information

For further information, and to have your name added to the Forum's mailing list, please contact: R. Eugene Rice (x37), *director*, or Pamela Bender (x56), *program manager*, aaheffrr@aahe.org.

What Is AAHE?

The American Association for Higher Education (AAHE) is the individual membership organization that promotes the changes higher education must make to ensure its effectiveness in a complex, interconnected world. The association equips individuals and institutions committed to such changes with the knowledge they need to bring those changes about. For information about becoming an AAHE member, call the Membership Department at 202/293-6440 x27 or send email to pwaldron@aahe.org.